ALONE I DID IT

TZURI KING

AUTHOR'S NOTE

To write this work, I consulted friends. Of course, I also used travel logs and images – my constant companions on all my trips. All the characters and names mentioned in this book have been changed, and I have added some colorful features for the sake of anonymity. Likewise, I also made up and omitted certain depictions and characters without distorting the truth of the main plot.

To my parents, Mom and Dad, who always encouraged me to follow my heart.

PART I

1
DAY 1

"No one has ever become poor by giving."

Anne Frank

March 27, 2016
Starting point: Ashkelon
Destination: Kibbutz Kramim
Distance: 70 kilometers

Many things have changed since the morning I embarked on my journey. Issues such as love, happiness, and family life took on a new meaning that intensified as I rode on.

Somehow, I happened to decide on taking the road precisely at the turn of the season, when the trees were changing their colors and the earth was changing its smell. I knew this journey would change me, both inwardly and outwardly, and I had been looking forward to that feeling for a long time.

It was nearly 06:00 when sunbeams started to peep

through the shutters, drawing a golden stripe over the window. I rose and acted mechanically, taking a shower, brushing my teeth, and putting on my cycling outfit – cozy, cushioned pants to help my butt survive the long ride and a white, DriFIT T-shirt imprinted with the trip logo on the front and a slogan on the back, "When was the last time you helped a fellow human being?" which I wanted everybody driving by to notice.

I was all set, ready, and excited to go, my only wish being to get started, leaving my doorstep for the wide world. All the gear I had been toiling to acquire for long weeks was packed beside my bed. Peeping outside the window to check on the weather I was about to face, I smiled. I saw wet roads and blue, scarcely-clouded skies, promising a clear morning following a rainy night.

My experience from similar trips had taught me that first steps are very significant. All's well that starts well, while bad starts are more challenging and do not always lead to the planned ending; they always require exceptional mental strength. I remember very well that attempt when I, due to spontaneous stupidity, decided to jog with a back-pack all the way from the beach at Ashkelon to the beaches of Tel Aviv. That idea enchanted me back then, yet it took me no longer than a thirty-minute run near Nitzanim beach to realize how shitty it was going to be. It was the hottest day of the year, with the humidity of a Costa Rican rainforest. By the time I approached Palmachim beach, I had run out of water, twisted my ankle, and had to beg rides with my tail between my legs after running 50km in sweltering heat. It made me as frustrated as Sisyphus.

Since that debacle, I had become more experienced and had learned my lessons. Hurriedly packing the last missing items – a cell phone, toilet paper, and some energy snacks –

I texted my best friend, Eitan, who had asked to join me on my first day: "I'm off. See you at the southern gateway of Ashkelon."

Then I sipped my hot, black coffee and devoured my porridge oats and yogurt that I had stored the day before in the fridge. Excitedly, I gave the street a farewell glance.

I live on the third floor of an apartment building in the Barnea Quarter, one of Ashkelon's oldest districts, on a hilltop overlooking the Mediterranean to the west and the Judean Mountains to the east, views that have always filled me with tranquility.

I went through the door to the landing, which was still dark due to the early hour to tackle the stairs, carrying my bike. With it weighing no less than forty-five kilograms, I had to struggle with each and every step. Many minutes later, I found myself in the street, as ready and thrilled as a boy before his Bar Mitzvah.

Just as expected, the weather was perfect, the air soaked with the familiar smell of wet soil and the forecast promising a clear day. It was still cold, so I put on several glowing layers of cyclists' winter clothing.

My excitement was so overwhelming that even the pigeons perching on the rooftops of Har Knaan Street, who cooed me "Good morning!", seemed to be observing me as if they knew that I was on the verge of a great adventure. Closing my eyes, I let the earbuds deep in my ears pound my head with the sounds of Infected Mushroom, one of my favorite Israeli bands. Inhaling two lungfuls of fresh air, I mounted my heavy bike with a somewhat eager heart, and then – I charged on!

Since it was still very early, most of the streets were deserted. Riding along, I passed by the packs of newspapers and water bottles waiting in front of the local grocery store, and the still-closed post office. It already felt that the Sunday morning frenzy was about to begin. How lucky I would be to skip it all, I thought to myself.

My bike felt heavy but kept steady on the road, feeding me with a familiar wanderlust, that addictive desire to ride into the unknown. Suddenly, I started recalling moments from my previous trips, making me wonder why I didn't go on such trips more frequently. Apparently, the answer was that if I did, such a journey would have felt less enchanting, and therefore not have thrilled me so strongly. Actually, I cannot tell exactly which way is better.

Ten minutes later, I was out of Ashkelon, riding south on Route 4. The road was perfectly clear, as if somebody had carefully cleared it for Day One of my journey. At about 07:30, I met Eitan at the city's southern entrance.

He was a kibbutznik, a Yemenite with dark, curly hair, and though he was my classmate, he hadn't changed much since we had gone to the same religious high school in Kibbutz Yavneh. We had shared some dreams, such as traveling around the world the way we had sixteen years ago, flying to Australia and New Zealand, where we had some unforgettable experiences.

Another dream we shared was about opening a hostel on some alpine crest. Since our high school days, we had always ridiculed the way vital issues such as money, love or sex were so minimally addressed by those who educated us – that is, our teachers and parents alike. In this respect, we offered each other a sympathetic ear.

"Morning, buddy! What's up? Been waiting long?" I asked Eitan while dismounting.

"It's all good!" he replied. "I only got here a couple of minutes ago. You know the way it works in a kibbutz when you need a ride. It took ages to find the keys in the secretary's cabinet. But never mind, we sailed through. What about you? All set? Did you see how lucky we are to skip the rain?"

"Yeah, very lucky!" I agreed, suggesting we should take a selfie on the foggy roadside.

A professional photographer, Eitan accepted immediately, taking his camera out and shooting a series of pictures. Then we rode on to Sderot, a town where we expected my parents to be waiting for us with a small breakfast.

Eitan rode an ordinary city bike, unfit for a fast road ride, so we traveled at a convenient speed of fifteen to 20kph on average.

We were still on Route 4, on the outskirts of Sderot when my cellphone rang. It was my mother, eager to know my whereabouts and when I expected to arrive at the meeting point.

At first, I had wanted to just forget about my mom and dad, since on this trip I was on my own and my parents had nothing to do with it. Yet I hesitated, knowing that my parents – my mother, in particular – would respond over-dramatically, which I wanted to avoid.

After a twenty-kilometer ride, we reached the agreed meeting point, and my parents were already looming on the horizon. They were difficult to miss, especially my mother, whose highly emotional character drove her to cry out loud.

"Tzuri! Tzuri, we're here! Can you see us? Well done!" she cried, waving her hands.

They were standing at the bus stop where they had already set a makeshift breakfast table. I remember laughing endlessly at that surreal scene: two brown, wooden trays bearing rows of ten identical triangular sandwiches, each of different flavor, wrapped in plastic bags, alongside one yeast cake, sesame cookies, bananas, apples, two four-packs of yogurt, a pile of at least twenty of my favorite British snacks, namely Mars bars and Kit Kats, and, finally, a silver thermos filled with coffee, ready for pouring.

"Please, Mommy, don't be so over-dramatic," I begged her, telling my parents that Eitan and I only planned to spend a few minutes with them, though I thanked them carefully for the abundance of food they had brought.

"Didn't you go a little overboard with the food?" I had to ask, noticing the incredible feast.

"Well, grab as much as you can, I don't want you to run out of food on the road," my mother replied, concerned.

After spending a couple of minutes on the consumption of carbs in the form of sandwiches, cakes, and cookies, Eitan and I somehow managed to force all the chocolate my parents had brought into our saddlebags and, just when we were about to ride off, my parents wanted me to give them a few minutes more.

"Well, Eitan, are we off?" I asked my companion.

"I'm ready when you are," he replied, putting his helmet on.

After some hugging and kissing with my parents, we rode off, entering the town of Sderot. We kept riding south toward Kibbutz Ruhamah. Upon leaving the town, Eitan asked me a question.

"Do you remember the song we used to play whenever we wanted to feel like we were abroad for a while?"

"Sure, it was that hit of the Balagan band… what was its name?" I struggled.

"It was 'Abroad' sung by Dana Berger," Eitan replied, starting to hum the familiar tune. Riding alongside me on the curb, Eitan found that song on his cell phone to play us all the way through the Western Negev hills.

A few minutes later, we rode by Ariel Sharon's ranch, Kibbutz Dorot, and Kibbutz Ruhamah, approaching the crossroads before Beit Kama junction. All the while we had been yelling out loud the refrain, *"You probably won't come, but this is unimportant; imagine it's abroad, and that's okay."*

Traveling on the southern roads during the first few hours of our trip reminded me somewhat of my six-month journey across Europe several years earlier. Yet this journey had an entirely different purpose from any journey I had made since then. On those journeys, I was completely absorbed in the trip itself, detaching myself almost completely from the outer world.

I had decided to do this trip on my own, with no escort car. Despite being a great help and providing confidence, an escort car also makes you seriously dependent on external factors and forces you to worry about many more things, such as finding the driver's food and accommodation, as well as fueling the car, which significantly increases the trip's logistical problems and expenses.

This time, my purpose was to generate an altruistic discourse – to make people think about when they had done anything for their fellow man recently. I appropriately named this trip the Heart to Heart Journey as I put it in the fund-raising leaflets I planned to hand out along my route:

When was the last time you did anything for your fellow man? When was the last time you paused your daily business to give your fellow man a thought? I am neither preaching to you nor criticizing you. Rather, I am motivated by a genuine wish to make our society more open-hearted and generous.

The leaflet went on, declaring, giving, helping, and contributing to the community is an amazing source of satisfaction.

This trip stood for all the values that are the focus of my daily life: protecting the natural environment, a healthy way of life, and social solidarity.

This would be the very first time a cyclist had ridden around Israel over the course of several weeks. I was starting from Ashkelon, riding south to Mitzpe Ramon, and would go all the way to Eilat.

From there, I planned to turn north toward Jerusalem, Katzrin, Nahariya, and Haifa, then turn back to Ashkelon, covering a total distance of about 1200km. During the trip, I hoped to raise as much money as possible in aid of needy families and homeless people. How would it work?

Everyone who wanted to donate could make a money transfer to a special bank account or pay me in cash on meeting me during the journey. One could also donate through a PayBox application, available on any smartphone. The donations would be transferred to a special account on the app, allowing me to buy necessary items for the needy.

The trip itself: I would ride on the peripheral highways of the country, carrying all my food with me, plus clothing and camping equipment, and sleep outdoors except on days when I would pay my family or friends a visit. This was to minimize costs so that the bulk of the donations would reach those unfortunate families and homeless people who could use any possible help.

That day's schedule was to reach Kramim, an unusual kibbutz where orthodox and secular Jews lived together, realizing ideals such as conservation, tolerance, and ortho-dox-secular cooperation. My plan was to spend the night with my good friends, Shlomi and Daniela, and start off the following morning for a long, challenging ride to Mitzpe Ramon, 100km away.

I was riding with Eitan, to the sound of Metallica's

"Nothing Else Matters" on his cell phone, a song we loved and found calming. Then I realized it was a grave mistake to have scheduled a lecture for that night. I couldn't have imagined how much energy this riding would take and that upon reaching my destination, my top priority would not be speaking to a crowd, but rather to eat and get some sleep. However, since I had already scheduled the lecture, I had no choice.

At 12:30, we made it to Beit Kama Junction.

"Buddy, I do appreciate your coming along. It was too short! Too bad you can't ride on with me," I told Eitan.

"Too damn bad. It was great fun, though this ride's made my butt sore as hell. I can't figure out how you'll keep going like this for another three weeks," he replied, massaging his behind.

"Why don't you join me again later on?" I suggested.

"I doubt it. You know – work, wife, kids, and all that... actually, you don't," he replied with his usual sarcasm. "But I'll try my best, and if I can, I'll let you know."

I waited with him for his bus to arrive. When it did, we shook hands like two businessmen striking a deal, a gesture I always found odd among friends, and concluded our farewell with a warm hug.

It felt as if we had been riding together for an entire week, rather than five hours.

Once his bus had gone out of sight, I crossed Route 6, heading east toward Sansana Forest on the slopes of the Judean Mountains. Here, I planned to rest and eat a little, but since it was a transitional season, the weather was rather whimsical. That afternoon was hotter than usual, so I had to let my body adjust itself to the effort, avoiding overstrains right from the start. Therefore, my planned schedule guaranteed a gradual increase in strain. Experience of many years had taught me that it takes careful planning and addressing the whimsical forces of nature – namely the weather – to survive such a journey.

Against it, one is powerless. Thus, I had prepared and spared neither money nor effort in obtaining high-quality equipment and scheduling start-offs when the weather was as friendly as possible.

Route 3252, leading to Kibbutz Kramim, is a scenic road. Starting in a small valley surrounded by green wheat fields that make the road look wild, it ends with a steady, steep climb toward the community of Sansana, located on the ridgeline and surrounded almost entirely with Aleppo pines.

While I was slowly pedaling uphill, my mind started running through ways of gathering all my energy for my first lecture of this trip and convincing my friends to make donations to enable me to complete it. I had no idea what I'd plunged myself into or how my audience would respond to the presentation I had worked so hard to make.

The idea of speaking to a crowd of strangers felt awkward and challenging, and I became overwhelmed with anxiety. I remember wanting nothing but to get that lecture over with so that I could focus on riding to Eilat. It felt like a pain in the neck that I wished to get over as soon as possible.

I arrived at Kramim 70km later, toward 16:00.

I have known Shlomi and Daniela since we had gone to the same elementary school. A couple of years before, they had left Kadesh Barnea, a community located on the Egyptian border, with their children, to start a new life in Kramim. I could always communicate with them and whenever we met, whether on a trip or desert weekend, we bonded strongly. They always kept an open house, always amazing me with manifestations of their generosity. I was so happy to have friends like them, already familiar with my numerous eccentricities, so it warmed my heart to know I was about to see them. Arriving at their home, I rested my bike against their wall and knocked on the door. Answering the door, Daniela couldn't believe I'd made it with all the equipment I was carrying.

She immediately started helping me with the sound system for my lecture. Meanwhile, the smell of her vegan dinner provoked my already mounting appetite.

At 21:00, I set off for the local club, hoping to see some real crowds there, since it was important for me to drive home the purpose of this trip to people. Despite my great excitement, my weariness started to take its toll, and my thoughts were split between the lecture and next day's uphill ride, during which I was about climb all the way to Mitzpe Ramon, braving the wintry weather – as I was about to find out the hard way.

The lecture was successful, collecting several hundreds' of dollars in cheques and money transfers despite technical mishaps such as power outages, screen failures, and software bugs throughout the lecture – as usual. Somewhat dispirited by these annoyances, I realized there was nothing I could do except learn from my experience and hope to avoid them next time.

After the lecture, I spent some time with Shlomi, my old friend since I was seven years of age, laughing our way down memory lane, while talking of plans for the distant future. The lighthearted atmosphere was only enhanced by the hot tea and Daniela's quite addictive homemade cookies. We went on dreaming together about motorbiking through northern India, a dream we will probably realize someday.

Just before retiring to my bedroom, I presented to

Shlomi my next day's route, as well as the challenging weather I expected to deal with. Next thing I remembered, I was getting up in the dead of night to pee. Then I was back in the cozy bed, where fatigue combined with the silence to knock me out, with the light – and my shoes – still on.

2

DAY 2

"That man is richest whose pleasures are cheapest."

Henry David Thoreau

March 28, 2016
Starting point: Kibbutz Kramim
Destination: Mitzpe Ramon city
Distance: 100 kilometers

At 05:30 and near 0°C outside, it was extremely cold for a desert morning even before the chill of riding in the wind started to take effect.

Shlomi's and Daniela's warm hospitality restored the energy I needed to ride on. Putting on all the thermal clothing I had, I took a sip of my strong, black coffee and took my leave of the people of Kibbutz Kramim.

I felt good about Day Two of my Heart to Heart Journey, though my legs felt a little heavy, which was not unfamiliar to me. Turning my eyes to the skies, I found it to be blue, with tints of azure, orange and white, especially in the east, where day was breaking, and I smiled. If I had known what weather and physical challenges this day had in store for me, I would never have grinned so much! Luckily, I didn't, so I didn't bother to think about what might go wrong. Instead, I focused on the here and now, trusting that when I reached each bridge, I could cross it.

I had been looking forward for a long time to cycling through this remote, desert part of the country, mentally preparing to be almost completely on my own. The area beyond the Beersheba-Mitzpe Ramon line is sparsely populated and has very few facilities useful to a cyclist.

Therefore, for this trip, I had to obtain the best cycling and camping equipment available in order to sail through challenging conditions. It takes a lot of adventuring and survival skills to undertake such a project and, of course, the ability to adapt to the desert's challenging weather and natural conditions – not to mention a high degree of physical fitness.

I also believe that confidence and general knowledge are keys to the success of such a trip, just like any enterprise involving uncertainties and countless accidents. This is exactly what Day two of my trip was like.

When I left Kramim that morning, the forecast promised an easy day. However, nature had her own plans, which ido not always match ours. Near Ramat Hovav, a strong wind got up, making me realize that something bad was building up. Thirty minutes later, the sun was hiding behind dark clouds and the temperature dropped.

Wind has a very powerful effect on a cyclist, making it the number one enemy of all cyclists, regardless of cycling experience. Riding on Route 40, heading for Tlalim Junction, I felt the wind intensifying, which usually meant that some rain was about to join the fun. I love wintertime and rain always makes me feel lively, like it's the best show in town.

However, my love was put to the test once I neared Kibbutz Sde Boker, when the rain started whipping me my face with a force I hadn't felt for a long time.

I instantly decided to make a stop at the first possible shelter to change into more appropriate clothing. As if the wind and the lashing rain weren't enough, a few minutes later my lungs and eyes started taking in an irritating mixture of thick desert fog and sand.

"Dammit! What the fuck!" I mumbled from under that balaclava that separated my skull from my helmet, leaving only my eyes exposed. Although I never thought to yield and stop, the conditions became increasingly challenging, and it really made me pissed to go through such an ordeal as early as Day Two.

Withdrawing into myself, as I did whenever I faced a challenge, I decided to break this project into many minor goals, conquering them one by one. So now I looked ahead, searching for my first minor goal – any road sign or traffic sign, or some dry hill next to the road.

Riding a 45kg bicycle against a nearly 100kph wind is difficult. It is a challenging aerobic exercise, involving a lot of concentration. I had to firmly grasp the handlebars and stay fully focused so as not to drift into the middle of the road while pedaling. In the raging wind, the heavy bike was hard handle, and I made no progress, no matter how hard I pedaled. This, of course, was a deceptive feeling, and I was sure it was the struggle with the wind gradually exhausting me.

Forward visibility became so poor that I could see no further than ten meters in any direction.

"Come on!" I kept pepping up myself, attempting to

restore my rather shattered fighting spirit. "There must be a gas station nearby. Dammit, there's got to be!"

After about half an hour of head-on struggle against the wind, I was all too happy to see the Tlalim Junction gas station, which was engulfed with whirling sands. I dismounted right at its entrance and rushed inside for shelter. Taking my coffee kit out, I started brewing a cup of coffee with tons of sugar and preparing a bowl of yogurt and muesli to refuel before riding on. I was definitely exhausted but had yet to ride another 50km uphill to Mitzpe Ramon, my Day Two destination. I knew I only needed a few minutes to recover.

While the coffee brewed, I turned my cell phone on and immediately saw many unread WhatsApp messages, mostly encouragement from friends and relatives. Yet one message dumbfounded me; it was from one of my swimming group from a couple of years ago: "Hi, Tzuri, hope you're well. I've been following you on social media. Please give me your bank account info, so I can donate 1000 USD for your journey now. BTW, I'd like to donate some money to you every couple of days, so don't you dare to break down and quit! If you need anything, just tell me. Take care and come home safely. P.S. We're having a triathlon event in a couple of weeks, so hurry up. Ehud."

His message put a big smile on my face, making me forget for a short while about my semi-breakdown and the raging weather. I remember how that message infused me with strength even more than the coffee and muesli combined, so I texted my sincere thanks back to Ehud.

Then, putting my cell phone into the back pocket of my shirt, to sip my coffee, I had a revelation. All of a sudden, I realized that people were actually following my trip, and some did care about it. Although I planned to interest as many people as possible, the hard evidence of my plan starting to work astonished and thrilled me, making me decide that, no matter how tough it might get, there was no way that I'd stop!

The plan I'd been working on for a long time actually worked! I felt like an artist whose masterpiece was starting to take shape. Checking the donation bank account, I learned that the balance had doubled since yesterday, reaching 3,000 dollars!

"Yes!" I yelled, excited. "Yes! I'm making it!"

"Are you okay?" One of the convenience store workers was showing an interest. He was a chubby guy with a goatee, wearing a black uniform and a red baseball hat and was in the middle of arranging chocolate snacks on the shelves.

"Yes, it's a milk and honey life!" I reassured him.

"Superb, bro. Tell me, are you positive you want to ride on right now? Have you seen what's going on outside?" he asked, drawing on his cigarette.

"Definitely. I won't be stopped by some rain and dust. In the worst case, I can set up a tent and spend the night on the roadside."

"Well, what can I say? Be well... and can you give me some of whatever you're smoking? You look absolutely stoned."

He eyed me as if I'd just landed from another planet, and then sure that I had lost it completely, he nodded his head to indicate that he'd be happy to watch my stuff while I was in the bathroom.

When I returned, he was posing for a selfie with my heavy bike between his legs, a cigarette in one hand and his cell phone in the other. I watched him and laughed myself silly at the sight. When he finished, he asked me for a selfie with him. I accepted, naturally.

Noticing the time on his cell phone screen, I learned that I had already spent an hour in the gas station, so it was time to move on.

The winds were still raging, and the dust was still whirling madly. I couldn't make out the horizon, and the storm didn't seem to be dying down. Checking the weather radar on my cell, I was happy to learn that most of the rain had already passed over, which meant the storm would soon subside.

Encouraged, I immediately set off on Route 40, heading for Sde Boker, my last stop before Mitzpe Ramon. The ride was still rough, and I was sweating like a marathon runner in mid-August in all my layers of clothing. I decided to stop after every thirty minutes, to take a rest for a few minutes or until I started shivering – whichever came first – and then ride for another thirty minutes.

Pedaling kept me warm, so the sweat absorbed by my clothes did not affect my body temperature. It only bothered me during the stops, when the wind hitting my sweat-soaked clothes made my body temperature drop, my teeth chatter, and my body shudder disturbingly, as if I'd lost control over my system. I decided to shorten my stops to overcome this.

I was riding on a well-maintained and broad road. After I turned left, heading for the Nahal Havarim trail, the road wound to the left, starting a 70km climb to Ein Avdat Canyon. The climb was not easy for me, so I shifted into the lowest gear possible, letting my feet propel me slowly but steadily throughout the climb. I maintained the routine with a few minutes of rest once every thirty minutes until I made it to Ein Avdat Canyon.

Then, the skies started clearing – at last! – letting the warm afternoon sun caress me. It felt like I was gradually thawing out. Mitzpe Ramon was still a 25km-long climb away. It is about 900 meters above sea level. At Ein Avdat's gas station café, I made a stop, ordering the largest cup of the strongest coffee they had. After stuffing my mouth with an energy snack and some dates, I mounted my bike again since I wanted to reach Mitzpe Ramon before nightfall.

Aware that from now on the ride would be slower due to the many climbs, combined with my increasing fatigue, every minute mattered. Most of the Sde Boker to Mitzpe Ramon road runs between rugged hills with sparse vegetation and golden rocks, which makes the black road look like an alien body winding through the landscape. Usually, during long, exhausting rides, I try to enjoy the wild landscapes engulfing me, but this time, I just withdrew into myself, thinking of nothing except my immediate goal: reaching that day's destination quickly and safely.

Toward 17:00, I arrived at Mitzpe Ramon, accomplishing a 100km ride. Stopping at the curb, I took a selfie next to the town's name sign and then rolled on until the first square. I needed some hot food and a drink before choosing where to camp that night.

At the city's business center, by the main road, I spotted an old wooden bench in the middle of an unkempt lawn. Using the very last hours of daylight, I decided to call it a day and prepared to stop for the night. I dismounted my bike heavily. My legs were stone-hard, and my face was coated with a thin layer of dust from that day's ride.

First, I took off my sweat-soaked clothes, spreading them on the bench to dry. Next, I took off my raincoat and then my shirt. My black balaclava had turned beige from the desert dust. A few minutes later, an old man approached, asking if everything was okay, telling me there was a hotel nearby if I needed a place to stay. Thanking him, I reassured him I was fine, just a little tired after riding.

It made me smile to think I looked so alien to the local urban landscape. As a matter of fact, it felt good to realize that I had finally entered the phase of my trip where I faced the forces of nature, and it may become a journey into my soul.

While my clothes were drying out, I went to the nearby diner to order hot lentil soup, a large dish of hummus, and three hot pitas. Their smell invaded my nostrils, giving me a few minutes of goose-pimples. It was only then that I realized how hungry and completely exhausted I was, with no energy left at all.

I decided I must do everything I could to regain my strength before nightfall, when I planned to set up camp somewhere and go to sleep. My previous trips had taught me that sufficient sleep and good nutrition were essential for restoring energy before facing the next day's challenges.

While eating my last pita, I decided to look for a camping place on the north side of Makhtesh Ramon wall, on the Sculpture Trail, with a view of the crater. When I gathered my clothes, they were still damp from my sweat, but I had no choice and started looking for a spot protected from the wind and the cold desert night, preferably with a beautiful view. After a couple of minutes of exploration, I found the perfect spot: a small hollow about ten meters away from the edge of the main crater and fifty meters from the trail. In front of me spread a panoramic view of Makhtesh Ramon.

When night fell, the storm, which had been raging all day, died out. Under the faint starlight, the crater offered a stunning view. The moon slowly rising from the east tinted the crater bed, or so it seemed from my tent, with surreally dark hues. That evening was mystically transformed from a physical and mental struggle with nature, to some supernatural connection with that primordial creation. It felt like some infighting was going on: my exhausted physique, craving some rest, struggled with my psyche, which was crowing ever stronger, inspired by the wilderness surrounding me.

I felt as if my body, worn out by the last two days' efforts, was practically melting away under the moon. At the same time, I was restoring my mental energy, anticipating another day of challenging rides and endless roads, which might bring new insights.

At 19:00, I set up my tent and started to prepare for the night. As a precaution against thieves, I locked my bike to my tent pole. This way, anybody who planned to claim it would also have to take my tent and my person with him. To be on the safe side, I also brought all my stuff inside the tent, leaving nothing outside but the bike and water bottles.

I guess my tent was probably the most important item on all my journeys. It was a resilient, high-quality, four-season tent, 90cm wide and 100cm high, perfectly suitable for me with enough room for one person with equipment, resistant to rain, hail, and strong winds, fitting any possible weather in Israel. After using a two-season tent on short trips, I realized I need something more resistant. The next quality level was a five-season tent, used by mountaineering expeditions dealing with snowstorms and subzero cold.

When I'd completed my camping preparations, I had time to text all my relatives and friends, reassuring them that I was okay and informing them of my location. I also had to update my social media followers about my condition, total location accounts, and my destination for the next day. Communicating my messages was essential for the fund-raising.

Once I was done with the updating, I sat down on my small inflatable mattress inside my tent and wrapped myself up tight in my sleeping bag. Then, fastening my headlamp to my head, I updated my travel log, as I always have whenever I can:

I have just accomplished a 100km-long ride in six hours of cycling through challenging terrain and weather, in the remote yet beautiful Negev Plateau. On this trip, I have had to endure devilish winds, incessant rain, and got so fed up with dates that I nearly threw away my whole pack.

I somehow felt as if I had to pass some kind of test before Nature let me into her great desert as if she wanted to drive it home to me who runs the show, and gosh, I loved it! I loved the challenges the elements threw at me since I truly believe that fortune only puts us to tests that match our powers. Therefore, we must rejoice at any such test, and the greater the challenge, the prouder we should be, since, deep down, we know we can make it, and it's only up to us.

After several hours of rather nightmarish riding, when I passed by Sde Boker on my way to Ein Avdat, I felt the wind slightly calming down. It was then I realized I'd passed Nature's test, so, for the time being, she allowed me to ride on, south, toward Eilat. Right now, I'm lying on my back in my small tent with a big smile on my face. Maybe my brain's overwhelmed with endorphins, which makes me write all these hallucinations. However, seeing all that sympathy from people all over the country, and receiving all these donations, I feel a great satisfaction and excitement that I haven't experienced for a long time!

I closed my log, putting it in the same bag that I use to keep my copy of Murakami's *Kafka on The Shore* and dived deep into my cozy sleeping bag. My experiences of the two previous days and my expectations of what this trip had in store for me kept me from sleeping.

Despite my exhaustion and drooping eyes, a lot went through my mind, such as ways of cycling better the next day, the 160km trip to Eilat and, above all, whether I was capable of hitting the goal I had set myself: traveling the planned route within 22 days and raising at least 20,000 USD. All that kept bothering me, and the jackals howling nearby only enhanced my unrest.

The silence outside and the cold finally lured me out of my tent, taking me to the edge of the crater to gaze at the horizon. Then and there, it didn't bother me. I was barefoot, shivering, and practically naked, except for my underwear. I just let nature engulf me; I was puzzled by my indifference to the 1°C cold surrounding me.

At that very moment, I recalled what I had once read about Native American culture. Unlike Western culture, it assigns all creatures, large and small – be they microbes or mammoths, blue-blooded royalty, or blue-collar laborers – the very same significance in sustaining the universe.

After nearly freezing to death outside, I rushed back into my tent, zipping it tight-shut and falling fast asleep, as only a desert night allows you to.

The next day, I was up at 07:00 to a morning even colder than the previous night – so cold that I filled the air with steam whenever I breathed out. I unzipped my tent to look at the landscape, only to see blinding sunlight filling the colossal crater. I knew the sunrise over Mitzpe Ramon was famously beautiful, but this scene was like nothing I had seen since I first embarked on this journey. It felt like the world's most magnificent show, staged especially for me.

The sky started turning bluish with not a cloud in sight,

which promised a rather warm, rainless day. Though mesmerized by the sight of the rising sun, my ass still felt cramped and as stiff as the desert rocks, and my legs started aching from the last two days' riding, mainly in the quadriceps.

I crawled out of my tent to do some stretches and yoga exercises, to help me wake my body up after my long sleep and prepare it for another day of physical strain. Between exercises, I packed up my stuff, getting ready to ride on south.

I was nearly finished when I noticed a small cloud of dust approaching from the west along the trail leading to Mitzpe Ramon. Guessing it was just some vehicle, I ignored it and went about my business. A few minutes later, a small, blue Suzuki Samurai stopped next to me.

"Good morning!" The driver opened her front window, greeting me in English with a strong local accent.

"Good morning," I returned the greeting. "To you, too," I added in Hebrew.

"Gosh, how surreal! I took you for a tourist! So, what's your game? There must be very few local nuts who'd be camping and cycling out here," she replied, eyeing my bike.

"Well, I'm one-hundred percent made-in-Israel. May I ask what you're doing out here at such an early hour?" I enquired, stirring my brewing coffee.

"Well, I have a few days off, so I'm just off to the desert. By the way, I'm Maya. Nice to meet you."

"Would you like a sip of my coffee?" I asked her, stirring it.

"Thanks, I'd love some." She accepted, turning the engine off, and hopped out of her car.

Raising my eyes from the coffee pot, I noticed that Maya looked fabulous – a tiny, perfectly-shaped ass in perfectly-fitting jeans. She must exercise a lot, I thought. Jogging or dancing? Maybe yoga? She wore blue jeans, a black fleece, and Australian-made Redback boots in a yellowish hue that blended with the desert hues. Her dark hair was covered by an orange-and-black striped scarf.

Her smiling, freckled face made her look cheerful and optimistic. Still, I remember that I couldn't figure out what business she had being in the desert all alone so early in the morning.

"You look all dressed and set up to conquer the wilderness. Or maybe your thing is just riding in your Jeep?" I observed.

"I still have to figure out the details, but I'm certainly not planning to go back to Tel Aviv soon," she clarified.

"Here's your coffee. By the way, I'm Tzuriel. Nice to meet you," I introduced myself.

"Thanks. So, what are you up to, with your bike and stuff?" she enquired, closely examining my bike.

"Long story. In short, I'm on a trip around the country, raising funds for needy families and homeless people. I left Ashkelon a couple of days ago, heading for Eilat, and plan to get back to Ashkelon in a couple of weeks, a few days before Passover."

"Wait a sec! That's totally crazy! You mean you're riding around the country on your own?! No escort? Who carries your food and water? Aren't you afraid?"

"No escort, on my own, carrying all my food and water with me." I confirmed her suspicions.

"C'mon! Get real! You carry it all in these small bags?! You mean this is all your stuff?! That's insane! Gosh, it's so cool! To be honest, it's exceptionally unique of you – to fear nothing at all!" she giggled, "and I thought I'd met my share of loonies... Wow, you must have some fascinating adventure stories to tell," she remarked playfully. "Listen, sorry for running into you this way, first thing in the morning. You seem to be a lone wolf, in a good way. Am I right? Well, if I'm standing in your way, I'm off."

"Not at all, it's okay. I could use some pleasant company. Regarding the lone wolf thing, you aren't the first to tell me that, so who am I to argue?" I replied with a touch of mystery.

It took me no more than a few minutes' conversation to realize that Maya and I were singing the same tune, even though I still couldn't get what exactly she was doing there at 07:00 in the morning, but I chose not to pry since I didn't care. However, I found her absolutely intriguing, graceful, and naturally great-looking, which is always nice in a girl.

I made another round of black coffee for two, and when she brought a pack of addictive Tim Tam biscuits from her Jeep I thought to myself that she was my kind of woman.

"Would you like one?" she offered.

"Would I like one!?" I laughed. "Are you kidding? If you don't eat up the whole pack, I will! Tim Tams in the middle of the desert is one of the best things in the world. Give me two of those..."

We drank our morning coffee and enjoyed lively conversation for a few minutes, but then an awkward silence fell, only disturbed by the sounds of the desert and us sucking the Tim Tams.

Suddenly, she broke the silence, "How about joining me for a few hours' walk today? You can put your stuff in my car, and we'll get back when you like. There's some lake nearby I'm dying to see, and, since it looks like it's going to be hot, it'll be really cool to take a dip... you look like a swimmer, so what do you say to that?" she asked with a naughty smile.

"Gosh, sounds inviting, but I planned a really long ride today, and I don't know if it fits in my schedule"

"C'mon, Tzuriel! I'll give you more Tim Tams if you come along!"

Laughing loudly, I gave in: "Well, I'm convinced. But it's only for the Tim Tams – clear!"

We secured my bike to the Jeep roof, placing my stuff in her vehicle, and at 08:00 we started toward the lake. She tuned her navigation app to Mitzpe Ramon Colored Sands, and it told her they were a ten-minute drive away.

The parking lot by the lake was shrouded in an unusual, awe-inspiring silence. Maya got out, walked a few meters the other way, and climbed up a big rock, where she just stood for quite a few minutes, gazing at the horizon. She was definitely going through something, I thought, wondering once again what drove such a woman to such a place at such a time.

While she was away, I updated my social media followers about my location.

"Will you come to the lake with me? It's over there, a few minutes' walk away." She pointed.

"Yes, I'll be right there, just let me send some messages," I told her.

Instead of waiting for me, she just descended toward the water, out of sight. When I caught up with her, that small yet colorful pond displayed all its splendor to me: the crater wall right next to it was embedded with colorful sand. Some of the sand fell into the lake, adding a touch of orange to the strong turquoise color of the clear water.

"I need to take a pee. The coffee's starting to take effect," I told Maya. "Can you keep an eye on the stuff for a few minutes?"

"Sure, you're free to go."

When I got back a few minutes later, she was out of sight, which sent alarming thoughts through my mind – namely Maya running away with my stuff. This sent me sprinting toward the lake. Reaching the spot where we had parted, I was relieved to see familiar black fleece, a black balaclava, and a folded pair of jeans resting on the rock, and next to them, a pair of familiar boots.

"Will you make me wait for you all alone, in the deep water?" I was surprised to hear a shout from the middle of the lake.

"What the hell are you doing out there?" I cried back, realizing she was only in her underwear. And I thought I was the loony one...

To plunge in or not to plunge in, this was the question I presented to myself. Since I knew practically nothing about her, my mind sounded the alarm.

Well, a woman I had met only a few minutes ago was asking me to join her in the water, where she was practically naked... it sounded interesting enough. However, I'd already had my share of adventures, and my planned around-the-country journey promised me more than enough thrills. Besides, just then, I didn't feel the urge for a woman's tender touch although in my everyday life I'm up for it. As had happened on previous trips, here, too, I had all the excitement, joy, and satisfaction I needed from nature. Thus, when I meet good-looking women, I don't always feel attracted to them, and Maya, too, despite the charms she'd tried to use on me today, left me indifferent.

She got out of the water and started walking toward me. Once I realized properly that she wore nothing but a white bra and panties, I called to her, "Okay, you win again! I'm coming, stay where you are!"

"Excellent. Hurry up, the water's great!" she replied, swimming back to the middle of the colorful lake.

Well, if she's going wild, so will I, I thought to myself, undressing down to my boxer briefs, which somehow blended with the desert hues perfectly.

Swimming toward her, I met her in the middle of the pond.

"Well, I see I was right when I called you a swimmer. By the way, you look gorgeous in these red briefs. You really blend with the desert," she laughed, adding, "Do you always swim with strangers in the middle of nowhere?"

"Do you usually seduce innocent strangers in the middle of nowhere?"

"Yeah, right... you're the embodiment of innocence," she taunted me.

She seemed to be teasing me, the way she stretched her breasts on the water. I struggled to ignore her body language, yet I was repeatedly hearing warnings: "Keep away, don't fall for it. Something here looks too good to be true."

After about thirty minutes of chatting and swimming, we waded out of the lake at the same time, saying nothing, only examining each other. No doubt there was something in the air. Maya, observing my physical response to her, just smiled silently. Feeling slightly embarrassed, we dried ourselves, got dressed, and started walking toward the Maale Ramon hike.

Hiking in Makhtesh Ramon was refreshing after two days in the saddle. Realizing I was not going to ride that day, I started thinking about sleeping arrangements and what I should do next. Eventually, we got back to the spot where her car waited.

"Tonight, I'm staying at the town's guesthouse. It'd be nice of you to drop me there," I told her.

"No problem, just guide me there and we'll say goodbye, and maybe we'll meet again, someday."

"What are your plans, Maya? Any ideas about where you want to go from here?"

"Nothing specific, but I think I'll drive on to Eilat, where I have things to do for the next couple of days. How about swapping numbers, to keep in touch?" she asked as she drove.

"I'd love to. Just get me to the guest house, so we can say goodbye properly."

My friends had told me a lot of good things about that Green Backpackers guest house, about a four-minute walk away from Camel Lookout Hill, near Mitzpe Ramon. It was a very special, international-style place, situated on the cliff overlooking the basin. I was surprised to hear the receptionist addressing me in English and noticed that most of the guests were overseas tourists.

It was a warm, family establishment with a small, carpeted lobby, resembling a private living room. A bookshelf packed with travel literature stood behind a sofa. The wall facing the main entrance was covered with a huge map of the globe, stabbed with hundreds of pins marking the guests' places of origin from the last couple of years. Next to it was a kitchenette for guests to make their own meals.

Entering the lobby, I saw tourists on their laptops and smartphones, while others sat outside on hammocks and chairs listening to world music and drinking beer and coffee. The receptionist showed me my room, which had three bunk beds, letting me choose my bunk.

Naturally, I chose a bottom one. Judging from the stuff in the room, it was already occupied by another two tourists.

After I had arranged my bags under my bed, I went outside to lock my bike, where Maya was waiting for me, and we went to have a farewell coffee.

It was already past 18:00 and the sun was no longer shining over Mitzpe Ramon, so the temperature had dropped significantly, which made us want to get to the café as soon as possible. Once we got there, we swapped numbers and a long, warm farewell handshake, but not before I thanked Maya for the ride and the walk.

However, as I turned back to the guest house, I saw her Jeep stopping by me, and she lowered the front window to ask: "Tell me, lone wolf, are you heading for Eilat?"

"I am. First thing tomorrow morning I start out for Shittim, and, hopefully, reach Eilat in two days."

"Fine, just take care of yourself, okay? And drop me a word once in a while... don't be shy." She smiled at me from under her wool cap. Waving goodbye to me, she blew a brief kiss into her car air, and then drove on into town.

When I got back to my room, the cozy bed sent me into a long and pleasant sleep.

3

DAY 3

"The journey, not the destination matters".

T.S. Eliot

March 30, 2016
Starting point: Mitzpe Ramon city
Destination: Shittim
Distance: 73 kilometers

I set my cell phone alarm to 05:00, long before sunrise in order to enjoy the sight of the sun rising over Makhtesh Ramon, one of the world's most beautiful landscapes.

My roommates were still sleeping, so I cleared the room and repacked my many bags outside to avoid disturbing them. It was only by 06:00, after having a light breakfast, that I crossed the road, quickly reaching the edge of the crater.

The sky started to assume the magnificent orange, red, and even yellow hues of sunrise, which even spread to the sparse clouds dotting the sky. It was terribly cold and, since I had forgotten my gloves, my frozen fingers struggled with the camera.

Spotting a large rock, I sat down on it. Then I spotted a few other freaks who had got up early enough to watch the sunrise from the cliff. I guess it was the first time any of us had enjoyed such a spectacle.

Toward 07:00, I jogged back to the guesthouse to get warm and started my final preparations for crossing the Makhtesh. My immediate challenge was the steep descent to the crater. Since the temperature where I stood was only about five degrees, I put on every clothing item available, expecting the wind to lower the temperature to zero inside the crater.

I planned to get to Shittim that day, a tiny community about 72km south of Mitzpe Ramon. It is a kind of Israeli ashram, one of a kind in the country. Since it is situated next to Route 40, one of the country's most remote routes, I had to make a stop there. From Shittim south, there were neither human settlements, gas stations where I could get water, nor even bus stops to shelter me from the scorching sun. Because of that, I loaded my bike with nearly 15 liters of water for drinking, brewing coffee, preparing meals, brushing my teeth, and – when I got lucky – indulging in a brief, makeshift shower from a bottle.

I parted from the guesthouse staff and the tourists I had met there, rolling over to Route 40, which ran across Makhtesh Ramon. The descent was as freezing as I expected it to be, the cold penetrating every square millimeter of my skin. Yet I cared not about the cold, but only about the view unfolding before me as I dashed to the bed of the crater. The crater walls, tens of meters high, rose suddenly north of the road, tinted brown and yellow by the rising sun. The serpentine road cut through the rocks and formed a composition only nature can create: the black, man-made asphalt with the white line in the middle seemed to fit almost naturally in the golden desert land.

For a few minutes, this view weakened a little of the effect of the cold biting me through my coat. It even thrilled me enough to scream all the way down. The GoPro camera mounted on my helmet documented every single second of the descent, and only ten minutes later, when it was all over, did I turn it off.

After making a stop to take off some layers of clothing, I rode on. I had cycled for fifteen minutes on a completely deserted road overlooked by hills, the colossal Makhtesh Ramon cliff rising behind me, when I suddenly spotted two dots advancing toward me along the road. Unable to discern them, I assumed them to be pedestrians or motorcyclists. This unusual sight made me speed up, and then I learned they were cyclists just like me, dust-covered and loaded with saddlebags. I was pleasantly surprised to see them.

As soon as we met, I realized they were foreigners, so I asked them if they needed some help since they didn't look very well, to say the least, their lips looked parched with thirst. They turned out to be Czech tourists traveling from Egypt to Tel Aviv. Both were tall, their brown hair turned grey with the dust they had gathered on the roads. They had off-road bikes fitted for road trips, with broad, dusty tires, and bags stuffed with cyclists' equipment and spare parts such as tubes and spare tires attached to the rear of their bikes. In addition, they wore windbreakers and long bike pants. All that indicated they had been traveling through really remote areas with no repair shops.

We got off the road, putting our bikes aside. A short talk with them revealed they had been ill-prepared for a desert trip since they were now suffering from dehydration. Right away, I let them drink their fill and even filled all their water bottles, asking whether they needed anything else. At that moment, I ignored the consequences of carelessly going on with less than a liter of water for a two-day ride.

Only a few minutes later, it struck me what a mess I had got myself into; so while the Czechs were having a rest, I looked for a way out. I had only two options: either ride on with only a little water, or ride all the way back to town, dealing with the short, yet very hard climb to get a new supply of water, and then descending once again into the crater.

Trying to avoid the impression of regretting offering my help, I told them that if they started off right away, they would reach the town within an hour and find sufficient food and water supplies. So, I headed back for Mitzpe Ramon.

I felt so damn foolish giving away all my water and forgetting my own welfare. Luckily, it had happened near a human settlement. Had it happened at a greater distance, I would have been in really big trouble.

After exchanging cellphone numbers and email addresses for sending each other our photos, I pointed out the shortest way to Mitzpe Ramon and we said our good-byes. I couldn't wait for them to set off so that I could follow them. Since they seemed to travel fast, I had no problem trailing them without them noticing me.

An hour later, I reached Mitzpe Ramon, luckily spotting a gas station right at the entrance to the town. Refilling my water bottles, I started off again toward Route 40, hoping to reach Shittim as soon as possible since I was now two hours behind schedule. I struggled to dispel the bad feeling I had because of the blunder with my water, trying to focus on the here and now.

It was warmer now than it had been earlier that morning, which allowed me to ride in short leggings and my
yellow shirt with the three one-direction back pockets
located a little above the waist. Cyclists like these pockets
because they allow you to stuff them with necessary items
you can take out while riding. I stuffed mine with energy
snacks, my cell phone, and headphones for music to pass
the time. I spent the entire day on Route 40, which took me
across the wide Wadi Paran and the notoriously steep climb
out of the wadi.

I believe this climb is a must-do for every challenge-
loving road cyclist. The combination of the silence in the
wilderness, the steep slope, and the narrow road that leaves
very little room for error can put your stamina and riding
skills to an enjoyable test. The steep descent to Wadi Paran
was the most trying of the day, making me roll down at
about 60 kph. The speed didn't trouble me since my bike
had strong disk-brakes that are more reliable than the traditional rubber pads. What did trouble me was the wind from
the wadi, threatening to blow me off balance.

After about a fifteen-minute descent, I reached the last,
steepest part and saw a steep road climbing up 500 meters
to the south. This indicated that I was traveling at a good
speed. Judging from my previous trips, I concluded that I
might reach Shittim on time, despite the morning delay.

That road was the Mitzpe Ramon-Eilat highway, part of
Route 40. Climbing at a very steep gradient from the Wadi
Paran bed, it goes south and then east toward Paran cliffs
and Ovil plain. Later on, I learned that Ovil had been some
biblical guy who had tended King David's camels.

Riding uphill, I also observed the fissure along which
the road ran. One could hardly overlook the ancient, white

limestone rocks south of the road, and the younger and harder brown and beige rocks north of the road.

Reaching the top, I had to stop for a few minutes to regain my normal pulse, while also checking the distance left to Shittim, my remaining water, and the general condition of my bike after having put it through an extreme descent and an extreme climb. I carried out a technical check-up at least once a day to avoid unpleasant surprises.

According to my maps, I had 20km to go. I was determined to make no stops until I reached Shittim and then decide whether I should stop for the night or ride on. When I reached my destination, it was 30°C, so I desperately looked for shade and a little water to cool down a little. The rest I had there made me forget about the morning blunder of giving away my water to the Czechs. On the other hand, it made me terribly hungry. I could think of nothing but food.

I reached for the only available food I had at that moment – a banana and an energy snack – devouring them mechanically, not bothering to chew. My robot-like responses to such circumstances amused me.

The eating made me oblivious of three young people approaching me. One was a guy wearing a pair of psychedelic-colored Sirwal pants with Rasta braids covering a slim, naked upper body all the way down to his ass. Next to him walked two Nordic-looking women in their twenties.

One of them, too, had long Rasta braids, while the other's hair was short-cropped. The latter caught my attention right away as she reminded me of Demi Moore as Navy SEAL G.I. Jane.

One could hardly ignore their scanty clothing. Both girls wore very short jeans, hiking sandals, and thin T-shirts that barely hid their bra-less breasts.

"What's up, dude?" I asked the Sirwal guy. "Got a light? I need to light my camp gas burner."

"Sure, brother, here, with love," he replied, handing me a gigantic Zippo lighter. "What's your game? Where are you going?" he enquired sitting down next to me. His odor was an awful composition of sweat and incense, making me wonder how the two girls failed to smell it.

"I'm on my way to Eilat where I plan to give a lecture in a pub. If you happen to be there, be my guest, and your two friends as well," I explained. He translated our conversation into English for the two foreign girls, who were busy rolling up fags for all of us.

"Would you like to join us?" asked the short-cropped one in English with a heavy German accent.

"Umm... join for what?" I asked, slightly laughing.

"For a joint, of course. What were you thinking?" The guy made it clear.

"I don't know," I said. "Let me think it over for a few minutes. I'll fill you in."

Once they realized my thing was not smoking and drinking, we went our separate ways.

The owners of the hostel still had not given me a clear answer to my request to stay for the night and so I made up my mind not to waste time and rode off on Route 40 while there were daylight and traveler-friendly weather.

On my trip's Facebook page, I informed my followers that my next destinations were Uvda Airport and Shaharut village, one of Israel's most remote communities. I also texted my family, informing them of my location and telling them I was about to ride another 36km south on Route 40, and then turn onto Route 12.

The trip to the airport proved to be shorter than the ride earlier that day. The further south I went, the better the weather, which increased my speed. This seriously boosted my morale, and I was already dreaming of plunging myself into the Red Sea on the beach at Eilat. Even then, I was haunted by questions about how I would sail through the lecture scheduled for that Friday in a newly-opened pub.

This time, I decided to take no chances and resolved to get there better prepared and less exhausted than I had been for the lecture I gave in Kramim. To be on the safe side, I had scheduled the lecture for late Friday night, planning to reach the city by Friday morning and to have enough time to rest and prepare. However, as I learned later on while riding to Eilat, on such a journey you should always have a plan B.

It was 14:00 already, and I still had a few more hours' riding to do before reaching my night camping site near Uvda airport. Reaching Kibbutz Neot Smadar, I turned right, leaving Route 40 for Route 12, one of the best scenic roads in Israel.

The country's southernmost road, it runs nearly parallel to the southern part of the Jordan Valley. It offers the traveler a variety of landscapes, from the dusty desert plains near Uvda airport to the magnificent peaks of the Eilat Mountains with their hues of brown, black and light yellow against the background of the Red Sea and Gulf of Aqabah, making it the perfect setting for a trip.

Cutting through mountains, rising to nearly 1000 meters above sea level, this route descends sharply before climbing steeply between the mountains and finally reaching Eilat, Israel's southernmost city.

The view of the Gulf of Aqaba peeping through the mountains is so breathtaking that, whenever I travel there by bike or car, it feels surreal. The combination of the shining blue sea and the Edom mountains surrounding resembles an artistic masterpiece rather than a natural landscape. All those cliffs, ravines, and steep mountain trails with their intoxicating beauty always manage to take me away from my here and now for a moment.

After a few minutes rest, I set off for an easy, fun ride. The not-too-scorching sun and the cooling breeze allowed me to ride in my current clothing a little longer than usual. In addition, the road was nearly deserted.

Very soon, Uvda Airport's tower loomed on the horizon. Luckily, making one last stop before my destination, I remembered to read my text messages before turning my cell phone off for the night. It was Danit, a good friend and classmate from the New Media College of Tel Aviv, an extraordinary woman with an infinite, supernatural capacity to make everybody near her smile. Back in 2012, as classmates, we sat next to each other, which was perfect for us. We had even been nicknamed Max and Moritz.

For our teachers, however, it proved disastrous, and many times the teacher forced us apart due to Danit constantly interrupting the lectures and me always following her bad example. Her personal message on Facebook after my 108km trip definitely made my day. As usual, Danit was straightforward, caring, and humorous:

"Hi, sweetie, what's up? Listen up, very carefully, and don't argue! I've just read on Facebook you're near Shaharut, so Milly, my dear sister, who lives there with her life partner and their four adorable kids, are waiting for you. I've already told her you're on your way there. Start off right away. They have a fabulous house with such a view that you'll never want to leave. If I know anything about you, it will thrill you no end. So, if you don't want me to drive all the way over there and kick your little ass, and you know I always mean business, just give her a call to tell her you're on your way.

P.S. If you think I'm crazy, wait till you see her! So, c'mon, sweety, have lots of fun. My best regards to Milly.

Hugs and kisses, Danit xx"

On a little fork in the road near the main entrance to Uvda Airport, I turned left onto a road gently climbing among barren hills and dry waterways. I even spotted a deserted hotel, apparently under construction. The community was situated at an altitude of 550 meters above sea level, splendidly isolated on the edge of the Jordan Rift Valley cliffs, west of Kibbutz Yotvata. As if it weren't isolated enough, the road to it had a dead end. It was properly named after nearby Mount Shaharut.

I reached it a moment before sunset. I had to cycle into Shaharut slowly due to the short, steep climb just before the entrance, and as I entered the community, I noticed how perfectly the local houses blended with the environment and that they were constructed in environmentally friendly, local materials.

About 300 meters before the entrance, I could see the residents' yards, where I observed not only ordinary farm scenes such as haystacks, chickens, rabbits, horses, donkeys, and goats but occasional camels as well. This is definitely a unique place, I thought. Once I realized this must have been the most unusual spot in the country that I have ever visited, I also knew I had fallen in love with it.

Milly greeting me with a huge smile in the main square. "I guess you're Tzuriel, judging from Danit's description," Milly declared, stretching out her hand to me.

"You must be Milly, I presume. So, just before I forget, my kindest regards from your sister," I returned her welcome. "Well, sorry for just dropping on you out of the blue, but your sister made it an offer I couldn't refuse. You know what she's like. I'm much obliged -"

"Oh, yes, I know very well what she's like. Come on, you've nothing to be sorry for. Do you really believe you're bothering us? You're the main event in this hellhole for the whole millennium!" She smiled, beckoning. "Come, let's get home, it's getting cold."

While following her, I noticed the Edom Mountains to the east, and then, as if it were a special prize I had won for sailing through the challenging ride all the way from Mitzpe Ramon city, a magnificent sunset started to unfold in front of me. The mountains were slowly decked in dark, royal crimson. Stopping for a moment, I watched the dying day's laser-like sunrays pierce the Jordan Rift Valley cliffs, and eventually hit the ridge across the Jordanian border. That spectacular sunset, the likes of which I had only ever seen in art galleries, was a scene to cherish for a lifetime. After following Milly for a while, I had to make another brief stop to gaze at the mountains with only the Arava Valley coming between me and them.

"Your house offers the same view?! I mean, this is obsessively mesmerizing, do you realize that?!"

"Actually, the view from our house is even better. Come see for yourself," she smiled, relieving me of my backpack.

The path leading to Milly's house was marked with two rows of pebbles. It didn't offer the slightest hint of the view awaiting me from one of the most beautiful and unique houses I have ever seen.

My year-long journey to Nepal and North India left me with indelible, lifelong impressions. It gave me not only thousands of photos but dozens of acquaintances and experiences. Situated among the world's highest mountains, Nepal has developed its own peculiar culture that has tourists see it as some outlandish paradise.

I went on that journey to get over a hard time that had felt like a slap in the face. One day, coming home from my reservist military duty, I found that my girl had run off with another guy. More than merely hurting my ego, it drove me to feel that I was a disappointment to my family, best friends, and people in general. Only in hindsight can you see how you managed to recover from such a crisis. However, right after recovering from it, I booked a flight to the remotest and highest place on Earth to get as far as possible from my native places and culture, and, most importantly, from humans, to allow myself plenty of time.

A good deal of my current occupation was inspired by my experiences in Nepal. I tried all the best-known treks available in that country, such as the Around Annapurna trek and the Everest Base Camp, considered by many to offer the world's most magnificent scenery. However, it was neither the treks, the sight of the more than 8000-meter peaks, nor any snowcapped lofty mountain that made the most indelible impression upon me there.

Nor was it the frightening psychedelic adventure I had in Varanasi, on the banks of the Ganges. There, in the world's craziest city, I was tormented by the most unpleasant hallucinations of myself in an Indian prison, as well as by visions of endless kaleidoscopic displays. All that resulted from just one "special mushroom." Luckily, I survived since my companions knew how to handle that situation. Still, I will never forget that Lassi Bhang (Lassi, mind you, is an

Indian yogurt, not a dog) gotten from a wily, smiling, Indian waiter in broad daylight in one of India's most crowded alleyways. It was even more shocking since I only expected it to make me feel good, like a glass of wine.

However, my strongest, most life-changing experiences there were not at a tourist site, but rather in one of the world's backyards where nobody wants to live, let alone travel – a sort of poorly-lit abyss on shifting ground, where I had to muster all my mental strength to survive. It was the orphanage in Pokhara, Nepal's second-largest city.

In the spring of 2009, after landing in Kathmandu, Nepal, I took a bus ride for several hours to Pokhara, the starting point of the famous Around Annapurna trek. Checking into a cheap, yet nice downtown guesthouse, I fell asleep quickly, due to the bumpy, long, and exhausting ride.

Rising the next morning, I felt in perfect shape, bodily, and mentally. My small room offered a surprisingly clear view of Lake Pokhara with a beautiful reflection of the Himalayas on its surface. I could also observe the world-renowned Machhapuchhre, or Fishtail Mountain, rising nearly 7km above sea level. Its name refers to its extraordinary, fishtail shape that attracts hikers and photographers from all corners of the globe, even though climbing it is forbidden due to its local sacred status.

After taking a brief shower, I went down to the lobby to ask where a decent cup of coffee could be found early in the morning. The receptionist sent me to some tourist hub where he promised I should get what I wanted.

A five-minute walk along the main street, crowded with shops offering souvenirs, clothing, and, of course, a hell of a lot of mostly poor-imitation camping brands, brought me to the café. I immediately realized why the receptionist recommended it of all places. It was crammed with tourists, most of whom were easily-recognizable Israelis. It felt like just another Tel Aviv café, complete with small round tables invading the pavement, a bar where the waiters got the dishes, and the latest Israeli pop hits in the air.

Sitting down in the corner, I ordered a black coffee and a piece of apple pie, suddenly realizing I'd had nothing to eat since yesterday afternoon. A couple of Israelis sitting next to me recommended a camping gear store across the road. I wanted to buy some items necessary for the Annapurna trek, which is more than 200km long and offers some challenging sections.

Finishing and paying for my coffee, I started off for the store. On my way out of the café, a rather colorful Israeli guy passed by. His long, brown hair was gathered in by a purple rubber band. He was wearing dark glasses and a wide-brimmed hat. He stopped for a moment to stick notices in Hebrew on a notice board, while two local kids stood by him. Curious to read his notice, I approached the board.

"What's up, buddy? I see you're a newcomer, judging by the fresh laundry smell of your clothes. By the way, I'm Abraham."

"Yes. I only landed in Nepal yesterday. I'm fine, thanks," I said, confirming his suspicions.

"I see you're reading my notice very carefully. Does it have any appeal for you?" he asked, taking his dark glasses off.

"Looks interesting. What have you got to do with it, and where is it?" I enquired.

"Nearby, only fifteen minutes' walk away. I'm a volunteer there, helping the locals run the place and recruit more hands." Instead of replying, I read his notice again and then noticed the kids Abraham was holding by the hand.

A few hours after lunch, I changed my plans and paid a

visit to one of the most depressing places I had ever
happened upon.

The orphanage was in a two-story building with outer
stairs. Its walls were gray – most of the paint already peeled
off – and spotted all over with black mold stains. It stood in
a dense forest at the end of an uphill trail on a hill overlooking the city, its balcony offering an extremely close view
of the Himalayas. It felt like the most powerful manifesta-
tion of Nepal's nature. The majestic natural view against the
dull manmade view produced a contrast I could hardly
absorb.

Upon entering the building, Abraham told me I had
made it just in time for supper. He asked me to let him know
of any problem I had, warning me not to get too emotional
about unpleasant sights.

The sun was nearly down, and the darkening building
and surrounding forest only aggravated the depression
atmosphere. I noticed about ten boys and girls, aged four to
twelve, sitting on a bare concrete floor and pieces of a rug
scattered here and there. Since the building had no power
supply, they had to light candles all over the place after
sunset. They just sat on the floor in a circle, wearing their
pajamas – the only after-school clothing they had – waiting
obediently, in perfect silence, for a Nepalese volunteer girl
to serve their supper.

The very first thing I noticed about them was their eyes,
the desperate melancholy of which one could see all too
clearly by the faint candlelight. Never before had I seen
such sadness in children so young.

The moment I saw them, the first thing to cross my mind
was how the hell could any human being be so sadistically
twisted to make them so sad?

The sight enraged me so strongly that my right eye

started to itch. At first, I struggled to hold back my tears, but they broke loose like champagne from a bottle. All of a sudden, I found myself standing amidst the children, bursting into tears. Luckily, the poor lighting did not allow them to see how badly this foreigner had lost his self-control. However, Abraham saw my shame and immediately walked me out onto the balcony.

"It's okay, buddy, it happens to us all. You'll get used to it. I go through it about once a day. And you lasted longer than most of the visitors who break down and leave in less than a minute. Are you still interested in volunteering?" he remembered to ask, offering me a cigarette.

"Thanks. You know, you volunteers are doing colossal work here in every respect. Can you even grasp how great your work is?"

I stayed there for nearly six months.

First of all, I stashed all my trekking and climbing equipment under my guesthouse bed and started looking for a room closer to the orphanage. A search of several hours brought me to a cool, tourist-friendly guesthouse owned by a Dutchman who had married a Nepalese girl back in the 1970s and had never got out of Nepal ever since.

Then, after I had bribed a local immigration official with a couple of hundred rupees, my tourist visa was extended by another couple of months. My days there turned into weeks and, eventually, I found myself continuing Abraham's work. That man's sacrifice for those children defies description.

Just like him, I and another three British and Israeli volunteers served as those kids' parents, for all practical purposes. Finding additional volunteers, funds, and equipment proved to be of no lesser importance. A few months later, that place turned, in a way, into another home for me, as we volunteers practically ran the place.

One Israeli volunteer I shall never forget (her name was May) arrived in Nepal just a few months after completing her military service as part of her grand tour of the Far East. A tall and light brunette, with smooth hair falling to the middle of her back, she always wore her hair loose, as well as Salomon mountain shoes, slightly torn jeans and a North Face black down jacket. She hiked around a lot and was a regular outdoor animal, always using the best quality clothing and gear. Yet her large, brown eyes and her permanent smile gave her face a gentle look.

Occupying a tiny room in the orphanage, she stayed there 24/7, making an immense sacrifice for the children. Yet I suspect that she, too, was eventually affected by the depression so common among the volunteers.

She and I were perfectly in tune with each other and enjoyed each other's company. It became our daily custom to have a cup of coffee and a piece of homemade cake in the local café at 21:00. We just had to forget the orphanage routine and feel like tourists for a while. Still, I had constant pangs of conscience for spending 100 rupees a day on my supper instead of buying a week's supply of food for the children with it.

Eventually, with summer nearing its end and giving way to autumn, the flow of tourist-volunteers dwindled, and even the Israeli ones went away, leaving the orphanage with only a tiny staff. Little by little, we, the hard-core volunteers, sadly realized that we would have to leave.

Autumn, with its rain and cold, affected the children, turning them even gloomier despite all our efforts to cheer them up – at least for a short while. When we succeeded, the satisfaction kept us going and doing our holy work. One gloomy, wintry evening I spent in the orphanage made me contemplate the life I had led until then.

Under the house rules, lights were out at 21:00 sharp, and I, like all staff members, had to leave for the night, except for those allowed to sleep there. When I was about to leave for my guesthouse, ten-year-old Arjoon, the toughest kid in the home, suddenly grabbed my fleece coat sleeve, begging in broken English, "Can you please stay a few more minutes? I don't want to sleep alone."

Astounded by the melancholy in his voice, I took a deep breath and stared at him. I whispered back, "Dear Arjoon, I didn't hear what you just said."

He kept begging with a whisper, "Please don't go, it's cold and it's so dark, I'm afraid from the dark."

Luckily, the dark didn't allow him to see how hard I took his request. It just drove me so crazy that I needed to take a breath of fresh air on the balcony. There, I let myself curse and damn these children's heartless parents for bringing them into this world and Nepal's indifferent government for doing nothing except letting tourists like us finance and staff their orphanages. I even blamed God Almighty Himself for all the evil and suffering He had created in this world. With such a God, I wondered, who the hell could believe in Him? Calming down, I came back in. Asking no permission, I grabbed two blankets and lay on the floor next to Arjoon, letting him place his hand in mine.

That night, I didn't get any proper sleep. Lying on the concrete floor, I reached the decision to leave Nepal since I felt I was losing my mind. At the same time, I also vowed to help my fellow humans whenever I could. To this day, that decision seems like some supernatural enlightenment to me.

The next morning, strangely enough, that promise felt most natural, as if it had been deep down inside all these years, just waiting for me to carry it out. That night on the cold floor and the contemplation it generated made an indelible impression on me.

Arjoon only wished for what almost every Western child takes for granted, such as caring parents and clean clothing. Yet the anguish in his eyes showed that his wish was unattainable, which robbed me of my sleep that night. I clearly remember how sad I felt upon realizing how little justice and compassion this world offers – how I, my friends and family, as well as all Westerners, take such rare treasures like a normal family and clean clothing for granted.

Rising that morning before the other volunteers came in, I went straight to my guesthouse room to get some sleep. Two days later, I parted with them in a traditional Nepali farewell ceremony; the locals decorated my neck with a garland of flowers and giving me a certificate. Grabbing a cab to the bus station, I took a long ride across the Indian border. My next stop was the holy city of Varanasi.

My stay in Nepal gave me a most powerful experience that affected me many years later, as well as during my Heart to Heart Journey.

"It is only with the heart that one can see rightly; what is essential is invisible to the eye."

Antoine de Saint-Exupéry, *The Little Prince*

April 4, 2016
Starting point: Community of Shaharut
Destination: Eilat
Distance: 84 kilometers

I cannot forget that morning in Shaharut when I got up to start another day's ride. The previous day's grueling 120km ride, including the climb back to Mitzpe Ramon after I had given the Czech riders my drinking water, finally took effect. My body felt cramped and stiff, especially my butt, biceps, and quadriceps. On my early awakening, I was hungry and thirsty, so I stretched out one hand to grab a water bottle I had left next to my sleeping bag, while my other hand groped for the mashed energy snack stuffed into my saddlebag pocket. I devoured it the moment I found it.

Having hit the sack early, I got up before dawn to see the sunrise many claim to be quite a sight. Judging from the fogged window, it was pretty cold outside. A few minutes later, once I had wiped the condensation away, the sunrise revealed the houses. Once again, I was impressed by how perfectly the houses blended with the desert environment. Maybe, I hoped, it indicated the nature of the local people as well. Driven by this hope, I started preparing for that day's ride. Outside the room, day was breaking slowly.

I usually sleep with only my underwear on, or completely naked, to let my body breathe and rest after intense cycling, but the previous night had been cold enough for me to sleep in my training pants. Before I went onto the balcony to watch the sunrise, I also had to put on my black down jacket, as well as my gloves and balaclava.

Since Milly and her family were still sleeping, I tiptoed through the living room all the way to the balcony looking east. All of a sudden, my right leg cramped so painfully that I fell and was completely helpless as my entire body was wracked by a sharp pain. That muscle felt like a rock stuck inside my leg.

"Ohhh, dammit!" I let out a yell, nearly waking up the household. Luckily, I was right next to a wall when it happened, so I leaned against it and stretched my leg, which ended the pain in a few seconds.

I kept advancing to the door using a penguin walk, which is quite normal practice after a few days of intense exercise in a row. The moment I looked at the view from the balcony, all I could say was, "Wow..." into the cold, desert air.

It immediately reminded me of Danit's text message about the magnificent view from her sister's house. She was correct. The sunrise tinted the landscape with a divine symmetry, blending the colors masterfully into a brown-reddish mixture that gradually tinted the cliffs several hundred meters away to the east. This kaleidoscopic spectacle affected me so strongly that I had to ask myself in a low voice, "How in the world can I leave such beauty and serenity in a couple of hours?" But, succumbing to stronger drives, as I did every morning throughout this journey, I was to embark on another challenging ride.

The yard was littered with kids' toy cars and poufs, and it also had sofas arranged in an open rectangle around a small table. This outdoor seating corner was shaded by an arbor that protected it from the scorching midday sun. It was supported by poles from which hung pots of geraniums and other flowers that I could not name. Behind an east-facing sofa was Milly's small rock-enclosed kitchen garden where she grew spices and tea herbs. At a closer look, I saw mint, basil, and lemon verbena growing there.

The left wall of the house faced east and had three long windows that let natural light into the spacious house. Opposite the windows I could see a roughly circular swimming pool carved out of the desert bedrock, painted blue, blending perfectly with the hues of the natural rocks arranged around its edge.

All these elements combined to turn the balcony into a breathtaking scene, especially at this perfect moment with the rising sun just starting to shed light on the desert and Jordan Rift Valley rocks.

Sitting down on a sofa, I noticed three small palms between the pool and the rocks. This suggested a water source nearby. Gripping the table to avoid another cramp attack, I rose slowly and made my way to the pool to sit down by its edge.

That morning was, as usual, very cold starting off, but I could hardly feel it, being too intoxicated with the desert silence. The only sound was that of my own breathing. All I lacked to make this morning perfect was a drink of hot coffee or tea.

While my thoughts were wandering to other realms, I suddenly heard little footsteps behind me. They belonged to Milly's six-year-old son, Yonatan, a lovely boy whose long hair partly covered his face. He wore a yellow Capoeira-Club shirt painted with two figures doing this Brazilian martial art dance. While he was approaching me, I noticed the boy was smiling shyly, as if trying to tell me something.

"Mom asks what do you like – black coffee or strong tea?"

"Strong tea will be perfect. And please tell her I thank her a lot!"

"Fine," the boy replied, running back to his mother and shouting my choice to her.

A couple of minutes later, he was back with a small glass teapot filled with dark-brown tea, mint, and lemon verbena leaves floating in it. Its fragrance reminded me of the tea one can only get in the army or on great treks.

Yonatan joined me on the sofa and for a few minutes, we just sat silently, sipping hot tea, and staring at the cliffs that descended sharply toward Route 90 and Kibbutz Yotvata, situated right below.

"Will you stay with us until Saturday?" Yonatan surprised me.

"Sorry, I must be off today."

"Why?" He looked at me, somewhat offended. "My friends' band will play here tomorrow, and they're cool! I'll take you to their gig. Besides, Mom told me that what you're trying to do is very dangerous."

"It is," I smiled at him. "Mom's right. But whenever I take on a project, I must complete it. It's a matter of principle for me, never to quit before the job is done. You, too, should never quit if what you do is important for you, even when it seems risky or stupid. If you have a cause you believe in, see it through," I concluded, pouring us another cup of tea.

"But what if you have an accident? Who will take care of your fatherless kids?"

I had to pause for a moment before answering in an attempt to avoid giving him an answer he might find too confusing.

"Well, I don't have any kids. Someday, I hope I will," I said, praying that he would change the subject.

"Why don't you?" he persisted. "Find a nice girl and have some, just as my parents had me."

"Look – over there! See how the sun's rising across the Jordanian border! Amazing, isn't it?" I tried to change the subject. His response proved me successful. "Let me ask you a tricky question, Yonatan." I exploited my success. "What do you like better – watching the sunrise or the sunset?"

"I like both. I don't care whether it rises or sets. You know, I like eating apples with chocolate spread, even though Mom tells me that it tastes bad and it's unhealthy. You boomers always keep nagging us! I'm old enough to know what I find tasty without you telling me! I can't see why I can't like both things!"

"You're right, Yonatan, you can like both things, and it was a very clever thing to say. Who says you must always choose? This is what's totally wrong with us boomers. We're masters of ruining everything that feels nice. You know, I'll feel very bad about going away today. You're such fun!" I declared, placing my arm around his shoulders. "Shall we go inside? It seems your mom has made you some breakfast."

As I rose to limp toward the house, I observed how sad I'd made Yonatan by saying that I was going away. He lowered his head a little and fiddled with his shirt. I stretched out my hand to him, smiling, asking him to join me. We headed for the kitchen together, Yonatan looking disappointed and downcast.

By 08:00, I had loaded my bike with all my heavy gear and was thrilled to be starting the last day of the first leg of my journey. It was to end that afternoon in Eilat, 84km away.

I texted my location to whoever may be interested, including, of course, Koby, my friend who lived in Eilat and had arranged my lecture for that weekend.

I didn't expect a terribly rough ride to Eilat, knowing it would be a descent to sea level most of the time. However, it did have some steep climbs, especially near the Ein Netafim Crossing and Mount Yoash. Another expected source of excitement would be the sight of the fence along Route 12, which runs along the Egyptian border all the way down to Eilat.

Yonatan helped me walk my bike to the community's main street. Then, right before I mounted, he asked suddenly, "But you will come on visits, right?"

"Well, if you and your mother invite me, I'll do my best to visit you together with your Aunt Danit, who I really love, okay? C'mon, give me a big high-five and wish me luck!"

With a big smile, showing a row of tiny teeth, he struck his palm really hard against mine. After giving Milly a long hug, and hugging and stroking Yonatan on his head, I set off. I was back in my good old bike saddle again, riding down the Shaharut access road, and then riding on at a low speed along the Shaharut-Uvdah Airport highway.

After a 10km ride, I saw several figures at a distance. They definitely resembled hikers rather than cyclists. Judging from their large backpacks, I concluded they were hiking an Israel National Trail. Stopping by them, I saw they were a merry trio of two boys and a girl in full hiking kit complete with a black guitar the girl carried tied to her bag, and an abundance of pots, shoes, and clothing items hanging from the heavily-packed bag of one of the boys.

After we exchanged each other's adventures, the hikers wanted to try my bike a little before I rode on. Meanwhile, one of them brewed up a strong, cardamom-flavored black coffee for all of us. I learned that they had started their hike in Eilat a couple of days ago, heading north. That moment, I made myself a promise to walk the Israel National Trail someday. I had heard only good things about it.

We insisted on a farewell selfie as was expected, of course, but this task proved trickier than expected. My wide bike and their large bags did not allow all of us to occupy the same frame, so we had to improvise. Finally, after a series of rather funny repositioning, we all managed to squeeze ourselves into one selfie.

After they went on their way, I took an energy snack out of my saddlebag and set off. I rode on, chewing on my snack bar, my cellphone playing Ehud Banai's super-hit, "One Ha-Agas Street." Looming on the horizon was the barren, flat Uvda Valley.

Route 12, running across the valley, is commanded from the west by Uvda Cliffs, while the Timna Ridge and Shayarot Cliffs rise east of them. Route 12 had been the most pleasant part of the trip so far, and the idea of reaching Eilat that evening kept me going strong. I rode fast and could feel my body was becoming gradually accustomed to the extreme strains of such a ride. I was getting into shape little-by-little.

The road was deserted, and my legs were already free of the morning cramps, so I could cover a greater distance. In addition, the sky was cloudless blue, the sun shone brightly, and the cool morning wind was still blowing, minimizing my sweat.

Yet there was a fly in the ointment. I noticed that my sprocket cluster was clinging, and the gear shifting wasn't smooth. Though it was nothing serious, I planned to go to a bike repair shop in Eilat to take care of the problem. Riding with no stops for tens of dozens of kilometers, I reached a sign in all three languages of this country – Hebrew, English, and Arabic – marking the beginning of the Eilat Mountains. This certainly deserved a stop for a few landscape snapshots, with the sign as well as without it.

While the coffee was brewing on my burner, I examined my bike in search of the source of the problem. A few minutes' inspection revealed that the rear derailleur had probably gotten damaged during one of the last few days' many stops when the bike had fallen to the ground.

The rear derailleur, attached to the frame by a metal hanger, is essential for the bike's smooth operation. It shifts the chain to the sprocket fitting the speed selected by the shifter, which is on the handlebar. The command is trans-ferred from the shifter to the rear derailleur through a cable stretched all the way to the rear.

Even though I could ride on with a slightly twisted derailleur, it compelled me to be extra cautious for the next couple of hours as I was about to enter a dangerous area with poor cell phone reception, in close proximity to the Egyptian border, with a weather report predicting extreme heat.

I prepared carefully for a hot ride. First of all, I poured the contents of my two-liter water bottle into the bottles fitted on the frame. Then I replaced my head bandana with a neck-shading baseball hat. It was decorated with the

Nature Valley energy snacks logo, a gift from General Mills that imports them to Israel.

About a week before I had embarked on this journey, I had contacted this food giant, and they had offered their sponsorship. I asked them for 200 energy snacks, which they agreed to provide right away, as well as some items of cycling clothing. Three days later, hats with their logo on the front, especially designed for hot weather cycling, were delivered to me. I concluded my preparations for riding through the Eilat Mountains, where the temperature had already risen to forty degrees, by applying a thick layer of protection cream on my face, especially my nose. I carefully avoided applying the cream above my eyes. Experience had taught me that once your sweat flows down your forehead, it carries away the protection cream. This mixture of sweat and cream stings the eyes terribly, forcing you to make a stop to wipe it off your face.

After ten minutes over a low fire, the coffee was finally ready and while drinking it, I spotted the Sayarim Valley on the horizon behind me, a seven-by-five-kilometer valley south of Uvda Valley. Most of it is off limits, being used as a military firing zone. I crossed it, riding along the practically deserted Route 12 with only occasional army vehicles driving slowly by. It seemed that the boundless plains and the majestic silence all around made drivers relax and drive slower, usually with all their windows rolled down.

Suddenly, the silence was broken with text message alerts from my cell phone attached to the handlebars. It meant that I had regained reception and was now picking up all the messages my phone had failed to receive while off or had no signal. I had twenty new text messages, four of which deserved my attention, encouraging me to reach Eilat as soon as possible:

Good evening. I hope everything is going well. I just remembered you telling me, a few weeks ago, that you needed a solar charger, so I will send you one by mail order. You can collect it from Eilat's main post office. Let me know when you get it. Take care. Ehud

Hi, stranger! How are you? I hope you're well, doing nothing stupid like diving into lakes all of a sudden... 😊 Well, let me know if you're alive. Maya (the one with the Suzuki Samurai...)

What's up, buddy? Where in the world are you wandering off to, you crackpot! I'd love to join you for a couple of hours, how 'bout that? I thought about bringing along a grill, some beers, and some fine meat, so we could stuff ourselves silly during one of your outdoor nights. Text me when you get this. So, take care and have tons of fun! Bye, Amikam

Good Morning, Tzuriel. I am Tom Stein, an Israel Channel Two reporter. I heard about your journey, and I'd love to talk to you about a story for the weekend news. Please contact me ASAP when you read this. Thank you, have a good day and take care. Tom.

It was a few minutes past 12:00 when I had repacked my coffee kit into my front bag and was ready to go. The ride was easy and despite the desert heat, I felt in good shape. The heat seriously affected me only when I made stops since there was no headwind.

I tried to save water, drinking no more than one liter per hour's riding. Thousands of hours in the saddle had taught me that this should suffice. So far, this rule had worked perfectly.

On my way south, I passed many top-secret army bases, and the entire area was sealed off with a huge amount of barbed wire perimeter fences. The ride turned gradually harder, which meant I was already riding through the Eilat Mountains. Another indication was the altering skyline: the boundless plains of the Uvda and Sayarim Valleys gave way to lofty mountains, rising from 600 to 800 meters above sea level. I started seeing all around me the familiar brown, black, beige, and occasionally yellowish hues. When I caught occasional glimpses of the Red Sea, I enjoyed the scenery even more.

On the other hand, my pulse was rising, and my bike was making metallic clinking sounds, especially during steep climbs when the frame had to bear most of my weight. During the descents, I just rolled down, letting my legs rest before the next climb. Meanwhile, my mind focused on the recent messages, and I started running through answers to every individual message. My eyes, however, feasted on the present and, whenever I completed a wide curve, I caught a few-seconds' glimpse, through a ravine, of the Gulf of Aqaba in all its splendor, heralding the end of that day's ride. Such moments gave me the greatest thrills of my journey so far.

And then disaster struck.

Taking me completely by surprise with a loud, metallic, terribly dispiriting sound, my rear derailleur snapped and was dragging behind the frame on the road like some corpse being abused. Stopping right away, I bent down to examine the right side of my rear wheel.

"Dammit! Dammit! Dammit!" I yelled. Too dumbfounded to realize what deep shit I was in, I mounted again right away in an attempt to complete the climb. When I failed, I had to dismount, resting my bike on the ground for an immediate damage assessment.

"What unbelievably deep shit!" I cried. "Did it have to happen here of all places, in the middle of nowhere, with no cell phone reception? It can't be true!" I kept mumbling.

In a moment, despair got the better of me, making me believe that my entire project was ruined and that I'd have to tell all my followers I had to quit midway because my goddamn hanger had snapped just an hour's ride away from Eilat. What a disgrace – to go home defeated because of my amateurishly arrogant carelessness! I found it so difficult to accept that, from this moment, the trip was over.

From there, things only got worse. On top of my frustration and anxiety, the dry-sauna, hot, windless air of April 2016 indicated the arrival of the year's first heatwave.

About five meters away was a guardrail and a ditch separating Route 12 from the national border fence. In an attempt to calm down, I rested my bike against the guardrail and stepped a few meters away. Spotting a little rock by the road, I sat on it, taking off my hat and shirt and pouring all the water I had all over myself. It successfully cooled down the burning frustration and despair in my blood.

Suddenly, I recalled a TED lecture by a guy who survived a plane crash. He described how he started getting out of his deep shit the moment he stopped asking why it was he, of all people, and started asking how he could find a way out.

When my pulse was finally back to normal, I tried to embrace his strategy, stop feeling sorry for myself, and start thinking how the hell I could start riding again ASAP.

While I was having this enforced rest and trying to think of a way out, I heard a rockslide across the Egyptian border. Taking it first to be caused by a local ibex or rock hyrax, I soon realized my mistake and saw a guy with an AK-47 (Kalashnikov) running down toward me. At first, I could not believe my eyes, since there was little chance of encountering Egyptian soldiers here, and they had no reason to rush at me anyway.

However, he soon started shouting at me in Arabic, which got me edgy, making me jump to my feet and run like mad for cover toward a concrete wall about 50m away. Abandoning my bike, all I wanted at that moment was to watch that soldier from a position of cover. The Israeli Army had erected these walls after some serious terrorist attacks had taken place near Route 12. They offered some protection against gunfire from across the border and prevented terrorist incursions.

With adrenaline rushing through my blood, sweat blurring my vision, and breathing very heavily, I couldn't figure out what the soldier was trying to tell me. I decided to freeze and hold my breath, just to hear what he was shouting. Looking at the last spot where I had seen him, I figured out he was holding a plastic water bottle in one hand and his sling-less brown rifle in the other hand.

Suddenly, after shouting at me for a while, he rested his gun on a rock, gesturing to me to approach by pointing at the water bottle. Eventually, the penny dropped: that soldier was only trying to help me – a human trying to help a fellow human in distress. Feeling really awkward, I started walking back toward my bike, where the soldier stood. That guy – twentyish, wearing green fatigues with a beige camouflage pattern – approached the fence, continually talking to me in Arabic. I could only make out "water," "please," and "hello."

That made me burst out laughing as I put my shirt back on. Realizing that at last I understood him, he threw the bottle over the fence. The bottle, landing in the middle of the road, rolled toward me. It felt surprisingly cold when I picked it up. I guessed he had just taken it out of his outpost's fridge.

I opened it immediately, poured the water over my head, and gulped the remaining water passionately. The cool water had the instant effect of boosting my morale, so I pulled my notepad from my handlebar bag. I had brought it along just in case I needed to write anything down. I wrote, in English, the following:

"Thank you so much for your help and the cold water! I hope that one day we can meet up again without a border between us. ☺ "

Pulling that page out, I wrapped it around a small rock in order to throw it to him over the fence. Then I showed him with gestures and a few Arabic words that I wanted to throw something. He smiled at me and gave me a thumbs up to tell me it was okay by him. Flying over the fence, the rock rolled to his feet. It was only a few seconds later that he understood my message, judging from his smile and gestures. Then, we said goodbye to each other with a few words in English and gesticulations.

He kept watching me for a few minutes while I tried to fix my bike, and then climbed up and went out of sight behind the crest.

At 15:30, I still had no way out and every second was a critical delay. It was still disturbingly hot, and I started reconciling myself to the fact that I would not reach Eilat by bicycle. The only solution was to just walk on in the hope of either getting a ride or regaining cell phone reception, which would allow me to ask my friends in Eilat to come rescue me. The last thing I needed was for the lecture scheduled for that night to be canceled.

I started climbing, walking at the roadside, pushing the rear of my bike with one hand while holding the handlebar with the other hand. Every now and then, I looked back for a car that might be my deliverance. Meanwhile, I repeatedly checked my cell phone reception, which was lost for several hours. I hoped to regain reception when I reached the top of the climb, the highest point in the area, so I could contact Koby.

After an exhausting walk along Route 12, which itself emitted intense heat, I came to a bend in the road. Taking the bend, I spotted a vehicle: a fancy white Mercedes with light mustard leather seats was sitting in the road, its engine and powerful climate control running. The driver, spotting me, lowered his window right away. As I approached the vehicle, I could smell the strong fragrance of sage. The climate-controlled, cooled air was spreading.

"Is everything okay?" he inquired.

"Well, life isn't perfect. Generally speaking, I'm all right, unlike my bike," I informed him.

"Have some, be my guest." He offered me a bag of peanut butter snacks, then turned the engine off and got out to approach me.

"I'd love to give you a ride to Eilat," he apologized, "but my boss and his family are hiking right now along the canyon, and I have to wait here for them. Would you like some water or food?"

"It's very kind of you. I have enough water, but food's always welcome. Is there any chance you could let me make a call? For some reason, my cell phone has no reception."

"Yes, sure. Here, call whoever you need to call while I get you some sandwiches from my portable fridge in the trunk. What would you like, tahina or tuna?" Handing his cell phone over to me, he approached the trunk.

"Tuna would be perfect. Thanks!" I replied as I dialed Koby's number.

Figuring out my situation instantly, Koby just asked his boss permission to leave work and five minutes later informed me that he was about twenty minutes' drive away. I slowly and cautiously disassembled my bike, removing the bags, wheels, and saddle, so that everything would fit, with a little assistance, into Koby's vehicle. The heat took its toll on me. With my body as hot as fire, I had to move as slowly as possible and avoid any strain. Eilat being just 22km away and the fact that somebody was on his way to rescue me re-motivated me to complete my journey.

About thirty minutes later, Koby's white Hyundai Getz reached the parking lot where that fancy Mercedes and my dusty bike stood side by side. He got out and we hugged each other tightly. The sight of a familiar face in the midst of all my troubles reassured me that, eventually, everything would work out just fine.

"Listen, Tzuri, all the way here, I tried to figure out whether you're more of a crackpot or a genius," he confessed, blasting my shoulder blades with a hell of a friendly pat.

"Thanks, Koby, love you too," I returned the compliment.

After five minutes' struggle, we managed to stuff all my belongings into his tiny car, which nearly burst. Just before we set off, the chauffeur in the Mercedes kindly pushed another four sandwiches, still wrapped in plastic, into my hands.

"Well, seeing how you devoured them before, I thought you could use some for the road," he explained before asking once again whether I needed anything else. I care-fully remembered to thank him for his help, wish him a good day, and make sure I had returned his cell phone.

We reached Eilat at 17:00, a few minutes before Amin's closing time. Amin's was a bike shop offering excellent service and a variety of gear – a local landmark, in fact. Luckily, it had a repair department as well. I had called ahead to explain about my trip and my situation, so when I arrived, Amin welcomed me with a big smile and a cup of cold water. He had one of his staff come to greet me. He explained that my bike was rare and the broken part was the hanger. Since every individual bicycle has its own hanger, the repair would take more time and be more expensive due to unusual and necessary adjustments that needed to be made. He was very well aware of the urgency and therefore asked his staff to repair my bike immediately.

About an hour later, I was in Koby's place in central Eilat, having locked my bike outside and brought my stuff into the room where I was staying that night. I was able to shower off the mountain dust and recall my adventures of the past few hours and days.

Only under the cool water did I realize that I had traveled 300 challenging kilometers, gathered a 5,000-dollar donation, and was overwhelmed again with the thrill that I had felt earlier during that trip. A few seconds after I dried myself, I fell asleep on the bed wrapped only in a towel.

"Feeling better?" Koby shouted eventually from the other room. "How do you like your coffee?"

"I am. Strong, no sugar," I called from my bed.

"C'mon, siesta's over, you lazy bum! Take a sip and let's hit the town! I told the guys in the pub we'll be there by ten. It's a newly-opened place. They're waiting for us."

"What's its name?" I asked, sipping my coffee.

"The Brewery, in the new industrial zone. They're really nice guys. They serve homemade beer, too."

The friendship between Kobi and I went back all the way to my childhood in Kibbutz Alumim, while he grew up in nearby Kibbutz Saad. Our families had immigrated to Israel from the UK in the 1960s and had kept in touch since then. Every Jewish New Year, his family would walk all the way to our house for a festive dinner, which was quite an exciting celebration for both our families.

I had my own special reason to get excited about it, namely, Koby's younger, pretty sister, who had happened to be my age. She made me feel like no other girl did back then, but I guess it was just an unfulfilled teenage romance. I fell out of touch with Koby over the years, but I always knew he would be there for me in case I wanted to visit Eilat or needed a recommended trip destination.

When preparing for this trip, I had asked for his help, which he granted willingly, especially with arranging this lecture and contacting his local acquaintances of the last twenty years.

When we arrived at the pub, it was already open, though deserted. The bartenders had just started polishing the beer and whisky glasses and placing them on the proper shelves. Judging from the gleaming furniture and exposed electrical wires, it had opened quite recently.

Most of it was painted dark brown. The bar was surrounded by chairs, and the interior was dotted with small round tables, each with a pair of chairs next to it. Opposite the bar was a five-by-two-meter brown glass window that offered a glimpse of the distillation process and the tall, silvery, stainless-steel containers used for storing the beer during and after the brewing process.

I spent a few minutes setting up the projector and loud-speakers for my lecture, and about thirty minutes later the potential audience started filling the place. When we counted at least fifty people inside, some sitting and others standing, I was allowed to begin.

It felt strange to be speaking in such a place. I was used to speaking to audiences comprising only those interested in my message. But this time, only some of the crowd had come to listen to me, while others just came to have fun, having no idea about my lecture at all. I realized I was facing quite a challenge, with a lot of interruptions and distractions.

I began with a clip documenting my travels around the world, followed by a detailed description of my Heart to Heart Journey and the reason why I was in Eilat that evening. I tried my best to focus on my subject and speak loudly despite the frequent distractions of people who left the place to smoke or go to the bar.

Realizing that it was beyond my control, I decided, as I was speaking, to conclude my lecture that very moment and to appeal the people's sense of compassion – and start collecting donations.

The applause and cheers from Koby and his local friends reassured me that, despite all the disturbances, I had managed to reach out to my audience, and I was right: some made immediate money transfers, while others wrote me cheques.

After taking some pictures for social media, I ordered a beer at the bar.

"Good evening." A short, smiling, silver-haired man of about sixty years old, spoke to me in Hebrew with a heavy French accent.

"Good evening to you, too. What's up?" I greeted him with a handshake and nodded to his lady-friend who stood behind him.

"I'm Moshe. I and my friend Michele enjoyed your speech very much. Sorry for not introducing her. Meet Michele." Stepping aside, he presented her like his most precious possession.

"Hi, Michele. Thank you for your kind words. Are you tourists? Can I buy you both a drink?" I suggested, noticing as I spoke that there was at least twenty years age difference between them.

Michele slipped a tiny piece of purple paper into my hand. It bore some unclear English words. She was a little taller than Moshe and wore black, high-heel shoes with a blue evening gown that accented her feminine curves. She was carefully made up, especially around her almond eyes, and her hair was gathered in a bun. I definitely remember thinking she could not be Israeli. Hardly any local girl would go out looking like that.

"What's this?" I wondered, raising my hand with the note.

"Our Eilat address," Moshe told me, pointing at the note in my hand. "This is where our yacht is anchored, and we'd love to take you out on a cruise for a few hours tonight or tomorrow. You can bring along a friend or a girlfriend if you wish."

Michele's almond eyes were trained on me and her note. I remember how awkward I felt then: two perfect strangers had just hit on me out of the blue, asking me to join them on their yacht. That awkwardness felt familiar, and I suddenly remembered why. This is exactly what I had felt when Maya lured me into the pond near Mitzpe Ramon.

"I really appreciate that, and I'll do my best to come tonight, or tomorrow," I lied, hoping they'd fall for it.

"Good. We'll be more than happy. Here's my number. Just give me a call when you're on your way, so Michele can pick you up from the marina. You know where it is, right?"

"Yeah, sure." I lied for the second time that night.

We said goodbye, shaking hands, and they insisted on following the French custom of kissing three times. They left the pub with all the patrons' eyes following them.

"Do you know them, buddy? They look like a really odd couple," the bartender said casually.

"I've no idea who they are. They just listened to my

lecture and then came up to me to ask me to join them on their yacht."

"Really? Go for it, dude! The way that lady looked at you, you shouldn't turn her down." He wiped a glass with his towel and went on. "Go for it, you've got nothing to lose. At worst, you can just walk away if you don't feel like it."

"These bored married couples aren't my type, and besides, I stay away from women with partners. I think I'll pass. I admit she looks really good and definitely takes care of herself. You can't deny that," I giggled, sipping my beer.

"C'mon, don't be such a killjoy – let it go! They're all about having fun and you only live once! By the way, there's a saying, 'the gods send nuts to those who have no teeth.' Fits you perfectly, man!"

We both laughed and he refilled my glass of beer. After sitting there for another hour, I decided to go for a walk around town, so I told Koby, sitting with his friends across the bar, that he needn't wait for me since I'd take a cab back to his place. That Friday night, the streets of Eilat were crowded, and many tourists were there following the sun. My opinion of Eilat had changed over the years.

When I was a child, Eilat was notorious for being a place of loose morality and dirty fun. Gradually, the more I'd grown acquainted with the people of that town, I changed my mind about it, eventually falling in love with it. Now I have a couple of good friends there and I try to visit them every year. The intoxicating composition of the brown Eilat Mountains and West Jordan Mountains, with the (actually blue) Red Sea always makes me smile; it also offers, of course, the delights of the Red Sea itself, with its crystal-clear and transparent water and rich marine life. It also has a splendid seaside boardwalk.

The moment I reached it, I sat down on a bench to look

around. On my right was Eilat's main shopping center, Mall Hayam, and opposite it, the seaside hotel strip. This time, I'd come here to have some time alone. I was having to get used to all the crowds around me after a week-long solo ride.

The change felt just too extreme. Now, I enjoyed the whistling wind in my ears, and the comfortable weather in general. I also noticed the ripples around the anchored boats, and the gentle, calmingly monotonous breaking of the waves against the shore. It was a few minutes past midnight. The local and foreign weekend tourist rush had started.

I started answering every individual text message I had received recently. First, I happily granted Amikam's request to join my trip. Then I posted on social media a report about my successful fundraising lecture, thanking all those who had contributed to it. The donations total didn't yet show a significant increase, though I hoped to see the sum grow in a few days when the bank transfers had gone through.

My ass was rock hard with cramps. Whenever I sat for over five successive minutes, my leg muscles cramped in unison as if trying to tell me something, so I had to stand up every few minutes to relax my legs. After doing so, and after a short walk, I came back, spotting in the distance a familiar-looking vehicle in a lit parking space. Cautiously approaching it, I stuck my nose near the driver's window to inspect its interior. Once I spotted the orange balaclava with the black stripes on the driver's seat, it dawned on me: it was Maya, from Mitzpe Ramon.

"Why don't you come visit us in Switzerland? I guess you could ride all the way from Israel in a couple of weeks," Jessica, a Swiss tourist, suggested the day we went our separate ways on the balcony of a guesthouse in downtown Varanasi. We had first met in North Nepal, where she had been traveling with her red-haired friend, Lisa, and a couple of German friends. We made friends, and from then on, the two swiss girls, along with another fellow from New Zealand and I, traveled together.

Jessica was twenty-seven back then, a paramedic by occupation and a weekend professional mountaineer. Her fingertips were always covered with bandages and the time she had spent swinging from a rope on Himalayan cliffs had given her face a nearly permanent tan.

I could not help being attracted to her since her good nature and flexible, shapely body convinced me she was exactly my type. Her hair was smooth and blond, combed aside so it didn't need much care. She was shorter than me and had a small, tight butt, and perfectly shaped arms and legs.

She reminded me of Robin Wright's character in The Princess Bride. What fascinated me about her was her contrasts: her love of extreme outdoor adventures, with her exploding sex appeal that just crushed my heart. It wasn't long before we started getting better acquainted and spending more time in each other's company.

It was Jessica who persuaded me to travel to Europe. Before that, I had come back to Israel after spending nearly an entire year in the Far East.

When I got back, I had a little extra money. So, succumbing to yet another outburst of wanderlust, I embarked on a different, difficult, maybe even life-changing journey. While I was preparing to meet the challenge of a

cross-Europe cycling trip, I still entertained the hope of the
mistress of my heart back then surrendering to me and of us
starting a new life in Switzerland. Life, as usual, proved to be
something that happens while we plan other things. I took
the heartbreak that the European tour did to me quite
badly.

I designed and underwent a special training program for
that journey, consisting of several weeks of cycling 100km
north each day, sleeping in a sleeping bag in a tent in Tel
Aviv's Hayarkon Park, and then cycling another 100km back
south the next day.

One such cycling trip was quite unforgettable. When I
was near Beit Kama Junction in the Negev, I faced a north-
westerly wind blowing at 60kph, filling the air with a lot of
dust. It made riding insanely challenging, especially with a
35kg bike. Just as I was about to call my younger brother,
Gidi, to pick me up, a nice guy driving a brand new, silvery
Mazda stopped by and started to chat. "Hey, what's your
game? Are you nuts? Need something? Water? Some dates?
A ride? I'm a cyclist, too, but on some days, you just don't
ride!"

Had he only known how many times I'd heard these
words, he would have laughed himself silly. However, this
encounter drove me to fight on. I started to realize that I was
undergoing a transformation some people might find difficult to understand. It made me understand that an extreme
cycling trip also required another kind of preparation of the
mind.

My planned trip was to fly to Athens, assembling the
bike after landing, and riding from the airport for 500km all
the way to the Ionian Sea between the Adriatic and the
Mediterranean. There, I would take a ferry to Brindisi,
Italy's southernmost port, and from there ride north

through Italy via Naples, Rome, Tuscany, Milan, and across The Alps all the way to Switzerland, where I would spend about a month. Then I planned to turn south, toward Geneva and across the border to France, where I planned to ride for another thirty days. My final destination was England since I intended to visit my relatives in London.

I traveled to Europe with just four trunk bags and a small backpack. Such an international cycling trip is called touring in cyclists' lingo. On such trips, you must never fully stuff your bags. In my experience, and as other travelers had taught me, breaking this rule always makes trouble for you since you must always make room for items you buy while traveling. Besides, unpleasant surprises may compel you to get rid of some of the gear you brought along.

The front bags contained the heavier items – food, utensils, repair kit, a camping stove, and water. The rear ones contained the lighter items: my clothing, sleeping bag, and tent.

I've often been asked how to choose what clothing to take. Well, it very much depends on the individual cyclist, but in short, take as little as possible. I settled for just a fleece coat, a raincoat, a balaclava, two pairs of thick socks, and another pair of thinner socks for riding. I also packed three pairs of waterproof pants and trousers for riding in heavy rain, as well as two sets of tights and Dry-Fit shirts for long rides, one thermal shirt, a pair of flip-flops, and training pants to wear for cozy sleeping during cold nights.

Eventually, this, too, proved to be too much, and after a week of riding I had to discard several unnecessary clothing items.

Back then, before it was stolen from Arlozorov Railway Station in Tel Aviv, I had a 4500 Trek hardtail mountain bike. It only had a front shock absorber. Keeping its second-hand frame, I replaced all its tires, shifting mechanism, and sprockets. This trip required not only new equipment but also a different mindset.

I expected this journey to involve camping and sleeping in unusual places such as deserted building sites, remote train stations, forests, and parks. There was another challenge of equal importance: maintaining necessary hygiene, using the limited number of utensils I took with me. Failure to keep clean, poor-quality food, and insufficient sleep during the trip would get me flown home with a high fever and a bad stomach. In short, such a solo ride required a different strategy and tons of confidence and optimism.

The night before departure, I could not sleep, going to the bathroom every thirty minutes, constantly checking the time and inspecting my gear several times to make sure it was all set. I was at the height of my excitement and saying goodbye to my parents early in the morning proved difficult as well. When my father drove me to the airport, he suggested visiting me and spending a few days with me during my journey. I gladly accepted but could not wait to board the flight as I never knew how to handle family farewells.

As I said, my first destination was Athens, where I stayed with Tina, a twenty-nine-year-old local student in the faculty of education with a night job as a bartender. At first, I mistook her for a volleyballer, since she was taller than me and extremely slim, but after a little chat she told me it ran in their family. I met her on the Couch Surfing site, where tourists can find accommodation in local homes, free of charge, just out of mutual trust. It took her only two minutes after I had entered her apartment to say, "I must go, so here's the bathroom, there's food in the fridge. Here's your bed. Goodbye, I'm off, see you tomorrow."

Thus, all of a sudden, I found myself in the middle of Athens, in an apartment belonging to somebody I had only met ten minutes before and who trusted me with the keys to her house. It was astonishing. I mean, I was a complete stranger. Even the stories I heard about the legendary hospitality on such sites didn't prepare me for something so extraordinary.

Wondering whether I, my family, or friends would have treated a tourist who had similarly just arrived in our country, I had to admit, sadly – the answer was "No" with a capital N.

However, the next day I learned another lesson about local hospitality from a well-mannered and polite railway employee, smartly dressed in an Athens Railways uniform, complete with its logo on his hat.

"What's this long face about? If I understand you right, you plan to cycle thousands of kilometers," he remarked, laughing. "So why are you making such a fuss about an hour's ride to the next stop? Sorry, under our rules, you can't board this train with your bike."

To be honest, he was right, but it was somewhat frustrating. However, I had no choice but to ride to the next station along the line, where my bike and I could take a train to escape the bustling traffic of Athens. Traffic-wise, Athens is a disastrous combination of Tel Aviv, Jerusalem, and New Delhi. It is nearly as messy as the latter but without rickshaws, cows, and shitty streets.

For the last days of week one of my trip, I explored the least visited parts of Greece. I always managed to find these areas in every country and always found their landscapes, cultures, and people the most interesting. About a day after my departure from Athens, I had already ridden 500km west toward the Ionian Sea.

In those few days, I traveled through the central province of Attica and all the westernmost of Greece's thirteen provinces. Finally, I reached Epirus on the Albanian border, one of the least visited and – in my opinion – the most beautiful. What enchanted me the most were the deserted country roads running through high, green grassy hills along the coast.

Traveling north, I spotted a small fishermen's village once every couple of hours. In one such village, Astakos, I was lucky enough to enjoy the hospitality of a lovely local couple, Elena and Raul. They, too, had spent their lives traveling around the world. I had met them when they drove past me, in the opposite direction, about 20km away from their village. Once they spotted me, they U-turned and drove alongside me all the way back home. A cyclist riding into their village was a rather unusual sight. Though I didn't intend to stay at their place, I was moved by their hearty welcome and kindness. Anyway, there was no way I'd have turned down a chance to enjoy a bed, a shower, and a decent meal.

They lived on a scenic hill with a perfect view of the sea, which was only a kilometer away. Their balcony offered a clear view of the local fishermen unloading their catch every morning.

I remember how strongly I admired my hosts' way of life, even noting in my diary that if I could, I would have lived there for a while. I was so enchanted by that simplicity and tranquility that I completely forgot about the trip I had started. My hosts worked in a state-run tuna farm situated near the village that had a kitchen garden. Whenever they decided to go traveling, they just cycled far away until they'd had enough, and then cycled back home.

That evening, we all dined in a local diner where fish

was the main dish, and my hosts insisted on paying for it. Seeing how thriftily they lived, I was less than happy about it, but I soon realized it wasn't up to me. To this day, I have never eaten a fish dish matching the one in Astakos.

Astakos was 85km away from Igoumenitsa, the last Greek port before the Albanian border. I planned to get there that afternoon and take the ferry to Italy at midnight. Having a few hours to kill after I bought the ferry ticket,

I decided to treat myself to something tasty, so I bought some ingredients from the first grocery store I spotted. My camp burner was quick and efficient, giving the shakshuka my favorite texture, with strong red and yellow-white colors bubbling in the middle and an aroma that seriously stimulated my digestive juices. For my shakshuka, I used four eggs, two tomatoes, two red bell peppers, two cloves of garlic, parsley, a little olive oil, salt, and pepper. I devoured it instantly, and it sent me to sleep until it was time for me to sail to Italy.

After that bizarre, nighttime voyage from Igoumenitsa in Greece to its Italian partner, Brindisi, all I wanted was a cup of coffee and a few hours' rest. The ferry, as the main means of transportation between the two countries, mostly carried North African asylum and job seekers, along with some private cars and commercial trucks. It was a sort of floating bus terminal, with no privacy, no place to sleep; the only quiet space was the deck, leaving me exposed to the sounds and splashing of the waves breaking against the bow.

This is how I ended up wrapped in my sleeping bag on board a ferry, on a night voyage to Italy. I got no sleep at all due to the brightness of the night and the smell and salty spray of the Ionian Sea water breaking overboard and invading my nostrils. This served as a constant reminder of the real power of the sea. My only consolation and diversion that night was staring at the shining stars since I had to wrap up nearly all my body to fend off the cold wind, leaving just my upper face exposed.

Lying this way allowed me to contemplate many things, especially about how little of Greece I had experienced during my 500km ride through it. I vowed to return to that country, renowned for its excellent food and music. I also thought of the long ride ahead, wondering how Italy would like me. The rumors I had heard of that country's reckless drivers and its cyclist-unfriendly roads did little to boost my morale.

Exhausted by my long ride, I managed a little nap for about an hour, waking up to the sound of the ship's horn signaling that we had reached safe haven.

Most of Italy is mountainous, especially in the north, where the Alps and the Dolomites rise. Only a small part of it, between Venice and Turin, is flat, with many farms. Riding there was easy, but that wasn't what I had come for. The landscapes I longed to see were the mighty mountains separating Italy from its northern neighbor, Switzerland.

The weather on day one in Italy was unfavorable; the rain and Adriatic Sea winds relentlessly haunting me. In order to escape the lashing rain for a few minutes, I decided to take a bus. When it arrived, I realized that this ride was going to be a little adventurous. The bus was not designed to carry a cyclist with such a large bike and trunk bags, yet when the driver opened the door for me, he just smiled at me from under his huge mustache, saying a few words in the world's most beautiful language. I didn't understand a word, of course, but his tone and gestures made it clear that he was one of the good guys.

Not knowing a single word of English did not keep him from helping me. In a few words to the passengers, he probably told them he was letting me on the bus and if anybody didn't like it, tough luck. It felt embarrassing to be standing there in my short, dirty, cycling pants, leaves and mud stuck to my shoes and feet, my hands concealed by dirty gloves, clutching my bike loaded with waterlogged saddlebags.

After a forty-five-minute ride, when we reached a bend, I asked the driver to stop for me, and once again I received surprising help from him as well as a local woman passenger. This, too, made me wonder if I would have been treated the same in Israel.

In just a few weeks in Italy, I managed to ride over 1000km. Completing an ordinary climb just north of Genoa, on the Mediterranean Sea coast, I felt I was perspiring excessively. I knew very well that perspiration is part of any physical exercise, but this time I seemed to be perspiring even while resting, so I decided to have rest a little longer than usual.

With my pulse growing faster and my body temperature rising by the minute, I sought shade about 500m away, where I took all my clothes off except for my short tights. Reaching for the water bottle secured to the rear of my bike, I emptied it over my head, hoping it would cool me down, yet my body kept boiling like an overheated car radiator.

I started to worry. All this indicated that I was facing serious heatstroke. It could hardly be any worse as there were no human settlements within two hours' ride and the road was almost deserted. I kept sweating and felt like I was about to throw up my breakfast. To make things worse, I also felt exhausted, but I realized that I must do something soon or else I'd pass out and lose control.

I kept pouring water over my head and resumed riding, somehow managing to complete a small climb, then dismounted. Then, with my last ounce of strength, half-naked, I mounted my bike again. Gripping the handlebars with one hand and holding the bottle with the other, I poured water over my head. I hoped the wind would cool me down a little. Indeed, I felt a little better after a ten-minutes shallow descent. After I had thrown up my break-fast, the nausea ended.

After riding for about thirty minutes from where I had started, I began feeling sick, I reached a proper night camp-site at the edge of a grove by the main road. There, I set up my tent, stretched a rope between two trees to dry my water-logged and sweat-soaked clothes, and slipped into my sleeping bag. I had to rest for a few minutes. I can still remember how completely exhausted I felt that night.

Later on, strong hunger woke me, and I forced a few snacks into my mouth, drank hot, sweet tea that I boiled on my camp burner, and slipped right back into the sleeping bag to complete my recovery.

The next day, I was back in the saddle, yet I knew I would be facing a rough ride once I passed Milan, and so it was. Cycling on Italy's roads proved harder than anything I had done before, yet it was made easier thanks to the views of the snowcapped mountains and other landscapes on my way uphill.

I remember one such climb when I stopped next to a stone bridge covered with spots of green moss. Right after the bridge, a formidable cliff towered above the road with a yellow metal tap projecting out of it, just pouring water all over the road. I filled my water bottles and washed my face with it, wondering why nobody had ever stopped that water being wasted like that.

I saw many similar taps by the roadside in Europe that allowed me not to have to carry great amounts of water with me. Finally, I crossed the Swiss border, traveling along the

Paso del Stelvio – Italy's highest road and one of the world's highest – at an altitude of 2760m.

"What's up, Maya? I'm fine, thank you. Yes, still alive. I barely made it to Eilat, still exhausted, but getting better. Tell me, why do I see your old heap in this parking lot? Is there any chance you're around?"

"Hi, perfect stranger! Good to hear from you. What's up? You better not bad-mouth my SUV. Clear!? Yes, I'm in Eilat... unwillingly. Where are you, exactly? Send me your location on a Google Map and I'll come for you."

"Sending my location, Maya, but I still don't know why you're here at such an hour."

"Tzuriel, for one who's alone most of the time, you ask a lot of questions...just kidding, don't take it too hard. Actually, it's too complicated to explain by text message. Well, you nag, just stay where you are, I'm on my way."

Fifteen minutes later, I saw her approaching. For some unknown reason, I was excited to see her and all of a sudden felt shitty about being dressed like a bum in traveler's clothes and flip-flops, instead of more appropriate evening attire. I sniffed my armpit to make sure I didn't smell too much, wondering where this date might take me. I somehow read between the lines of her message that, for her, it was not business as usual.

The streetlamps only enhanced her seductive power as she walked toward me. Her black boat shoes and black elegant pants with visible creases accentuated her elegant steps. The northerly wind blowing against her long, white shirt made her nipples protrude. Her neck was adorned with a large collar, and on her chest, a small Tommy Hilfiger logo was sewn to her shirt. The wind blew her loose hair all over her face, and the contrast with her tidy attire looked seductive. But the moment she came near me, I noticed her eyes were red and that she had tried to conceal her unhappy face with her hair. I was right to suspect she had been going through hard times.

Without waiting for my permission, she crossed the border between our two personal spaces, letting me engulf her in my arms. The fragrance of her hair invaded my nostrils, intoxicating me with the smell of a high-quality hair product. I always had a weakness for fragrances, and I felt stunned for a while. While she was buried deep in my arms, I tried to practice a hugging technique I'd picked up a couple of years before: a clinch of at least twenty seconds, not too tight, not too loose. It's also essential to start very slowly and increase the pressure gradually. This goes, of course, for the release as well.

"Hey, where did you learn to hug like that?" Her voice was muffled as she was still wrapped in my arms.

"Oh, it comes naturally, an innate talent," I explained it away to her.

"You liar! C'mon, where did you learn it!?" she pressed on, pinching my waist.

"Well," I confessed, "I took a hugging course a couple of years ago. This helped me improve my embraces, especially when I embrace my dear ones. Why, did you like it? Does it need improvement?"

"Improvement? Are you kidding!? If I only could, I'd have asked you to never stop!" she protested, slowly breaking free from me.

When she faced me, I noticed the tears flowing from her eyes. Holding her hands in her pockets, she slowly shook her head, as if rejecting something.

"Honey, tell me what's the matter? I can't see you shattered like this, though you're terribly sexy when you're moist."

"Have you ever been called a complete moron!?" She scorned me, smilingly.

"Come on over here... let's sit down on this bench I adopted. Wait there, while I get you an ice cream." Pointing at the bench for her, I rushed off to the nearest ice cream bar.

A couple of minutes later, I was back with a cone with two scoops of ice cream, one chocolate and the other passionfruit. We stayed silent for a few minutes. I watched her licking her ice cream, unnoticed by her. When she finished it, her tongue had assumed a glamorous, orange hue against the dark night. She was definitely one of the prettiest women I'd met recently, I concluded. I was so caught up with her that, for a moment, I even considered abandoning this whole trip for her sake.

"How did you guess I'd like an ice cream, and exactly my favorite flavors as well?" she inquired.

"Well, Maya, for one who doesn't like to talk about herself, you're too damn inquisitive for such a time of the night. I know many things about you you're yet to discover."

"Good, one-nil to you! You're a kickass! Listen, I must get back to my hotel, so how about meeting me tomorrow? I promise to tell you everything, unless you already have an arrangement with another local girl."

We said goodbye, but not before we had decided to meet the next day at Dekel Beach, one of the city's iconic beaches.

I was quite speechless before she left since I still sensed some mystery about her.

Riding in a taxi back to Koby's place, I wondered why the hell I'd once again gotten myself in such a mess, after making a vow to stay away from women of her kind – that is, ambiguous and excessively attractive ones. Those as hot as fire from head to toe are those who burn you most painfully.

The next day, I accomplished many tasks. Collecting the solar charger Ehud had sent me, I was happy to find out it was the best in the market and would probably make my trip much more comfortable.

I was eager to get on my bike once again to rush north on Route 90 all the way from Taba Crossing on the Egyptian border to Fatma Crossing near Metula on the Lebanese border. I planned to cycle most of this 478km route all the way to Tzemach Junction near Lake Tiberias. I had many reasons to worry about traveling on this road. I'd heard so many warnings about the deadly curves of this road from friends who had traveled on it before, that at some point I just stopped listening to them. I just wanted to experience it for myself and assumed that having negotiated roads all over Italy, I could handle Route 90 just fine.

What really gave me sleepless nights was the weather. According to the forecast, there were several days of heatwave ahead all over the country. Usually, during a transitory season, the air temperature rises to extremes before resuming a normal level. However, the weather report for the next day was nearly 38°C in the shade, which meant over 40° on the road.

Well, this required special preparations. I had to buy special gear and would make a stop once every thirty minutes – or at least in every hour – to check my urine color, which is the best indicator of physical state. As I kept telling the children I trained in a sports club, "Orange urine means you're in ruins; if your urine is colorless, you're a damn kick-ass!" I remembered these words almost every day during my trip across the devilishly hot Arava Valley.

I felt flooded with the thrill of riding, and I spent the few hours before the early start next morning resting, reading *Kafka on the shore*, and texting:

"Hi, Maya, what's up? It was really fun yesterday, but on second thought, I think it's better to call our date off. I have a lot on my mind and too little time. Hope to see you again someday. Anyway, it was nice to see you again, especially when you were so close to me. So, take care. Bye."

I had really given Maya a lot of thought and doubted whether I should date her at all, so I decided just to call it off in a short message, without much explanation. This whole thing felt awkward, maybe because I suspected she was in a relationship and I really didn't want to get into a mess.

She failed to respond all day, which I found strange since, so far, she had responded immediately. This made me fear I might have hurt her feelings or shouldn't have called it off at all.

That afternoon, I was preoccupied with final preparations for the next day's ride, so Maya gradually became the least of my concerns, and I believed I would never see her again.

Or so I thought.

PART II

5

DAY 5

"Life is like riding a bicycle. To keep your balance, you must keep moving."

Albert Einstein

April 3, 2016
Starting point: Eilat
Destination: Kibbutz Yahel
Distance: 64 kilometers

"Space, the final frontier. These are the voyages of the Starship Enterprise, its continuing mission to explore strange new worlds, to seek out new life and new civilization, to boldly go where no one has gone before..."

That statement, opening every episode of Star Trek, an iconic TV series I admired as a child, had been on my mind ever since I started out along Route 90. This statement – as well as the philosophy presented in that series – had shaped my current character. More specifically, it bred in me a wanderlust and a love of great thrills that await those who dare to leave their comfort zones.

Though Route 90 was nothing like intergalactic space, it certainly felt like exploring unknown territory when joining it. Every heartbeat sent a shot of curiosity through my veins. A shiver ran down my spine when, perfectly in time, the Israeli rock-star Shalom Hanoch sang into my earphones, "Dressed in black she appeared – in the dark she was blazing. Queen of my fantasy came to me."

The sun was still concealed behind the West Jordan mountains and was about to appear at any moment, and I was smiling as that song ran through my head as I passed the checkpoint just before Eilat on Southern Route 90. I thought to myself – *Jerusalem here I come!*

I started testing the shifting mechanism during the first few hundred meters of the route to avoid surprises during the most deserted part of the Arava Valley, and I was pleasantly surprised by the smooth shifting of the chain between the sprockets.

Amin's bike technician had definitely improved my bike's performance, and the riding was quick and easy. The chilly, early morning air pierced my clothes, cooling me down a little. Still, I could already sense the intense heat expected later that day. I could see high clouds and practically feel the temperature rise by one degree every thirty minutes and the air growing drier, little by little. At sunrise, I started to face a mild north wind. Having already cycled here during triathlons, I was familiar with that wind.

Riding past Kibbutz Eilot, I noticed some unusual palms called Doum Palms. Unlike any other palm, the stem of the Doum splits into woody branches. Growing a few tens of meters away from the road, those Doum palms were majestically tall – nearly fifteen meters – with spiky, fan-shaped wide leaves, its top resembling a magnificent crown.

Later on, I rode past the date palm plantations of Kibbutz Yotvata, which stretches along the entire eastern side of the road. Dates, together with the iconic brand Yotvata Chocolate Milk, were Yotveta's main sources of income. The date palms were aligned in perfectly straight rows like soldiers on inspection, all the way to the Jordanian border, splitting the Arava valley right across the middle between the West Jordan Mountains and the Israeli Jordan Valley Rift mountains. The palm plantation made a green spot in the middle of the desert yellow and ran all along my northbound route.

Once in a while, a tractor pulling a cart full of farm laborers crossed the road. They seemed well-prepared for working under a scorching sun, wearing long, bright-colored clothing, wide-brimmed hats, with some even protected their face from the sun with a thin piece of cloth.

It was a few minutes past 08:00 and a few kilometers past the plantation when my cell phone suddenly rang, mercilessly interrupting Pearl Jam's hit, "Alive." I was so thrilled with the morning that I had forgotten to turn the cell phone off. Cautiously holding the handlebar with one hand, I pulled my cell phone out of the back pocket of my shirt. It was Tom Stein, the Channel Two reporter.

I pulled over to the curb, balancing the bike between my slightly spread legs. I was keen to avoid a long stop that might steal the precious cool hours of the day and planned to rest only when it was too hot to ride safely.

We talked for a few minutes, during which Stein very kindly demonstrated his interest in my project, listening most patiently to my explanations, and even suggested interviewing and taking some pictures of me. I was very flat-

tered by the channel's offer, although I had no idea how
they had tracked me down, and I gave him a brief description of my schedule for the next few weeks. We agreed to
talk again that evening in an attempt to make an appointment. Though I wasn't well-versed in the rather useful art of
PR, I knew it was critical for fundraising, which was what
this whole trip was all about. Making prime-time might be
really helpful.

After the call, I started thinking that meeting him might
prove somewhat impractical. Making a few hours' stop to
wait for a news channel crew was out of the question since I
planned to complete the journey shortly before Passover.
Well, I was proved wrong.

If I hadn't obsessed so much about meeting my schedule
at all costs, my project would have enjoyed much more
intensive public attention and, consequently, raised more
money. Still, I was doing quite well until then, collecting a
total sum of 8000 dollars, my final goal being about 20,000.

When the banana I'd bought yesterday had drowned in
a few good gulps of water inside my belly, I put my cell
phone in flight mode and got moving again.

My next stop was a few kilometers south of Kibbutz
Ketura, situated in the Southern Arava Valley, about 50km
from Eilat – a tiny green oasis in the middle of the desert-
yellow plains that Route 90 runs through. It was not yet
midday when the clip-on bike thermometer reached thirty
degrees. It was just another indication that the heat had
intensified enough for me to look for a shady place to rest
before facing the even more challenging route ahead.

Far away, I spotted a gray-haired acacia, a tree of the
legume family common in this part of Israel. It stood
upright and quite alone just a minute's walk from the road,
offering quite an impressive shade. Yet the shade was a kind

of mixed blessing since the tree's thorns could easily tear my tires, so I approached it very cautiously.

I carried out my routine: taking my clothes off to let them dry and a few lower back and leg stretching exercises with only my pants on. I noticed my complexion was getting tanned – that is, sunburned – since leaving Eilat. There were unmistakable tan lines on my mid-thighs and on both arms and ankles.

I liked what I saw yet decided to apply more protective cream and only wear long-sleeved shirts when riding during the hottest part of the day. Otherwise, sooner or later, my skin would start to peel off.

The hissing camp burner brewing my black coffee combined with the sounds of vehicles driving by got me into a resting mood. Spotting a large rock nearby, I decided to sit on it to avoid the thorny ground and turned on my Go-Pro camera as I did whenever I could in an attempt to document every moment of this journey.

A look at the map gave me many reasons to be proud of myself. I was making good progress, and the bike was in perfect shape. Therefore, calculating my daily advancement, I decided to change my plans and ride on, skipping the planned stop at Kibbutz Yahel, and only set up camp for the night the moment I felt exhausted.

Luckily, every community along my route had a shaded bus stop, and nearly all of them offered access to free water, so I could use my water quite liberally and suffer no water shortages during my sweaty ride.

The black coffee and energy snacks were taking their effect, and I felt all set for the last section before my long, midday break. By that time, my cycling shirt and sweat towel had dried completely. That 20cm by 20cm towel had become very handy to me on this journey. I stuffed it between the handlebar and the handlebar bag so I could use it to wipe my face whenever my eyes were irritated by sweat. However, sweat was part-and-parcel of cycling in that region; very frequently, it flooded every centimeter of my body like a rushing stream.

My capacity to sweat during extreme physical strain has never stopped surprising me, even after I became an experienced cyclist. The towel was always sweat-soaked after an hour or two of riding, and I frequently had to tie it to the rear of my bike, where I kept my solar charger.

I reached Yahel after 64km in sauna-like, dry weather similar to that of the Eilat Mountains. This time, on top of the heat and the strain, I also had to deal with a headwind as hot as a furnace channeling all its force at my face. However, except for the body heat and the fire-red face, there were no signs of physical distress.

The local bus stop made a perfect, shady resting place. I recovered there, cooled down, and planned my further itinerary for that day. I also used the resting time to read text messages and text my family my exact location.

All my emails that day consisted of quite similar questions regarding practical advice about preparing for such a trip, especially about handling such extreme heat. To avoid answering every individual message, I posted the following notice on my trip's Facebook page:

Hi, everybody. Right now, I'm on Route 90 and, so far, everything's going quite well. Temperature is nearly forty degrees in the shade, so I'm having a little rest to cool down before I ride on, and to answer the questions I've been asked for the last couple of days, such as how much water to take, how to deal with the heat, and whether you can cycle at all when it's so hot. All these questions have to be asked by anyone engaged in physical activity in extremely hot weather.

Following my long experience, I offer you these tips:

First of all, when there's doubt, cut it out. During hot weather, avoid any unnecessary risks, especially concerning water shortage. Once you've reached a watering place and you don't know when you'll reach the next one, drink at least a liter of water, refill all your bottles and load up with another liter! Carefully examine the map of the area in advance to learn the location of potential supply points such as gas stations, army bases, rural communities, and so on. Also, learn the locations of shaded places where you can rest – sometimes a rare piece of shade can stand between you and a fatal heatstroke. Plan your route accordingly.

Judging from my own experience on summer rides, take at least one liter of water per hour's ride. You'll also need water for cooking your supper (another half-liter for a trip of several days), and a further half-liter for keeping clean (showering, toothbrushing, and morning face-washing). The amount of water you'll need for the next day's ride depends on your distance from each watering place.

When I rode to Eilat on hot days, I carried with me between 10 and 12 liters per day. Further on along Route 90, I'm carrying less water knowing I can rely on communities and gas stations, thus avoiding overloading my bike.

Carefully watch body indications. The best indication is your urine color. If it grows dark, you're in really bad shape and it's advisable to make longer stops and drink more water. If you sense nausea, dizziness, or apathy, you're probably suffering from heatstroke or dehydration, so you must reach the nearest human settlement for treatment or call for rescue.

I'm here for any questions. In an hour, I'll be back on my

way north. Hope to meet you soon and thank you for all your supportive comments. Have a great day, y'all!

I didn't bother to check the time but I was eager to start off, and since my body had cooled down significantly, I liberally applied protection cream to my arms and legs, made sure my hat protected my face and the back of my neck, and pushed my bike back onto the road. When I got on the road, a truck rushing by blew its horn and the driver seemed to wave me goodbye, smiling like one who only crosses the desert under his comfortable climate control system could. It blew a powerful wind in my face as if from a colossal fan placed right in front of me, drying my lips and even slightly rocking my bike for a few seconds.

Only after the truck had gone did I fully sense the intense heat I was enduring. With a very sweaty and challenging 46km ride ahead, I hesitated for a second , but the next second, I jumped on my saddle smiling like an idiot who has no idea what a mess he's got himself into.

Well, I've always loved a challenge. Standing up to them is one of my daily sources of happiness and power. What makes life unexpectedly interesting – the moments that make life worth living – is exactly all those senseless challenges, such as writing this book, which I hope to complete someday. At that moment, I recalled the inspiring statement of some famous mountaineer. When asked, "Why climb Everest?" he replied, "Because it's there." The question of whether it should be attributed to the Briton, George Mallory, or the New Zealander who conquered Everest, Edmund Hillary, is still debated.

As early as one minute into my ride north, I had already realized that I was about to go through one of my most extreme heat-rides ever before I had even reached the Dead Sea, Israel's hottest region.

Making a stop in the shade of Yahel's bus stop, I carefully examined my route on the map and set that day's destination at Kushi Rimon Inn, known as the 101 Inn, since it was situated west of Route 90, 101km from Eilat. There, I planned to wash my hands with running water, fill all my water bottles, and maybe indulge in a cup of iced coffee before spending another night outdoors.

April offered me an increasingly long daylight time, which proved very useful. That day, sunset would take place at 18:05, allowing me a more relaxed ride with no reason to worry about nightfall.

I reached the inn at 18:30 in the early evening after the sun had set behind the Jordan Valley cliffs and the heat had subsided.

Oh, how I looked forward to that rest! By then, there was not an ounce of energy left in me. Though not dehydrated, I was completely exhausted by the heat and needed a sugar bomb of the unhealthiest kind available right away.

The place was filled with dozens of people, including some families. I asked a nearby family to watch my stuff for a moment and rushed to the nearest bathroom. First of all, I somehow forced my head under the tap, cooling myself this way. Closing my eyes, I maintained this awkward position for quite a few minutes. My skull felt the water's coolness instantly, projecting it all over my body until my shining, red-hot face regained its normal complexion.

Returning to my bike, I drank my hourly fill of water, and then another liter, to be on the safe side. I also had to check my urine color, since I couldn't remember the last time I had urinated, which was another sign of trouble. Five minutes later, I went to the bathroom to examine my urine, and the result was far from perfect. I'd lost a lot of fluids due to the intense heat and insufficient drinking, since I strictly rationed my water consumption. My urine, however, though not colorless, was not dark orange either, so I assumed I could make it in the current circumstances. All I needed to do was to constantly replenish my fluids.

I spent another thirty minutes at the inn and did another urine test with a better result this time. Now I could realize the wet dream (pun intended) that had kept me going during the last section of riding: the iced coffee. A couple of minutes after I had placed my order, the vendor served me a plastic cup with a black cap covered with clear water droplets due to the temperature difference. I grasped it gently, with both hands, like some precious gem, pressing it against my right cheek for a few seconds, then against my left.

The shot of cold pierced my skin like lightning, giving me a few seconds of goose pimples all over. Only after indulging in this cooling process with almost religious devotion did I insert the black drinking straw between my lips, and start to slowly draw the sweet, grayish liquid up the straw then down my throat all the way to my stomach.

It felt like a midsummer wildfire was suddenly extinguished. I was so relaxed that I was in a kind of sedated state for a couple of minutes. I can't remember how many minutes exactly I spent drinking that coffee, but I believe this iced coffee was the slowest-drunk ever in that inn.

Then I walked away cheerfully, pushing my bike east across the road toward the Jordanian border. Spotting a suitable site for my tent between the inn and the border, I started gathering branches and twigs for a campfire to keep me warm through the night and repel undesirable animals. The lights of the inn, about 50m away, brightened up the place a little, and the campfire burned with a small flame, exactly the way I wanted it to. I surrounded it with a wall of small rocks to keep the wind from extinguishing it and from blowing the embers in my direction. Little by little, the embers started spreading a pleasant warmth that made me sleepy. The bike was safely locked to the tent pole, all my gear was inside near the mattress and the sleeping bag, which were all spread out and ready to wrap me up for the night.

Surrounded by the dark, I trained my eyes on the fire, feeling isolated from my surroundings by the cocoon of warmth. To make it even cozier, I turned my Petzel head-lamp on. Its soft, white-bluish light illuminated my diary sufficiently. Leaning against a rock, I mindlessly let my pen run freely all over the pages while my thoughts roamed away, filling them with line after line:

It's been several years since I completed my tour of Europe, and I had quite a hard time getting re-accustomed to my country, especially explaining to members of my inner circle what exactly I had in mind. This bad communi-cation recurred during the days of preparation for the present trip, the Heart to Heart Journey.

I was so filled with the experiences from my previous journey that, in a way, they forced all mundane routine out of me, leaving me hollow. And there was only one way to refill myself: to succumb once again to my wanderlust, taking the endless road to the unexpected. Almost an entire decade of gathering sights, experiences, and a variety of acquaintances has left me an emotional billionaire in possession of a lifelong experience that has enlightened me about myself and my place on Earth.

That period taught me the art of boundless love and acceptance, of tasting whatever I encountered, of listening instead of speaking, containing instead of judging, looking around me instead of keeping my eyes shut, moving on rather than standing my ground.

Eventually, I realized that there are many ways to live this life; there's always much more to reality than meets the eye. When I decided to get off the wagon rushing along the beaten track, there were those who gave me an oblique look. Many of them couldn't figure out how I dared to part from them all of a sudden, asking no permission. This made me understand that I'd taken the right way, which didn't necessarily suit the rest of the passengers.

I woke up a few minutes later, lying on the desert ground and shivering from the cold. The warm campfire and the exhaustion of a 100km ride under heavy heat stress made me fall asleep in the middle of writing in my diary. Well, this indicated that it was time to hit the sack. I got up, brushed my teeth, removed some rocks from the campfire, and popped them into a shallow tunnel I had dug beforehand under my tent. I covered them over and restored the tent in place. After making sure everything was secured to the tent, I slipped deep into my sleeping bag and lay on my back staring at the tent ceiling, my mind absolutely clear of any thoughts. All I could hear was the gentle crackling of the simmering embers outside and an occasional car driving by while I was slowly falling asleep. I felt my eyelids grow too heavy to keep open and a few moments after I heard the last car, I was already in the realm of dreams.

Just before I fell asleep, I realized that the next day had in store a challenge as great as the one I'd faced that day, so a proper sleep was as essential for me as all the food and water that I had brought along.

6

DAY 6

"No one is useless in this world who lightens the burdens of another."

Charles Dickens

April 4, 2016
Starting point: Kushi Rimon Inn
Destination: Arava Junction
Distance: 82 kilometers

Only when I got up that morning, right next to Route 90, did I realize how soundly I had slept the night before. The air was as silent as it can only be in the desert – no traffic, with only occasional birds flying and tweeting in the air.

My tent flap opened opposite the Jordan Mountains, where the sunrise was expected at any moment. The tent walls were wet, probably the result of either rainwater getting inside or condensation from my body heat combined with the heat of the rocks that had I placed under the tent. They had certainly been effective enough to make me take my shirt and pajama pants off in the middle of the night.

Sitting up on my sleeping bag and unzipping the tent flap to let in the cool, fresh, morning air, I noticed that my whole body was moving heavily. Then a pain shot through my spine from my neck all the way down to my feet, a symptom of incessant riding for more than a week. Realizing that, I lay flat for another couple of minutes.

At such moments, I enjoyed letting all kinds of thoughts run through my head, such as wondering what might have happened if Maya had been there. Guessing the answer to this question made me so horny that I forgot my painfully cramped muscles and probed for and found my cell phone. While I was wondering what to text her, I remembered her elegant appearance during our recent date back in Eilat, which only aggravated my horny feeling. Counting to ten, I breathed in several times and put my cell phone down. I crawled out of my tent just as I was – naked, horny, and cramped. All my leg muscles, especially my ass, were terribly stiff, so I started doing stretch-and-release exercises right away. Little-by-little, I relaxed myself.

The sun had just risen above the ridge across the Jordanian border. With my coffee boiled, I continued my morning routine, namely stretching, drinking coffee, reading a few pages of Murakami, and preparing for the ride. I found *Kafka on the Shore* a hilarious growing-up novel. It really gave me an insight into that Japanese writer's head, thus serving as my refuge from the grueling routine of this trip and taking me mentally to places far away from my here and now.

I finished my preparations, making sure that all my water bottles were filled, and that all the gear was tightly secured, especially my intense heat clothes tied to the rear, ready to be used, and that my protection cream was in my handlebar bag, ready to be applied.

Once I started pushing my heavily-laden bike toward the road, I noticed an increased flow of trucks on it. One of them, with a trailer of rocks and sand, was leaving the inn's parking lot for Arava Junction. It slowly took the bend on the road and finally straightened up between the hard shoulder and the white line. Moving my eyes from my bike to the truck and back again, I had an amusing thought: my bike was just as heavily laden as that trailer and was just as cumbersome on the road. Just like the truck, it was practically incapable of doing a U-turn or traveling backward.

However, I felt that my load, though also heavy, was something more sublime than sand and rocks. It contained items such as compassion, charity, and non-judgmental acceptance of fellow-humans. Since then, I've nicknamed my bike "my truck." That day, I planned to reach the gas station near Aravah Junction, where I could get food and water.

The route there presented a moderate climb, yet my main concerns were the north wind, which was about to hit my face, and the heat about to set me ablaze.

A few minutes later, yesterday's pain – as opposed to all my other pains that morning, which I believed had gone – suddenly reappeared. A tiny spot next to my right knee, near the head of the fibula (where the hamstrings or knee cord muscles are connected to the lateral collateral ligament) started hurting whenever I pressed the right pedal of my "truck." Attributing it to incorrect footwork, I guessed that if I had been doing it for at least a week, pain was inevitable. Though not getting worse, the pain just didn't go away, constantly bothering me, as if I were running a long distance with a tiny rock in my shoe. Knee pain heralds trouble and trying to ignore the pain by shouting out song lyrics against the north wind did little good. Finally, I realized I must treat it at my very next stop, and that this was just another sacrifice I had to make for my project.

I was already past Wadi Paran and the greenhouses of Moshav Paran heading for the community of Tzukim, where I planned to make a long stop in order to apply muscle pain relief cream to my right knee and have a rest before facing the midday heat. I was almost completely sweat-soaked, and on some parts of the road, I had to ride with my helmet off, wearing only a hat, due to the heat. Wiping my forehead with my good old towel, I suddenly heard noisy music and the engine of a car tailing me so closely that I felt it was about to bump into me.

Without thinking, I pulled over onto the shoulder, gesturing the driver with my left hand to overtake me. A quick look back revealed a silver Mazda Lantis with dark lines of peeled-off paint on the bonnet and two passengers wearing black baseball hats seated in the front.

Instantly realizing that they were Bedouins in a hurry, I had no wish to delay them so I slowed down, pulling over even further to the right, hoping they would just overtake me and drive off. Instead, they just kept tailing me, which sounded alarm bells.

The road being empty, they had no reason to tail me. Finally, they moved over to the next lane but kept traveling in it. The guy next to the driver opened his window, holding a cigarette with one hand while moving his other hand to the music. Judging from the lyrics, I think it was an Eyal Golan number, though I couldn't be sure.

"Morning, buddy. Hey, what you doin'?" he asked.

"Morning to you, I'm riding my bike."

"No kiddin'." He took a puff and went on. "Say, buddy,

wanna join us for a tea and a hookah? There's a parking lot up ahead. How 'bout it?"

Pretending not to hear him, I kept silent. I had no idea why they picked me, of all people, to be their guest. It was hot and I was not in the mood for tea, let alone for stopping, so I just hoped they would go away.

Yet rather than letting go of me, they started tailing me again, following me north. Since I could not afford a confrontation with two Bedouins in the middle of nowhere, over 100km away from civilization, I decided to just stop and let them drive on if they didn't leave me alone soon.

Taking the central lane again, he resumed his questioning in a heavy Arab accent, "You probably take us for some Bedouin criminals, a bunch of thieves, right? Trust me, if we wanted to do something bad to you, we'd have done it long ago. But you look rather cool, a sort of cool looney, not worth messing around with. C'mon, it'll be okay. We'll stop and wait for you for a few minutes. Come, we're okay, trust me!"

Then, finally overtaking me, they disappeared over the horizon. I had no idea what parking lot he was talking about, but a few minutes later I spotted the sign for a parking lot east of the road next to a fallen soldier's memorial. I spotted their vehicle again when I was 500m away and had to choose whether to join them, risking some mishap, or ride on to the next parking lot.

What if they are, actually, okay? I stopped at the entrance to the parking lot. Why suspect them right away? It felt quite similar to my encounter with the Egyptian soldier on Route 12. Approaching the parking lot, I saw the two guys sitting, with a hookah and a camp burner going. They gestured to me to come closer. The strong scent of apple-flavored hookah tobacco hit my nostrils, cheering me up.

It only took me a few moments to see that I had no reason to fear them. They were brothers, members of the Krinawi family, one of the largest in the Bedouin town of Rahat. They were driving home from Eilat, where they worked, and only wanted to treat me to tea according to Bedouin custom.

For my part, I treated them to the Tim Tams I had bought in Eilat. This, it turned out, was the very first time they had tasted them. Judging from their responses, it wouldn't be the last.

After discussing local politics for nearly thirty minutes, we said goodbye, but not before I had apologized for my previous snobbishness. Forgiving me completely, they asked me to give them a call if I happened to drive by their place, as they'd love to meet me again. Realizing that I had no stuff on me, and wouldn't mind some, they gave me a thick joint stuffed with weed and drove on north to the sounds of Eyal Golan.

Right after they left, I took a look at the memorial. It must commemorate an unusual incident to have been erected in the middle of nowhere. I was surprised to find out that it was in honor of a Druze soldier who had died near Mount Nishpeh during a solo land navigation as part of his Special Forces training. His unit decided to mark the site of his death because, among other things, he was the only Druze soldier to join the Israeli Special Forces so far. I was so impressed that I sent a picture of the memorial to some of my friends who were doing their military service there.

It was a little past 12:00 noon when I started preparing my "truck" for the heat-stricken road. At the same time, I quickly checked the last series of messages. Most of them were mundane, some repetitive, yet they all made me smile and seriously boosted my morale.

If I followed my plan, within two days, I would reach Jerusalem where I would have a rest at the lovely home of my elder brother, Ari, his wife Shiri, and their six children, and enjoy a view of Temple Mount. I was looking forward to it, already dreaming of a decent shower and my sister-in-law's delicious food. Yet before that, I had to cover the entire section of Route 90 that ran along the shores of the Dead Sea, and then, naturally, its northern part.

Just as I was about to turn my cell phone off and put it in my handlebar bag, I received three message alerts. One was from Ehud about donating another 2,000 dollars and wishing me good luck. We'd become acquainted five years earlier when he had asked me to instruct him in lifestyle and fitness. It took us a short espresso in a gas station in central Israel and a ten-minute introductory conversation to completely understand and befriend each other.

Since then, we had been riding together on weekends, swimming in the sea on weekdays, and planning future adventures together. Ehud is practically a self-made man who, for the last twenty years, has been engaged in a global business that he rarely mentions. It was only recently that I had discovered his matchless generosity. I have never met anyone who has made so many donations to individuals and charitable organizations. Although we had become close friends, I was strongly moved by his generosity to my project and him sharing my vision.

The next message was from Maya. She was raging mad at me for standing her up to the point of wanting to beat the hell out of me. She also wanted me to send her my location on the map, which I did right away.

A third message was from Tali, my good friend and companion on my trip to Nepal. Following my route, she saw I was near Moshav Ein Yahav, where her parents lived, and texted me this:

Hi, Tzuri. What's up? Listen, you nutter, would I love to join you for a couple of hours! What you're going through looks like damn kick-ass! To the point: I see you're near my place, so ride into Ein Yahav – my dad's there. It's very hot, so have a rest and help yourself to a cold drink. Here's my dad's address and number. Have tons of fun. Hugs and kisses. Tali.

I first met Tali a few years ago during the around Anna-purna trek when a snowstorm pinned us down in the same guesthouse in the Nepalese village of Manang, 3500m above sea level. We were stuck there with dozens of tourists who had tried to reach Thorong La Pass, the highest point of the trek. There was no way into or out of the village due to the heavy snow. Since then, I have kept in touch with her, and we even toured New York City together when she was an El Al flight attendant and I was bored enough to enter the New York Marathon, the world's biggest running event.

Tali's message was just in time, so I texted her that I was on my way to Ein Yahav. It was already over 35° outside, and the peak was yet to come. I had already reconciled myself to the fact that I was facing very extreme weather conditions and that my progress would be hindered by the wind blowing along the Jordan Valley.

My next stop was 20km away. If I kept going at 20kph, I would reach it in a little more than an hour. However, after just ten minute's ride past the community of Tzukim, the heat was even more unbearable. The sun blazed right over-head, heating the black asphalt, which, in turn, reflected the heat straight at my face. I felt my body temperature getting dangerously high.

Realizing that my head immediately commanded my

legs to slow down, I took the earphones out of my ears just as Metallica was belting out their hit, "Master of Puppets" for me. I just withdrew into myself, focusing on my aching right knee, my sweat-stinging left eye, and the inferno into which I was riding. I was desperately searching for the strength to keep me going until my next stop.

I knew that I could not reach my destination in one piece if I insisted on riding at full force into the hot north wind, so I decided to slow down. It was about 14:00, nearly two hours after I had stopped to chat with the Bedouins, when I made it to Ein Yahav after making several stops in order to rest and cool my head and body with water. However, after another ten minutes' ride, I was completely dried up. It was as if I had never cooled myself down or drunk anything at all. During the stop, I changed my short-sleeved cycling shirt for a long-sleeved white one to protect my arms from the scorching sun.

The moment I entered Tali's house in Ein Yahav was unforgettable: my lungs were suddenly filled with cool air, cooling my sweat-coated body, and making me pleasantly dizzy. The moment I entered, I had to sit down and indulge in letting the coolness flood me. On top of that, the smell of scrambled eggs and fried onions hit my nostrils, making me drool and lick my lips, sending a flood of saliva down my throat. Tali's father, Michael, served me the lunch he had prepared especially for me like a waiter in a luxury restaurant. Laughing, he tried to chill my passion in his heavy South African accent, "Don't get so excited; it's just scrambled egg!"

After devouring the meal in half a minute, I told him all my troubles of the previous week. Saying nothing, he just picked up my plate and went to make me more scrambled eggs.

Michael had left South Africa for Israel back in the 1970s to become a farming pioneer in the Arava Valley, remaining there with his wife, Esther, to reclaim the desert and bring up their family. Over the years, I'd gotten acquainted with most of his family, especially Tali, due to her legendary and unforgettable smile.

Michael had now come back from the kitchen, carrying a large tray loaded with a larger dish of scrambled eggs; this time accompanied by fried onion and fresh parsley. With it were two bowls: one filled with tahina, and the other with a thinly-cut salad soaked in olive oil and lemon juice.

"Dammit, wait a second. I forgot your lemonade. I'll get it right away. Just eat up saying nothing, because I notice that you keep talking while chewing, which is very unhealthy. So just let me do the talking while you eat, okay? First of all, you can rest here; this is an offer you can't refuse. Secondly, I must say, you are a real nutcase, but if this is your kick, who am I to criticize?" He concluded with a smile, leaving me alone to relish the delicious dish.

At about 15:00, he walked me out and saw me off with a mighty handshake. Both his powerful handshake, as well as his rugged hand, attested to the fact that he was a true farmer.

While I mounted my "truck," Michael mounted a tractor, pulling a flat cart loaded with crates of vegetables and greenhouse irrigation equipment. "Take care out there, okay?" he shouted to me before starting the tractor and driving away eastward to the greenhouses.

When I stepped out from the neatly-trimmed hedgerow surrounding Michael's farm, I wondered why I hadn't asked him for a ride to Arava Junction, or at least to Ein Yahav Junction? After all, the difference between the room temperature and the infernal heat outdoors was too much even for a tough rider like me. Looking at the clip-on thermometer, I realized that the heat was far from subsiding: the reading was 39^0, and Arava Junction, my planned night campsite, was nearly 40km away, which meant at least three hours' ride before I slept.

However, since Michael had already gone, I mounted my "truck" and start pedaling slowly at around 20km per hour. Reaching Ein Yahav Junction, I turned right onto Route 90, where I sped up a little and was suddenly hit with the wind blowing south along the Jordan Valley Rift as if to remind me that I was only an accidental tourist in this desert realm.

The route ran straight, on and on, assuming different shades of gray and black with occasional trucks driving by. The West Jordan mountains stretched along the road to my right with the mid-April sun roasting me all over.

As I rode north, the landscape grew more desolate and the climate more inhospitable. My lips became dry and cracked and my sun cream was useless as the sweat flowing off me just washed it away. There were no signs of civilization anywhere except for a cluster of three communities far away in the distance, namely the Moshavim Hatzeva Idan and Kibbutz Ir Ovot. There was not even a shaded bus stop where I could rest and cool down a little.

The northern part of Route 90 has many slopes descending into wadis leading to the Jordan Valley. Each piece of the road forced me to slow down since the way out of the wadis was always uphill. Uphill rides, carrying a weight of 45kg when it is nearly 40^0 means enormous physical strain; therefore, they were my greatest fear. A little past sunset, I reached the gas station at Arava Junction. There, Route 90 split into a southern branch going to the town of Dimona city and a northern branch going to the Dead Sea shore.

I had mixed feelings at that stage of my journey. On one hand, I was proud of having just completed a challenging 172km ride. On the other hand, the people of the remote, inhospitable Arava Valley made me feel at home, showing me a lot of support throughout my trip in that part of the country, with some of them even donating some money to my project. Their support proved critical, so I was a little sorry to leave that unique region and its kind people.

Shortly before nightfall, I noticed a problem: the heat was not subsiding with nightfall. On the contrary, I felt that another heatwave was on its way. Only after darkness had engulfed my tent at the entrance of Wadi Tamar did it sink in that the day ahead would be hotter than any so far, and on top of that, I was about to enter Israel's hottest region, the Dead Sea area. The only silver lining was the firm hope of spending the next day in Jerusalem at my relatives' place, taking full advantage of their shower, sleeping in a cozy bed, and enjoying normal food rather than surviving in the desert on a combination of dried fruit, tahina, and sardines.

I set up my tent next to a small campfire banked with small rocks. That night, I decided to avoid heating my tent with heated stones under its floor as I had done on previous nights. I took my sweat-soaked clothes off to let them dry. Leaving only my underpants and flip-flops on, I examined the effects of the trip on my body.

What I saw was not too bad: the pain in my right knee, though not gone, had not grown any worse either. My hands had started to assume a strange, cycling gloves' tan, sunburned only near the nails while the rest of the hand remained relatively white. Any pain was mostly in the wrist, which took most of the strain of gripping the handlebars. On top of that, my lips were cracked, my lower lip had a large cut in the middle, and the skin on my arms and nose had started to peel off. Luckily, the rest of my face remained relatively intact, protected under the stubble I had let grow.

After sorting myself out, I walked toward the gas station, 500m to the east, where I replenished my water supply and regained cell phone reception. It was necessary to update my followers about my next day's route.

First, I sent my family my location on Google Maps, briefly notifying Maya where I was about to sleep and politely inviting her to join me with a wink emoji – a joke probably lost on her – and a detailed plan of my expected route. A few minutes later, my parents called, but I was too exhausted to answer and Mom pleaded with me in a long text message to skip the next day's ride and go to Jerusalem by cab instead. I didn't reply, sympathizing with her concerns, yet I was determined to complete my journey with no unnecessary interventions.

Then I called my brother, Ari, setting a time for him to meet me on the road going from the Dead Sea to Jerusalem and give me a ride back to his place. Checking the donations, I was pleasantly surprised to see the total now amounted to a five-digit sum; when I reached Arava Junction, it exceeded 12,000 USD. I started thinking about how I could use all that money. I planned to spend most on basic Passover food items for the needy, since the holiday was just around the corner. Coming back to reality, I checked several weather sites. All of them predicted a serious heatwave all over the country, especially in the east and south.

My greatest fear was ending this trip flat on my back, receiving IV fluids in an ER. To avoid this, I carefully examined my planned route, writing down the main threats that needed to be addressed: the major one, of course, was the heat, and then there was the traffic. A good deal of Route 90, which ran parallel to the Dead Sea shore, was bustling nearly all day with trucks and trailers, carrying all the minerals processed by the Dead Sea Works.

I was rather inexperienced in dealing with these two challenges at the same time, despite my overseas cycling experience. Therefore, I resorted to a desperate step I had never taken before – riding in the dark. Starting out before sunrise would allow me to avoid trucks almost completely, and also enjoy riding in temperatures of less than 30°. By the time I got back to my tent, the campfire had nearly died out and I could hear faraway the howls of jackals, or maybe wolves. They didn't bother me since I was preoccupied with the ride that lay ahead.

My eyes started to close while I was still walking to my tent, and when I crawled in, I practically felt my sleeping bag drawing me inside with a sort of magnetism. My only wish at that moment was to close my eyes, and I just fell on the bag. Without bothering to turn my cell phone off or close the tent flap, I fell asleep just as I was, in only my underpants and flip-flops, to the faint sound of crackling embers and occasional vehicles driving by.

In the dead of night, I woke up to the sound of a text message alert, somehow received in what I had mistaken as a no-reception zone. I was half asleep and, above all, needed to take an urgent leak. Only after relieving myself did I notice that my cell phone had been on all the time, resting on the ground, half-buried under the handlebar bag. The moment I picked it up, it ran out of battery juice before I could properly read Maya's two messages. One message was about her being on her way from Eilat to Wadi Tamar, while in the second one, she hoped I would be still awake when she reached me.

Learning my lesson, I plugged my cell phone into the

solar charger. Seeing it was only 23:00, I resumed my horizontal position, falling asleep mere seconds later.

My 2000km cycling tour to the Alps was over. I had traveled across Greece and Italy, all the way to the east to northern Italy's lakes region. Ahead of me lay the breathtaking Paso del Stelvio National Park on the Swiss border.

Reaching that magnificent park involved climbing Italy's highest road, 2760m above sea level, overcoming 48 bends, a 7-15% uphill slope, and completing over 3.5 hours' rough but fantastically unforgettable cycling.

Actually, I started the climb the night before after a mostly mental preparation. During the days before, I tried not to overstrain myself, and the night before the major climb I carried out a pre-marathon routine: a lot of pasta for supper, a long sleep, and an early rise. Well, it was a little difficult to sleep before my first solo alpine climb with no partner or escort vehicle.

"What if I get exhausted or need any help?" I wondered. Who would be there for me?

However, the next morning I rose full of energy like a coiled spring and after packing, cleaning up, eating, exercising, and taking pictures, I was ready to heed the mountains' call. The weather being cool and the sky perfectly blue. I put on my long, gray-and-bright-yellow patterned leggings, a sweat-wicking shirt, and long black gloves. Eager to conquer that mountain, I set off, amazed at the scenery, thrilled at my very first time traveling through an alpine pass and seeing landscapes that I had only seen from an aircraft window until then.

The road leading to Stelvio had made a name for itself among cyclists and motorcyclists due to its steepness and – even more so – its 48 bends that made it look like an endless serpent climbing to the peak. It has even been described by the popular BBC show, Top Gear, as the world's most enjoyable road to drive on. Every bend concealed a different kind of alpine landscape I had never seen before, and I wanted it to last forever.

Speeding up, I traveled uphill amid pine woods. Once I crossed the forest line – above which it was cold and snowy all year around – the landscape grew barren, with snow and snowcapped peaks all the way up. It was shaped like a colossal amphitheater that only Nature's hand could have wrought.

The road wound between small, picturesque villages, with small churches with steeples. Small stone bridges provided access to the main road. High above me rose the top of the cable car that carried skiers to the top during the peak season. With another bend behind me, I was already halfway through, with another 20 to bends to go. It was less arduous than I had expected. I practiced the intense-effort procedure, as I had gotten used to doing during my trips in Israel: eating an apple, a pear, or a Snickers bar every 45 minutes in addition to taking a few gulps of isotonic drink, and, of course, my ultimate anti-breakdown weapon – 1980s music.

This time, it was Irene Cara's turn to speed up my pulse to nearly 200 beats per minute as she belted out into my ears what became one of the most iconic songs of that decade, the theme song of *Fame*. Like many of my generation, I was addicted to the series, and that day I really indulged in the song, despite my failed attempt to turn my MP3 volume up just before the unforgettable refrain, "Remember my name, (fame!) I'm gonna live forever, I'm gonna learn how to fly (high!)..."

It swept me with a torrent of nostalgia back to the 1980s, giving me a slight shiver. Riding on, I could see in my mind's eye the actors running out of the classrooms onto the streets of New York to do what they love and do best – dance.

The slopes grew steeper than 10% and occasionally even exceeded 15%. Feeling the strain, I started talking to myself. By comparison, Israeli roads rarely have such slopes for longer than a few dozen meters. I was beginning to feel the effects of the near-3000m altitude. Despite the cloudy weather, I was sweating quite intensely. As a rule, at such an altitude, breathing becomes heavier and harder, and bodily reactions grow slower due to lower oxygen density, exacerbated by intense physical strain. I started drinking more frequently, once every 15 rather than 30 minutes.

I knew that the really hard climb would start at an altitude of 2500m – another strained, sweaty climb. This made me recall all the marathons I had run until then. One lesson I had learned from them was: until the 30th kilometer, it's just a warm-up. This suited my current challenge perfectly.

I will never forget the last 10km exhausting climb toward the Stelvio Pass. Despite my exhaustion, I had hardly suffered from my heavy breathing, my legs begging to rest, or the sweat mercilessly burning my eyes – due to the intoxicating sights all around me.

When I got back from Europe, my mother asked if I had suffered during that climb since, to her, the whole thing sounded like an endless nightmare. I instantly answered, "Not at all!" What I felt then was a bizarre combination of stress and pleasure flooding every single blood vessel in me, a sensation incomprehensible to anybody who has never experienced such a phenomenon.

I had only 5km to go to the pass, but the clouds started turning gray and the fog grew dense as if trying to engulf me along with any other driver, cyclist or motorcyclist who had come from far and wide to pay the mountain a visit. When I was just five bends away from my destination, I started to feel exhausted, my body begging me to dismount and walk the rest of the way; yet my mind commanded me to press on.

Suddenly, I saw the peak and the ski site right in front of me, a few meters away, and a big, triumphant smile spread across my face. At that very moment, the heavens opened, blasting me with rain and hail as if to literally cool down my exaltation. Yet all it did was to drive me to speed up on my way to the top.

"Come on!! Is that all you've got?!" I mocked the elements deep inside. "Sorry, it'll take more than hail to force me down. Try harder!!"

Once I had reached the top, the hail stopped and I was surrounded by cyclists on trim, hail-covered road bikes. When they spotted me riding uphill, they didn't know where the hell I'd come from. Approaching me, they started interrogating me about asking how I'd managed to over-come – with that same, heavy bike – all of Stelvio's 48 bends. When I confirmed their suspicions, they were speechless, giving me standing ovations and asking for selfies with me. A rare sensation of triumphant joy combined with an immense desire to express my gratitude to some entity started overwhelming me, yet I did not succumb to it. After a few minutes' rest, restoring my breath and changing into warmer and drier clothes, I had a craving to eat something... anything. Only then did I understand that it was my body that deserved my greatest gratitude.

I rode into Switzerland with immense hopes, and I wasn't let down. Its postcard-beautiful landscapes showed me that all the clichés regarding that country were true: it was not only fantastically beautiful, but also spotlessly clean, neat, and tidy, and everything there worked exactly to plan. Its landscape consists of millennia-old, enormous mountains and valleys. Traveling through these valleys is quick and easy thanks to the roads and railway tunnels running through them, serving one of the world's best train systems.

On Switzerland's roads, I traveled a total distance of over 1000km, including several steep climbs and descents, climbing two peaks a day, each as high as Israel's highest mountain, Mt. Hermon (which rises to nearly 3000m above sea level). Yet my craving for alpine scenery only grew stronger. I still remember the day I planned to reach Zurich, and it ended with a most exciting meeting with Jessica, the Swiss lady who had crossed my path in Nepal, and her friend, Lisa.

The night before, I happened to stop in a glade that made a perfect night campsite. At 22:30, the dark and dense fog had already reduced visibility to 5m in all directions. Zurich was just 30km away and I expected to sleep soundly, wrapped up in warm clothes and my sleeping bag. Unfortunately, the forest dwellers, particularly the four-footed ones, had other plans, and they instantly became curious about the newcomer.

Just as I felt my eyes close, I heard footsteps approaching and concluded they belonged to some animal. One by one, a few animals gathered in front of my tent flap and started sniffing it, the boldest even touching its walls. I realized that they had probably picked up the scent of some pasta or vegetable leftovers outside the tent.

Listening more carefully to the symphony of footsteps and sniffing noises, I concluded they were probably caused by various rodents, namely mice, big rats, and rabbits. Judging from the footprints I found the next morning, some larger animals, probably cats, foxes, and maybe even some hungry wolves, had paid me a visit later during the night.

Despite all that outside activity, I tried to get some desperately-needed sleep, but at least once every hour I was awakened by an animal rubbing itself against the tent or trying to displace my bike until I decided that enough was enough. Unzipping the tent flap, I turned my cell phone on, setting it on the most annoying ring available at maximum volume, while flashing my flashlight all over the place. This bought me some time, but later on the animals just went about their business, paying no attention at all to my special effects.

At some point, the sun rose, and I realized that I was about to reunite with Jessica and Lisa that very day. After packing-up, I set off immediately. When I was about 2km from Zurich, traveling along a bicycle lane through a rain-soaked forest, I saw the first "Welcome to Zurich" sign. A week before, Jessica, her friend and I had arranged to meet at this very place.

Riding a few minutes down the road just beyond a dense group of trees, I entered an open space. A woman wearing a bright, white shirt and riding a bike loomed on the horizon. Recognizing me first, Jessica stopped straight away, resting her bike on the ground and running toward me with a big smile. In addition to her white shirt, she wore blue jeans and flat blue sneakers. I only recognized her when she had come really close, and her Nordic beauty exploded in my eyes with full force. When our eyes met, I recalled how I had missed her beauty. She embraced me right away with a tight and very long hug. Her fragrance was extremely sensual and arousing, reminding me of the involuntary celibacy I had been practicing during the nearly three months since I had embarked on this tour.

Jessica bombarded me with short, funny questions, finding it hard to believe that I was actually in Switzerland and only half an hour away from her home. We chatted for a few minutes, holding hands, before switching to long embraces like two teenagers realizing they were nuts about each other. Finally, with an elegant wink and a slap on my cramped ass, she told me to chill out since we were not in India anymore and to start following her to her parents' home where she was staying.

"You better stop acting like some jungle savage," she warned with another wink just before we entered her home.

After a few days' rest, it was the weekend. For Jessica's family, this meant mountain hiking.

"Listen up! Tomorrow you'll come with me to visit Lisa's mountain chalet, where she works. It's a cool place in a fantastic location. Trust me, you won't want to come back."

"Okay," I promised. "Sounds great. What should I bring along and how long is the walk?"

"Nothing too hard for you. We'll spend the night in the chalet, so you shouldn't worry about food and sleeping arrangements. The place is in the canton of Valais, and the chalet' is several hours' climb away."

A mere twenty-four hours later, we were on a south-bound train, each of us equipped with a small backpack, some energy snacks, a raincoat, and a few dozen of Swiss francs for public transport.

Lisa, who we were visiting, was Jessica's close friend. I

had met her, too, on my Far Eastern trip. She was a very nice, red-headed, freckle-faced Swiss girl. Like Jessica, she worked as a paramedic but spent her summers in the chalet, waiting on guests, cleaning, and helping to manage the place. She chose to work there due to the high pay even though the hours were long and access was difficult.

Three hours after we had taken a cable car from the picturesque village of Kippel, we were hiking a trail with the kind of signposts you'll find only in Switzerland, including on every path the estimated time – down to the number of minutes – it will take you to reach your destination.

We kept walking at a devastating pace, which did not keep us from talking all the time and using every opportunity to take pictures. I let her lead and straggled about 5m behind. After a half-hour's walking, she suggested we speed up because the weather might surprise us at any moment and we were 2500m above sea level already. Jessica didn't allow us to rest, arguing that we should only rest when we got there and that we could talk and eat while walking, and so we did; we did not rest once during the several hours' long climb.

I was unaccustomed to long, strenuous walks, and found it a strain but, thanks to the previous months of cycling, I was fit so, all in all, it was a refreshing change.

Reaching a saddle between two peaks, we followed the left bend and entered a steep, narrow, and difficult trail. To make any progress at all, we had to climb over sharp boulders and stone walls wet with the mist descending from the peaks, then slide down from them on our butts.

"It looks bad," she said suddenly.

"What, the fog? Are you looking for an excuse to stop?"

"No, dummy! I can go on for hours like this, but you're gasping like some ninety-year-old! Are you such a pussy!? I mistook you for some Israeli war hero!" she mocked, adding right away, "This fog, with the wind that's just started, will bring either rain or snow. Didn't you notice the sudden drop in temperature?"

"Okay... but we're wearing only shorts and waterproofs. Why don't we jog to the chalet?"

Indeed, when we reached the top of the steep climb, the trail became broader and easier to walk along, and we started jogging at a steady pace. Jessica had to estimate the time to our destination since the fog concealed the faraway chalet.

A moment after she had pointed in that direction, the heavens opened, lashing our faces with torrential rain and wind. Within thirty seconds, we were soaked to the bone, yet kept laughing and encouraging each other to speed up. After running for nearly half-an-hour, crossing gushing streams, jumping over slippery rocks, and covering our shoes and exposed legs with mud, we stormed into the chalet loudly and dramatically. We got there just in time. Supper was being served to the guests who had arrived earlier.

They were shocked by the noisy interruption during the calm meal service. Our noisy entrance made the manager and Lisa come to see what it was all about. The moment Lisa saw us, she started yelling and jumping up and down. By then, those who hadn't yet noticed us could ignore us no longer.

A few minutes later, the staff members were busy helping us to dry off and making us something hot to drink. Lisa had been very anxious, fearing we wouldn't make it because of the rain. She showed us to her room, where we could change, and told us that all three of us would spend the night there.

Freezing cold, I cared for nothing except getting into dry, warm clothes, so I took off all my clothes instantly, forgetting that the two girls were in the room. They told me, laughing, that I was not in Israel anymore and this was not done in Switzerland.

"What's the matter?" I wondered. "Haven't you ever seen a naked man before? If my memory serves me, it happened quite a few times when we traveled in India together."

"No kidding! You must be a complete crackpot, but you're right," Jessica admitted, starting to undress as well. Meanwhile, Lisa had gone back to the kitchen to help with serving supper, leaving us to settle in. Lisa hung her clothes up to dry next to the fireplace, just where I was standing in an attempt to thaw out. The cold started affecting me, sending shivers along my spine. Examining Jessica's body, I observed that she, too, was shivering all over and couldn't stop her teeth chattering. She was so cold that she couldn't even get dressed.

"Shall I warm you up a little, Jessica?" I suggested.

"I'd love to," she smiled, approaching me quickly.

I wore only dry pants, while she wore nothing but her panties. Her shapely body shivered, and her efforts to contain the shivering accentuated her abdomen muscles. I noticed that she had the tan lines of a tiny bikini. She came near and pressed herself against me.

We stood this way for a few minutes with my arms around her, each enjoying the other's body heat. Her hair smelled strongly of rain and earth, and her skin felt soft and gentle. Meanwhile, we covered ourselves with a woolen blanket that we had pulled off the bed. Little by little, her goose pimples disappeared and her nipples, erect against my body, resumed their normal position.

We started to put on our clothes, which by now had

dried completely, and she gave me a look. "You look quite good naked! We should do it more often," she remarked with a somewhat embarrassed laugh, then added, "Hey, don't get excited. It won't happen again." She started helping me unpack our clothes.

I clearly remember that as odd as it might seem, there was no passion in the air, although both of us were stark naked. I guess the brain knows what body parts most of the blood should go to when we're freezing! I'm sure that had it happened at any other time, this episode would have had an entirely different conclusion, yet when we tried to get warm in the chalet, I still recalled the sight of her beautiful and flexible body from the time in India.

The evening sky above the chalet was perfectly cloudless, which let the temperature drop to nearly freezing. The chalet, situated in a small valley between two snowcapped mountains, was designed for self-reliance. Its food supply for one month was helicoptered in, its power supply was produced by large solar panels on the roof, charging a battery, and it received water from thawed snow. An LCD display near the main entrance constantly showed the battery charge level and the amounts of water and food left, as fed into the kitchen computer. This allowed for constant supply management.

When we had finally warmed up, we went downstairs to the heated hall, where some guests were playing cards while others enjoyed hot tea or quiet conversation. Despite the heating, you still needed warm clothing down there, since by nightfall, the outside temperature dropped to below zero and the windows overlooking the valley would become covered with condensation. During the day, however, they offered a fantastic view of the enormous valley stretching beneath the chalet.

After chatting with some Dutch tourists for a few minutes, I spotted a computer with internet access occupied by a German engaged in a skype chat. When he had finished, I took his place and checked my messages. Since I only had limited surfing time, I didn't bother to read most of the new ones.

The first one to catch my eye started with, "Hello from Nepal." The moment I finished reading it, I was taken far away from all my European cycling tour troubles to a period not so long before that – March 2009 – when, during that remarkable time that I had spent in Nepal, I had been alongside volunteers from all over the world, joining hands in pursuit of a noble cause: running and sustaining the Pokhara orphanage. The message was from Sanjib, a nice, thirty-year-old Nepalese guy, with some pictures of the orphanage attached.

First, he updated me about how life was there and then went on with a detailed update on the work that May and I, and another Israeli volunteer had done. According to him, we had managed to change the place dramatically. Thanks to the funds we had raised, management had hired construction workers, plumbers, and electricians to renovate the place and make it a lot less bleak and harsh and more homey. As a result, both the children's morale and their grades had skyrocketed, and the institution had grown to be popular amongst orphans.

He concluded his message by sending me a thousand thanks, begging me to pay the place a visit soon so that the staff could express their gratitude to me as well as to the other volunteers. As he put it, if not for our work the previous year, the institution might not have survived, and its children would have probably gone homeless. As I was reading the email from Sanjib, I was already conceiving plans to be carried out once I had returned to Israel. This whole trip suddenly seemed less important to me all of a sudden: my new purpose in life was to combine my love of extreme sport with some enterprises to raise funds for the needy.

I was so absorbed with reading and answering the message that I didn't notice the serious and even dangerous event that had taken place around me. The heating system had failed, and the temperature outside had dropped to ten below zero. There was no way the system could be fixed before the next morning.

Briefing me about what had happened, Lisa told me – slowly and with a naughty smile that we had trouble big time and I must put on more clothes and find some way to keep us warm and cheerful. I finished typing my reply hastily, promising myself to keep developing this idea after I had left the mountain.

Turning the computer off and getting back to the Dutch tourists' table, I noticed that it was, indeed, much colder and that we could see our breaths in the air when we spoke. Though I hadn't a clue as to how cold it could get, I started realizing it when I looked out of the window with the view to the valley. The rooftop perimeter lights were still on, clearly illuminating the chalet's immediate surroundings. This was the moment when I realized that the cold was no joke. I noticed that one of the streams that supplied the chalet with water had frozen and turned icy-white. The occasional mountaintop mist that condensed into dew and dribbled from the roof had frozen as well, forming icicles along the walls.

It was nearly 22:00 when people started leaving the hall. Lisa and I reached the conclusion that the wisest decision would be to stay in her bedroom under a blanket.

We were used to dealing with the cold in Nepal. When we had climbed mountains there, the temperature had dropped to twenty below zero, and we'd had to cuddle up all night long to keep warm. We even had our private jokes about it, which helped us laugh away the hours until we fell asleep. When the thermometer on the wall dropped to nearly minus one, we resorted to this strategy in Switzerland as well. I took the left side of the bed, Jessica the right, and Lisa squeezed in between us, all of us covered by a large duvet and another two woolen blankets. Every second outside the blanket was a struggle for survival.

It took about fifteen minutes under the duvet, specially designed to deal with extreme conditions, for the cold to subside, and thirty minutes later we felt cozy enough to fall asleep. However, I didn't get much sleep due to my room-mates. Both Lisa and Jessica had showered just a few minutes before the heating broke, and the scent of their liberally applied shampoo and body lotions filled the entire room, including the under-blanket space.

"Why am I on the outside instead of in the middle?" I suddenly wondered, quietly.

"A very good question. And why aren't you next to me? I won't mind you warming me up," Jessica remarked.

"You two...you're so immature! I can find you a room of your own and you get on with it if you like. Come, cozy up with me, you're nice and warm!" Lisa protested, pulling me near her.

It took me a minute of repositioning myself to get next to Jessica, leaving Lisa on the other side of the bed. Pressing myself against Jessica's back, I could hardly ignore the plea-sure it gave both of us. She, in turn, pressed herself against my pelvis, dragging my arm across her body. A few minutes later, all three of us had fallen asleep.

The morning sun's rays entering the room straight through the window heated the rather cold room a little. While Jessica and I were still in bed, Lisa was already busy preparing the guests' breakfast. Jessica was still fast asleep, and there was a little chance of her waking up. She was breathing softly and quietly, her blond messed-up hair partly concealing her eyes. The bright sunlight revealed that her lips were closed almost completely. With her right palm resting on my chest, her head rested on my right shoulder and our legs interlocked. We must have looked like a regular couple. Staring at her for a few minutes, I certainly thought that I liked what I saw. A slight horniness started creeping through my body, and I felt her body heat rising and her body responding to my touch. Considering the situation, I saw only two alternatives: either stay under the blanket, undress and pleasure her right then, or get out of bed and help the kitchen staff. Her body heat and being close to me felt like an even greater torment than the cold night.

All of a sudden, Lisa came in, ordering us to get up and prepare for breakfast instead of acting like a couple of rabbits who hadn't seen each other for years. Jessica responded with a juicy, Swiss-German curse.

After breakfast, all three of us took a little walk around the chalet, following a trail marked similarly to those I'd seen in Israel – with paint stripes on the rocks. Rising to a vantage point, Jessica and I stopped for a little chat while Lisa went ahead, leaving us alone. I wore shorts, since my long ones were still wet, a balaclava, and three shirts one on top of the other, while Jessica was properly dressed in clothes borrowed from Lisa. Lisa just wore her work clothes – smart jeans, a black fleece coat and dark glasses.

Reaching a staircase hewn in the rock, we stopped to enjoy the alpine view in front of us.

"Amazing! Such beauty... no picture could ever capture it," I observed.

"Right, but last night was even more amazing. It was really fun sleeping with you, especially this morning," she whispered in my ear. Her wind-blown hair concealed half of her face while her dark glasses concealed her brown eyes. Removing them slowly, I noticed her flowing tears and running nose. Suddenly, she came near and kissed my lips. We stood there, cuddling tightly.

"I enjoyed it, too. It felt perfectly natural, as if we did it every day," I replied, inhaling her scent. "I didn't notice you were awake this morning," I went on. "Did you have the same feeling I had?"

"Sure, I was looking forward to it. Why did you take your hand away? It felt very nice," she remarked, pressing the palm of her hand against mine.

"Well, I guess we'll have to do it again," I replied, searching for a response in her shining eyes. Yet she failed to respond as I expected her to. Instead, she pierced me with such a look that I had never before seen in her eyes, and then she looked down at her walking boots as if to signal that it was our last goodbye. Her sudden sadness affected me as well.

We walked on for a while, holding hands, and it suddenly hit me why she was moved so strongly: this whole scene was a combination of silent consent and her peculiar attempt at telling me, over the course of several hours, that it was probably the last time we would spend together.

All three of us stopped for a group picture next to a large cross bolted into a mountain peak near the chalet. Setting the camera timer to ten seconds and resting it on a rock, I rushed to take my position between the two girls, and all of us put our arms around each other.

"Just like last night," Jessica remarked suddenly, making us all laugh.

"Too bad it only lasted one night. I'd have loved to spend another couple of nights like that," Lisa commented.

Jessica and I exchanged looks, our jaws dropped with astonishment, making us look like gaping fish.

Lisa pressed on. "Do you really think I didn't hear you talking to each other in bed? And Jessica, after the talking... I know what you were up to -"

"You're such a liar, Lisa! There's no way you could have heard anything through your own snoring!"

"Jessica, you promised me she'd hear nothing!" I joined in the teasing, clenching her palm even harder with mine.

"Lisa, you're dead meat! I can't believe you were right next to us, saying nothing!" she burst out, making us nearly choke with laughter. After taking a couple of selfies taking turns to hold the camera, we started walking back to the chalet, accompanied by our laughter echoing off the mountains around us.

7

DAY 7

"Some people want it to happen, some wish it would happen, and others make it happen."

Michael Jordan

April 5, 2016
Starting point: Arava Junction
Destination: Jerusalem
Distance: 147 kilometers

Darkness engulfed the Arava junction. Only the gas station's lights faintly illuminated the mouth of Wadi Tamar. Some of the light entering the wadi helped me find my way when I went out to take a leak. Crawling out of my tent, I'd had two surprises: first, a hot wind was blowing, predicting a heavy heatwave, and second, my campfire was still burning even though I thought it was extinguished the last time I checked. It made little sense.

I stood for two minutes with my eyes closed, enjoying the emptying of my bladder and waiting for it to eject all the fluids I had drunk the day before. I tried to check the color of my urine, but the lights of the gas station proved too faint. Then, when I set off toward the tent which was at the end of the jeep trail, I noticed her.

She was in a sleeping bag, on a mattress about a meter from the fire. I approached her, touched her back gently, and whispered her name to wake her up. She turned around slowly, revealing eyes half-concealed by her balaclava and messed-up black hair.

"Good night to you, too!" I greeted her.

She smiled, waiting a few seconds before replying. "I see you didn't read the message where I told you I was coming after you from Eilat," she said, sitting up. I was totally surprised by her presence, once again, in the middle of my trip.

Whenever I saw her, I realized why she attracted me. There was something between us that defied verbal description, but it was definitely in the air. I brewed herbal tea for two and we spent an hour sitting by the fire. Maya did most of the talking, sharing what she had been through during the previous weeks, showing me pictures of the hospital where she worked, her friends, and the places she had visited all over the world. Being rather emotionally overwhelmed, the silence and the fire made her sleepy again very soon. While she rolled over the photos on her cell phone, I checked the time and saw that it was a little after 01:00. Soon, I thought, it will be morning.

"Look," I explained to her, "can we continue this conversation some other time? I must get up soon and I've got a hell of a challenging day ahead. Anyway, you can't sleep out here! You sleep inside, I'll sleep outside!" I told her, pointing at my tent.

"How nice of you, but there's no way I'll let you sleep outside. Why can't we sleep together?"

Smiling, I arranged the hair behind her ear. "Are you sure about that? Remember, I have a great challenge to face tomorrow, and I doubt whether I'll get much sleep with you next to me."

"We'll never know unless we try, will we?" she teased me.

"Maya, it's surreal! First, you entice me into a lake, half-naked and now you want to share this tiny tent after an acquaintance of no longer than five hours!"

Hearing me out, Maya opened up her Jeep to let me move all my stuff from the tent to her car. After lining the tent floor with our mattresses, I spread my sleeping bag over them while Maya brought a large summer blanket carefully folded and packed in a white cloth bag from her jeep.

"I must inform you," she declared, preparing to sleep inside the crowded tent. "Any man sleeping next to me – and there have been very few–" she added quietly, "has to be really close to me, or I won't be able to sleep. You've been warned!"

She entered my tent right after she had emptied a bottle of water on the fire, putting it out almost completely despite my request to let the embers burn to ward off reptiles. Then, locking her vehicle with her remote central lock, she zipped up the tent flap.

"Is that a threat!? C'mon! Move your cute little butt over here. I must get some sleep!" I told her, pulling her under the blanket. It smelled like freshly-washed laundry.

We lay next to each other under the blanket, listening to the wind beating against the canvas and the occasional cars driving by on Route 90. At least the jackals had stopped howling by now, but we could hear the crackling embers all too clearly. She moved close enough that I could feel her breath on my face, and my hands touched her belly. I was aware, as well, of her ribs rising with every breath.

"Who are you, Tzuriel?" she whispered suddenly.

"Do you want a short answer or a long one?" I tried to talk my way out of a long discussion.

"Just give me any answer!"

I didn't since I was not in the mood for a heart-to-heart that night. It was never the right time. I was never in the right mood. So I just waited for her to fall asleep so I could fall asleep right after her.

"Will you write about this? I mean about the two of us?" she inquired.

"Where do you think I'll write about it? And when? I don't get it."

"In the book you'll write a few years from now, about your Heart to Heart Journey. What you're doing is far from trivial – insane even – and I just want to know if you'll mention me there."

"I really like your sense of humor in the dead of night! What book are you blabbering about!? I hardly survived my final high school exams in Hebrew, and the greatest piece of literature I can write is a half-interesting Facebook post, so a book's out of the question!"

"You're so wrong," she whispered, placing her right knee between my legs. "I've been reading your blog about your European tour and about the rest of your worldwide journeys. I think you underestimate yourself. So, just for future reference, I hereby authorize you to mention me in your book, whenever you decide to write it."

"I see we've shed our inhibitions. I like that. I already realized you've been following me. For your information, the law calls it stalking...and I really appreciate your authorization. I'll keep it in mind. So how 'bout shutting your trap and trying to get some sleep?" I asked as she laid her head on my right shoulder.

"Luckily for you, you're heading for Jerusalem tomorrow. Otherwise, I'd be nagging you for hours. Am I allowed one last question?" After a few seconds of silence, she went on. "Is it okay, under tent rules, to get a goodnight kiss?"

Without waiting for my answer, she just pressed her lips against mine for a few seconds of addictive pleasure. The touch of her lips felt as delicious as the very first, slow bite into an unfamiliar tropical fruit. It makes you want more. Right after, turning her head away, she fell asleep.

The next morning, I wrote the following in my diary:

Apparently, I've been through some transcendental experience during my trip. While I was sleeping next to a beautiful woman in the middle of nowhere – a woman I only recently met for the first time – it struck me that is far beyond any other trip. My thoughts are focused not on outdoor survival, travelers' gear, or getting from A to B. Instead, I'm experiencing a sensation probably shared by all travelers wherever they are if they are truly connected to nature.

It probably has something to do with the great open spaces around me, and this is why I'm addicted to it. It stems from riding a heavy bicycle for thousands of kilometers. It's more than just looking forward to sunrises and sunsets, crossing rivers and lakes, walking through dense forests and grasslands, or conquering desert roads, mountaintops, and endless plains. It's about something more existential.

Listening to Maya breathing, it suddenly struck me that as long as nature remains what it is, humans traveling through it will always feel this way. I guess this is how the great explorers and space pioneers felt, and perhaps each and every one of us who had ever faced any surprise nature has to offer.

My cell phone alarm went off at 04:30 when it was still pitch-black outside. That day, I planned to cover as much ground as possible before the worst of the heat, since the weather forecast promised more than 40° by midday. The day's planned route had two parts: the first, the 65km from Arava Junction to Kibbutz Ein Gedi and the second one about 83km from there to a just a few kilometers short of Jerusalem. I planned to "go wild," covering the entire distance in one stroke until I met my brother, who was to give me a ride to Jerusalem. That was planned to be the longest single leg of the entire trip and was to take place at the lowest point on Earth.

By then, Maya was gone. I guess she'd got up before me and driven away without saying goodbye. All she left me was her red floral blanket.

I spent fifteen minutes folding my tent, packing and securing everything, and checking the bike, including the headlamp and bike lights. Then I went to the nearby gas station and ordered a cup of coffee before starting the hottest day of the entire trip. The handlebar temperature display already showed 32° and it wasn't yet 05:00. I also noticed that the gas station's air-conditioning system was operating on full power, which meant I was about to run into risk yet again.

The heatwave expected during the ride along the Dead Sea shore required maximum attention to my bodily changes, down to the last detail. Under such extreme conditions, this is the key to success – and sometimes to survival as well. Swallowing my last gulp of coffee, I glanced at the West Jordan Mountains, still shrouded in darkness, and at the entire Jordan Valley Rift, which showed no sign of the sunrise that was expected in a few minutes. Making sure for the last time that all my gear was tightly packed in the trunk bags and checking the tire air pressure, the brakes, headlamps, as well as the front and rear lights, I put on my yellow vest as an extra safety precaution during the first two hours' riding, most of which would take place in the dark.

When my "truck" was ready to go, I took the right turn at the junction. It took me quite a few minutes to get used to the dark and using my headlamp. Riding for a few minutes, I passed the turn leading to Neot Hakikar. East of the road, I began to notice the yellow lights of the Dead Sea Works, which resembled some kind of megacity on the Jordanian border. Those distant lights not only illuminated my way but also made me feel more confident of being visible to the cars coming up behind me.

Route 90 was absolutely deserted so early in the day. Knowing that it would soon be bustling with trucks, I sped up in an attempt to get out of the Dead Sea Works zone as soon as possible. Thanks to the mostly flat road, I made good progress at an average of 25kph. My first stop before Ein Gedi was the Neve Zohar Junction, where a left turn leads to the town of Arad.

I felt the heat more keenly during stops, which I tried to avoid unless it was absolutely necessary to wipe the sweat off my eyes or to take a leak. The sun had already started rising above the West Jordan Mountains, tinting the Jordanian border – just where the mountain line met the horizon – with dark blue and white pre-sunrise hues. This indicated that the temperature, too, was about to rise and that I was in a race against time. I knew I would face big troubles if I failed to reach Ein Gedi before midday and this thought kept haunting me.

This time, I'd put on the shortest of clothing items I had:

a short, red, cycling shirt unzipped down to mid-chest, a beige baseball hat with a neck flap, and black padded tights already white with the salt my dried-out sweat had left on them during the ride along Route 90.

Reaching Neve Zohar Junction, I stopped next to the road sign pointing to Jerusalem and Ein Gedi. Happy with the progress I had made so far, I tried, in vain, to ignore the marked distance to Jerusalem: 107km. While I pulled my cell phone out of my black handlebar bag to inform my followers about my location and my next planned stop, the temperature reading on the handlebar already displayed over 39°. The north wind, which had just got up, brought no relief. The closer I got to the steep cliffs on the west, the more it felt like a furnace heating up, and there was not a breath of wind there.

The weather made me sweat that morning as much as on the final stage of southern Route 90. Humidity was high, probably because I was near the Dead Sea, and the right side of my face bore the brunt of the scorching sun. Whilst resting under the shade of the Neve Zohar Junction bus stop, I received several messages. One was from Maya, who thanked me for accepting her as my guest last night and for tolerating her despite her terrible nagging. All she wanted me to do was to take care and keep in touch and, if I happened to be near Tel Aviv, to drop her a line and she'd love to meet me.

The moment I moved it to the archive, I received another message with a picture of her wrapped in a white towel and her black hair wet. The caption under it read, "Are you coming?" with three wink emojis. She definitely knew how to make me laugh and was familiar with all my sensitivities. Thanks to her, I was distracted for a couple of minutes from the furnace that had just lit up around me and forgot that I was facing several hours of riding through the lowest point on Earth.

During those minutes, I recalled our long night by the campfire when she had revealed to me what she had been through recently. Grasping her steaming cup of tea in both hands, which smelled like wintertime, she told me how she had just broken up with Guy, her life partner of five years. The previous week, they had been in Eilat at a lawyers' convention in a last attempt to save their relationship, and he proposed to her. When she met me in Mitzpe Ramon, she was on her way to Eilat to meet him. With tears rolling down her cheeks, she confessed that she had accepted his proposal just because he had asked her, but that her passion for him had already died out. She no longer saw them sharing any future but had no idea how to break it to him gently enough.

I learned from her that they had nearly got married two years earlier, but postponed it for a while because he had just completed his internship in a law firm and was starting his own office. It was then that she started feeling that something was going wrong between them and sadly recognized that he was no longer the man she had known. This drove her to depression and to a psychosomatic disorder in the form of a skin rash. When her torrent of words stopped for a second, I offered her a towelette to mop her tears and running nose.

"He'd changed dramatically over the last couple of years," she went on. "He'd become preoccupied with work and money-making, forgetting about me and our future together. Now, you tell me: is a little attention and care too much to ask?" she asked, staring at me with tearful eyes.

The day before she visited me at Wadi Tamar, she had finally broken up with him in their Eilat hotel room, telling him that she was leaving him for good and was going back home, up north. It was exactly then – with perfect timing, as she put it – that she had received my message about reaching Arava Junction.

Only then did she realize where she really wanted to be – near a desert campfire, away from any judgment or questioning, surrounded by silence.

I recalled all that while chewing my energy snack and staring at the little valley stretched between me and the Dead Sea. Out of the morning mist, the brown West Jordan Mountains appeared in all their splendor, casting a giant shadow on the Jordanian territory. The Dead Sea stretched just below the feet of the mountains, a few meters short of Route 90, which cut its way south across the lifeless valley. The number of trees and blades of grass visible there could be counted on one hand. The whole place looked like a realm of desolation. Down the road, a little to the north, I saw the community of Neve Zohar, a part of the Tamar Regional Council – the lowest-altitude human settlement on Earth.

I was startled by a big, yellow Dead Sea Works truck driving by. It knocked my own "truck" to the ground. Since I'd grown accustomed to my bike falling onto the road, and since the bags cushioned the fall, I knew it would take more than just a fall to damage it. However, the noisy fall shook me back to reality, forcing me to prepare for the 40km to Ein Gedi.

I was still riding faster than usual, and I pedaled with all my might, knowing I had to cover as much ground as possible despite the heat since I would soon have to slow down due to the even more severe heat to come.

Approaching the archeological site of Masada, I made a short stop to take a few Go-Pro snapshots of the site, and also to devour two energy snacks. Knowing that without both snacks and water I could not survive this trip, I strictly rationed my snacks per stop and regularly bought new snacks whenever I reached a gas station. I would check their effects on me while I rode. On my last stop, I'd bought a few bags of peanut-butter coated nuggets. The nuggets tasted great, providing me with plenty of fresh energy, but the peanut butter coating was hard on my digestive system. In temperatures of 40°, it felt like cotton blocking my throat unless I grabbed some handy liquid to wash it down. My only option was to eat up the bag quickly and wash it down my throat with a few gulps of water. I decided to forget about peanut butter snacks from then on.

Another perfect snack for riding, which also compelled me to drink more, were pretzels. They seemed perfect for hot days due to their high salt content. On the one hand, their texture made them easier to digest and as opposed to the peanut butter snack, they were easier to pull out of the bag without making my fingers sticky. I decided to prioritize pretzels for the time being.

Examining the route to Ein Gedi, I realized that it offered no human settlements nor even bus stops where I could have some rest. The closest suitable resting place was the Ein Gedi Spa, a compound of hot pools and a private Dead Sea beach. This part of the ride concluded the crossing of many wadis such as Mishmar, Miflat, Harduf, Metzada, Asahel, and Tzeruya. Every crossing involved a descent into and a moderate climb out from the bed of the wadi.

On rainy days, these parts of Route 90 were impassable due to floods rushing in from the Judean Desert and the hills of Jerusalem, but on these infernally hot days, it was parched and totally lifeless. I could hardly imagine water filling the wadi a mere few months before.

After pedaling for two hours, something resembling a human settlement loomed on the horizon. I mistook it for Kibbutz Ein Gedi, forgetting that the kibbutz and the reserve, though bearing the same name, were two different places.

I was already dreaming of the longed-for rest to come. With just a little more effort, I thought, I would make it, completing this part of today's ride. It was only twenty minutes later that I, grunting and sweating all over after the long climb to the gate of Kibbutz Ein Gedi, realized how wrong I was. I still had another 5km to go before I could rest. The idea of having to pedal for at least another fifteen minutes frustrated and enraged me terribly.

My wishful thinking had made me miscalculate the route. During my military land navigation training, it was called "forcing the ground." Usually, it happens during night training, but it's quite possible for it to happen in the daytime as well. Under extreme conditions, your body has insufficient energy and oxygen. Your mind misinterprets reality, probably as a survival tactic aimed at providing your exhausted body with another ounce of energy.

I examined the map more carefully, hoping to discover that I had reached the reserve. Unfortunately, the "5" on the map indicated the number of kilometers to my destination.

Losing no time, I mounted my "truck" while exploding with a series of dirty Arabic curses, feeling that I had made a fool of myself.

Luckily for me, this section of the ride was downhill, taking me straight into the iconic Wadi Arugot. The short ride cooled me down a little and boosted my morale instantly: at the very entrance to the reserve, I noticed directions to a parking lot and a public toilet, which – for me – meant shade, running water, and a kiosk where I could expect a refreshing cup of iced coffee.

Indeed, I soon found a shaded wooden bench where I changed into dry clothes and spread my wet clothes out to dry. I now looked like a beachgoer, wearing nothing but my flip flops, jogging shorts, and an undershirt. The rest of my clothes were soaking wet, mostly with the water I had been pouring over myself, as well as my constant sweating.

A little past 12:00, I saw that the weather report was right: it was over 43° already – terribly hot. In addition, all my muscles had cramped up and my cracked lips bled occasionally. However, my spirits were high. Jerusalem was less than 90km away and my brother would be picking me up for a ride to Jerusalem. Therefore, I lay on the grass with only my pants on, enjoying the shade and letting my body recover before the next section of riding. It was expected to be longer and in even hotter conditions, but there would be more stops and places to rest; and when it was over, I hoped to enjoy a cold shower and rest on a real bed.

I noticed an endless stream of buses bringing tourists to the reserve, with a stopping place near the kiosk. Apparently, most of them had never experienced such temperatures and their response to the merciless heat was amusing from my shaded refuge. The Japanese, typically wearing their cameras on their chests, were resilient and kept up appearances. The Americans were louder, yet smiled all the time and seemed to deal with the heat more patiently. There were also a few Israelis who made no fuss about the weather and seemed to handle it just fine. I took them for local residents as only those used to such temperatures can feel comfortable there.

It was lunchtime by now and I devoured two energy

snacks, two cups of iced coffee, a Snickers bar that melted instantly in my mouth, and a 100g bag of almonds and raisins. To replenish my protein, I also ate a can of tuna. For dessert, I had a baguette with sesame spread on it and a hot omelet freshly made by Yossi, the kiosk vendor, who added extra fresh cheese and black olives. He even bothered to evenly cover the omelet with fresh tomato slices and to liberally sprinkle salt over it, just as I asked him to. Finally, he wrapped my sandwich in a special white paper wrapper and sliced it in two before serving it to me on a tray. It was one of my best meals for several days, and Yossi made the sandwich with such devotion and skill that it was one of the prettiest sights that day.

After licking the fresh cheese off my fingers, I went back to the bench where my "truck" and drying clothes waited for me. Once I was back in the shade, I resumed my horizontal position to get as much rest as possible before starting off for the second part of my daily ride. Ahead of me lay a long ride along the northern Dead Sea shore and then the climb toward Jerusalem. I planned a long rest there before riding north to the Golan Heights and Mount Hermon.

I hesitated between reading Haruki and writing in my diary. On the one hand, I had a few thoughts to record, but on the other hand, *Kafka on the Shore* served as a fascinating respite from everything that had anything to do with cycling. Finally, I chose the diary, fearing the book would put me to sleep and make me lazy. Unplugging my cell phone from the solar charger, I tapped the Play button.

I lay on my belly, my diary straight under my eyes, squeezing my body onto a 50cm by 150cm cloth to avoid the dirt and the prickly, brownish-green grass. All the while, the Gypsy Kings, one of my favorite bands, were singing in my earphones their version of Sinatra's "My Way," which got me in the right mood for writing. After writing a few lines, it struck me that the lyrics perfectly described how I felt in 45° of heat after nearly a fortnight of relentless cycling around the country.

At that moment, I deleted the last five lines I had written, replacing them not with the Spanish version of My Way, sung by the Gypsy Kings, but with the English one, "I've lived a life that's full, I've traveled each and every highway, But more, much more than this, I did it my way..."

When "My Way" was over, the Gypsy Kings started the livelier hit, Bamboleo. This was enough to start my automatic response. It surprised me, just as it had done on day one. Jumping to my feet, I put my clothes and shoes on, drank some water, secured all my gear, and kindly thanked Yossi for looking after me during my short stay at the Ein Gedi reserve. About five minutes later, I was riding my dusty "truck" toward the capital city of Israel.

I was very well aware of the challenging ride ahead but was determined to cover that distance that day no matter what, with no lame excuses or whining. Jerusalem was nearly 90km away, and my daylight time just four or five hours long. I decided to do my best to ride all the way to the point near Jerusalem where I was to meet my elder brother, making no stops.

My next planned stop was either the Kibbutz Mitzpe Shalem or the military checkpoint before the turn to Dragot Cliffs. It all depended on what exhausted me first: the extreme temperatures or the cramped feet due to that day's earlier ride. It felt as if my head was being fried – 44° in the shade meant nearly 50° under the sun. If not for the water I poured over my hat every ten minutes, I would never have made it.

During that ride, I went without a helmet since it only

concentrated heat on my head instead of diffusing it. On top of that, the dark asphalt was blazing with heat, reflecting the sun straight into my eyes. My skin felt roasted as well.

In addition to the desert heat, I also felt terribly lonely at that moment. The road was practically empty, and there was hardly a living thing around apart some vultures hovering, as if waiting for me to drop dead, and a few beachgoers on the remotest parts of the Dead Sea shores. After several (mostly unsuccessful) attempts at communicating with drivers by waving my hand, I was so exhausted and sweaty that I decided not to waste energy on useless movements.

Then, after another kilometer's ride, I found the best-tasting lemonade I had ever come across. Of all places, it happened to be at an army checkpoint situated on the left turn to Dragot Cliffs. I discovered it by sheer accident just as I completed the moderate climb from the Dead Sea shore area. It was manned by a couple of sweat-soaked, gloomy reservists. A few meters down the road was a shaded observation point offering a magnificent view of the South West Jordan mountains on one side of the road and the impressive Jordan Valley Rift Cliff on the other.

The drinks vendor approached me like an age-old acquaintance, gently placing in my hand an ice-cold lemonade in a disposable cup. "Drink it up. If you want another, just raise your hand. Pay me only if you like it," he suggested with a smile, getting back to work.

"Thanks a lot, but I didn't ask for it. How much is it?" I enquired. He didn't say.

After downing it in one fast gulp, I regretted not drinking it more slowly because pleasant things should be done slowly. I hesitated to ask for more in case I was pushing my luck. When I did approach him to ask for another, he was already waiting for me with another cup.

I couldn't help asking him, "What's your game, my friend? Do you happen to know me, to be so kind and generous?"

He looked sixtyish and sported a white, trimmed beard, a brown, wide-brimmed Australian hat, a white buttoned shirt, and blue farmer's shorts. On his feet, he wore dusty blue sandals. His skin was tanned as if most of his life was spent in the sun.

"Do I have to know people in order to be kind to them? You looked like one who could use some help, and one who has an interesting history, so why not?"

"Let me have the entire jar for twenty shekels," I told him, pushing the money into his hand and picking up the jar slowly without waiting for his permission.

"I knew you'd love the juice, so enjoy it. If you want some more, I'm over there," he told me, pointing to the checkpoint.

Taking off my orange jogging shoes as well as my socks, I rested my legs on the shaded bench. The shade protected me from the infernal sun,\ and all I could think of at that moment was lemonade. The view in front of me was a hazy cocktail of the blueish-gray, mirror-flat Dead Sea with upward hot air streams raising a mixture of dust, plastic bags, and birds taking advantage of the hot air to save energy.

I decided not to ride on, not because I shirked the challenge, but for the sake of the sheer pleasure of that moment and wishing it would last forever. It sort of carried me away from reality. Just as a flash flood restores life to a desert wadi, so that sweet lemonade restored me, raising my blood sugar, and flooding my mind with pleasant fancies. At a certain moment, I even fell asleep for a few minutes. Waking up, sweating despite the shade, at first I had no idea where I was, and then – what the hell? I was by the Dead Sea!

Noticing the Dragot Cliffs sign behind me, I remembered it all – the trip of our old gang a few years ago. We had slept in a Bedouin camp on top of the cliffs and it was hot as hell. This old gang of special guys had been together for at least twenty years, and we still made an annual trip south. We had formed our friendships back in our high school days and since then we always shared each other's friends, highs and lows, happy and sad family occasions, and selected episodes of Game of Thrones.

We had, of course, our reunions that usually took place in some Bedouin camp in southern Israel. I never failed to attend them and they never let me down, even if I sometimes felt out of place, especially due to the topics of conversation. There was the kids' stuff, literally – school and kindergarten issues, diapers, nightly changing, baby foods, circumcision, and Bar Mitzvah parties. And, inevitably, there was the boring marital sex life. I guess this is how a bachelor feels in the company of married men. Well, I could live with that on a yearly basis, and once the conversation drifted to those realms, I usually took my leave or just kept silent. Probably, since I'd chosen to follow a different course and conquered different peaks, it made sense that what mattered to them were trifles to me. Sometimes it seemed to me that I didn't speak their language anymore.

Having swallowed the last drop of lemonade in the jar, I emptied the cup into my mouth to get all the sugar it contained. I was back in the long, rough ride mode, having to deal with the last 70km (or less, if my brother picked me up earlier).

I had started to push my "truck" out of the shade when I saw the white-bearded man waiting for me by the road as if he had anticipated my actions. Since the first moment I saw him, it felt as if he knew me through and through, including what I needed and where I was heading.

"Take it," he said, handing me a 1.5-liter bottle full of chilled lemonade. "Use it during your toughest rides today. I'm sure it will be useful."

"Wow... I'm speechless. It'll be so handy, you can't even imagine how. I don't know how to thank you. How much do I owe you?"

"C'mon, forget it! What's this 'owe you' crap!? Just keep riding and doing what you're best at, and only you know what it is exactly. That'll do for payment, okay?"

Before I could answer, he patted me on the back, wished me a safe ride, and starting walking back to his kiosk.

I stood there for about a minute staring at the man walking away from me, grasping my handlebar in my right hand and the cold bottle in my left. I remember it as if it all happened yesterday.

Overwhelmed by his kind words and actions, I recalled a similar encounter I had had in France at the foot of a lofty mountain a couple of years ago. A really friendly French lady demonstrated true French hospitality to me.

Taking two gulps of the lemonade for the road, I pushed the bottle into my trunk bag for easy access and set off. All I wanted was to get through that day, so I resolved to make no stops whatsoever, not even for coffee or snapshots, replenishing energy and fluids on the run.

The temperature did not drop but didn't rise either, which allowed me to hope that from now on it could only drop. Indeed, after crossing Wadi Tur, I reached the Einot Tzukim Reserve, which borders Route 90, and noticed that the temperature had dropped to 35°. Once again, the weather report was accurate about the heatwave subsiding in the afternoon.

After nearly four hours I reached Megilot Junction, where the westbound Route 1 meets the northbound Route 90. It was during the very last minutes of daylight, long after the sun had set behind the Jordan Valley Rift cliff. Looking east, I saw that the sunset had tinted the entire Dead Sea basin with spring evening hues. The South West Jordan Mountains looked especially beautiful, assuming increasingly dark shades of orange and brown. It was all set against a background of azure skies with dark blue streaks.

I made a stop to take a sip from the now-warm lemonade and call my brother to ask if I should wait for him right there. The other option was starting the long ride to Jerusalem, climbing from 400m below sea level to 754m above it, in the dark, on a busy and very bicycle-unfriendly road. Receiving no answer, I postponed the decision and checked the donation account. It didn't look bright, and due to the frequent non-stop rides and my almost complete absence from social media, I had hardly collected any new money. This made me make a mental list of matters to address and to refresh the donation campaign once I was in Jerusalem.

Ten minutes later, just as I was about to start pedaling toward Jerusalem, my brother called to tell me he would pick me up in a couple of minutes. It was a heavy load off my chest.

An hour later, I was already taking a shower in his place in an attempt to wash off all the dust that had built up on me over many days. Then, just as I did in Eilat, I let myself relax and relish my momentous triumph over the lowest road on Earth, which I had conquered despite the extreme heatwave. Finally, when I started to cool down, it dawned on me that I was already halfway through my journey. Running water also flooded me with a great thrill in anticipation of what lay ahead of me and my "truck" in a couple of days: the roads of Upper Galilee and the Golan Heights, which offer Israel's toughest climbs.

I dedicated my first morning in Jerusalem to filling in blanks in my diary, texting my friends, and posting updates about my future route. I was so absorbed with writing that I didn't even notice that I had been sitting for hours in the best part of my brother's house, namely the balcony overlooking the Temple Mount.

My family managed to talk me out of my plan to resume my journey the very next morning after my arrival. Having not an ounce of energy in me, I changed my plans and decided to start again in two days' time, early in the morning, to make it to Mt. Hermon in two days, and rest there at my relatives' place.

Toward evening, I was back on the balcony, sitting on an oakwood chair painted white, gazing at the horizon. In front of me, on a little brown table, rested my diary. After watching the orange hues of sunset, I just let my pen and brain run free, and they eventually worked in perfect harmony, producing the following lines:

Facing the Old City of Jerusalem, I'm thinking of my journey, especially of lessons to be drawn from it. Usually, when your skin is soaked with sweat, and your blood flooded with adrenaline, you can't think normally. You only reach fleeting conclusions, and once every few hours, your life looks like some movie in which you direct yourself. However, these are the life lessons I've learned so far from this journey:

1.Whenever you're overwhelmed with either joy or sorrow, you must record it in any possible way, either by writing, photos or videos, in order to remember that intense emotion with a smile.

2.Sooner or later, every downhill will be followed by an uphill, and vice versa. And when it comes, hold on, since it will rock you.

3. Love thy neighbor – even the ones not such as thyself.

4. Smile at the world, nature, and all living creatures, and they will return your smile. My experience taught me it always works.

5. The human body is an amazing machine like no other in the universe. Just look after it and it will take you wherever you wish.

6. Good attracts Good, and Evil attracts Evil, so it's your choice where to be and what to attract.

7. When out in torrential rain with no roof in sight, the best response is to just close your eyes, breathe in, and smile. Believe me, it is a unique experience.

8. When all alone in the desert with no shelter under the heavens and preparing for sleep, no noises should alarm you if you are self-reliant and self-confident at that moment. Since all our fears are in our mind, they go away once our mind is clear.

9. Be attentive to the slightest noise your machine makes while you ride it, since, if not taken care of immediately, it might grow louder and result in damage beyond repair.

10. Experience taught me that all mothers, wherever they are, have that anxiety and care gene that is triggered by just about anything.

11. Whenever somebody dismisses, mocks or cynically derides your ambitions and dreams – and more often than not it is a man who has the confidence of a nine-year-old – he is consumed with jealousy and feels threatened by your success. It's a sure sign you took the right way.

So, to all those who kept asking me over the last weeks what kind of a dream I'm living in, let me tell you – this has been my most beautiful dream for years.

I was so caught up in writing that I didn't notice that it had become pitch dark all around me. My cell phone vibrated in my pocket, interrupting my line of thought. I was quite pissed off with this disruption in such a rare moment when all my thoughts were flowing smoothly straight onto the page. However, I finally answered.

It was Tom Stein, the Channel Two reporter. He wanted to know how I was doing and my location, and suggested that we meet for an interview. When I informed him that the following day I was bound for the Golan Heights and was currently in Jerusalem, we both understood that the meeting was out of the question, despite Stein's sincere intentions to give my venture some airtime. Unfortunately, during his call, I was too preoccupied with the Galilee and Golan Heights roads to think clearly. I guess that when you have to do everything on your own; it's practically impossible to see the bigger picture with a cool head all the time.

Right after the call, Gidi – my younger brother by five years – texted me to say that he would bring me all the items I had asked for very soon. My family, especially Gidi, had been helping me throughout this trip, providing me with all my needs, be it clean clothes, food, or cycling equipment. Whenever I lacked anything, we would make an appointment for him to bring the supplies. That day, I'd asked him to bring from my Ashkelon apartment all the energy snacks the trip sponsors had given me. To do this, Gidi, who worked as a law firm intern at Ramat Gan Business Center, had to ask for a day off.

When my parents immigrated to Israel from England, they were looking for the best place to start a new family.

They were very keen on coming to Israel at a very young age. However, after their very British wedding, my father changed his business suit for a kibbutz farmer's blue shirts, and my mother changed her high heels for sandals. They spent some time in a Hebrew school for newcomers in northern Israel before heading south and joining the ex-soldiers who founded Kibbutz Alumim. All of us grew up and were educated on that kibbutz. Back then, as I recall, the main values instilled in us were work ethics, a love of nature, and adherence to the Jewish religion and traditions.

Most of my elementary education took place in nearby Kibbutz Saad. Then I spent three years in a secondary boarding school in Kibbutz Yavne alongside youths from other areas. These were my first years away from home, as I only came home for weekends.

Alumim is part of the Religious Kibbutz Movement, started in Europe in the late 1920s by Hassidim who enthusiastically embraced Zionism – the belief that Jews must take action to establish their own independent country.

Located in the western Negev, by Route 232, it looks like a green oasis. Almost all year round it is surrounded by all kinds of seasonal crops: avocados, corn, wheat, peanuts, sunflowers, carrots, and potatoes. It also has several long chicken-coops a few hundred meters from the outer fence. Agriculture is still responsible for 70% of Alumim's income. Its reliance on agriculture, as well as the boundless open spaces where I used to roam as a child, significantly influenced my future choices in life – especially the decision to embark on my current journey.

The two "big cities" I visited as a child were Netivot and Sderot. Any trip to Netivot was an event requiring two-days' advance preparation, and we were allowed to wear our special-occasion attire. In the 1980s, a trip to Tel Aviv or

Jerusalem was a major, once-a-year event, involving all the people on the kibbutz who wanted to make sure their children safely set foot in Dizengoff Street, the Israeli equivalent of Fifth Avenue. For us back then, it was as exciting as flying abroad for the first time in your life.

Graduating from high school, I spent a year in a pre-military academy, then did my three years of military service as part of a Special Forces' anti-tank team. Those hard years taught me to accept discipline and authority, as opposed to the earthy rural paradise of my early life. On the bright side, it offered me the opportunity to befriend all kinds of guys from all over the country with whom I still keep in touch.

Military service during my early twenties had an incredible effect on me. My army experience – dealing with mud, cold, thorns, and on top of that selfish and sadistic commanders – wiped out many of the values I held before, as it did for many other combat soldiers. It also drove me to completely detest field trips, nature, and outdoor experiences – even the pleasant ones, such as the sight of springtime flowers. Whenever I started planning a trip, I recalled my army days of long walks in the cold with a heavy backpack, which always dispirited me. It was only many years later that I learned to love and feel at home in the outdoors, despite the feeling of human frailty in the face of the elements.

I once spent a month in the fascinating country of Costa Rica with Noa, my girlfriend back then, on board a Jeep. Back in Israel, I noticed that, unlike previous trips, this one had not been spoiled by any bad memories from my army days.

"Time has surely healed my wounds," I told Noa when we landed back at Tel Aviv Airport.

"A man reflects his homeland's image," she replied,

quoting the best-known line of late-nineteenth-century Jewish poet, Tchernichovski, "and no commander or military service experience can change that."

Later that evening, I spent some quality time with Ari and Gidi hanging around Jerusalem before embarking on my journey again. During that evening, my brothers kept asking me what they could do to make my trip as successful as possible. As a matter of fact, there was nothing special they could have done for me since, until then, it had all gone to plan in general. I only asked them to be available for rescuing me or bringing me supplies.

We spent most of the evening in the Mahane Yehuda market. At night, it turns from a bustling marketplace smelling of fish and spices into a nightlife hub. As soon as we got back, at about 22:00, I started my preparations for the following day's ride along Route 90, taking my clothes out of the dryer and making sandwiches. I also gave Gidi some unnecessary clothing items that had taken up precious storage space and increased my burden. My sister-in-law, in cooperation with my nephew, made me two liters of fresh pomegranate juice.

"You definitely know what I like," I flattered her.

For a cyclist, pomegranate juice is one of the best things to drink, not only due to its sweet and refreshing taste, but also because of its high percentage of nitrates, which improve circulation and food digestion. A couple of gulps of it during my northbound ride would significantly boost my energy when I felt exhausted.

Everything was ready for tomorrow. My bike was locked to the railing in the basement, my cell phone and solar charger were being charged, and my four bike bags were full of food and clean clothes, gently smelling of lavender.

Chatting on for a while with my sister-in-law and my

nephew, I hit the sack at about 01:00. However, my stomach bubbled with excitement and wouldn't let me sleep, and a particular nephew of mine snoring a few meters away didn't help, either. I knew this ride would be nothing like anything I'd had to deal with on the dusty southern desert roads, so I expected this trip to end in just over a week.

All of a sudden, while I lay on my back under the blanket trying to fall asleep, my thoughts drifted to Maya. I hadn't given her any thought for a couple of days. I recalled the night we spent together near Wadi Tamar when she told me that she'd started her residency in a Tel Aviv hospital. I wondered what was happening with her, and if she'd returned to her guy after all.

I grabbed my cell phone to check my recent text chats with her and, while I was checking, I recalled that the last time I'd texted her from Arava Junction gas station, the result had been our intimate night together by Route 90. That memory sent a warm, happy sensation all over me, helping me to fall asleep with my cell phone in my hand, right after I'd texted Maya about my planned route for the next day.

The night Jessica and I climbed from Lisa's chalet down to her Zurich house, we had a long talk about the future of our relationship, reaching the conclusion there just wasn't any future in it. Later on, Jessica invited some friends for a drink in the local pub, as if to celebrate our break-up. Once I realized she was preoccupied with her studies at that point and had no wish to plunge into an affair with an Israeli adventurer, all I wanted to do was get in the saddle again and ride far away.

I had mixed feelings about her that night. Although every moment next to her was great fun and a source of extraordinary satisfaction, I realized it had no future. I was building castles in the air. Thus, I tried to keep up appearances in order to part from her amicably and ride away south to France.

The next morning, Jessica's parents walked me to the bike trail near their house where they said goodbye. She herself wanted to accompany me out of town where we could say a friendly, calm last goodbye. There was no way I'd have given up what seemed to be my last chance of enjoying her company.

An hour's ride brought us out of town. The sun shining in a totally cloudless sky was hot enough to make us sweat. A mild sidewind was playing with Jessica's hair under her yellow helmet. We rode along a narrow asphalt road, just the two of us, through green meadows stretching all the way to small faraway hills that gradually grew into lofty mountains, the peaks of which were still snowcapped. I wore my usual cycling clothes – tights and a short-sleeved, yellow DriFIT shirt, while she wore knee-length blue jeans and black Nikes. I don't know whether she wanted me to, but I noticed she wore no bra under her tight, white top, judging from her visible white tan lines. Of course, the unrestrained movement of her breasts proved hard to ignore.

The silence only enhanced the passion in the air and, once again, she seemed to try to tell me she wanted something, yet didn't know exactly what or how to communicate it to me.

"I sense you want to kill me today," I remarked during a stop.

"You mean, with this top? I noticed you weren't very focused on the road, you naughty boy!" she replied, taking her helmet off, and then came near enough to remove my own helmet and breathe on my face.

"Thank you. Indeed, your top, as well as your bouncing boobs, did very little to help me ride straight," I explained and we both laughed.

"Well, crackpot, hug and kiss me and then drive your rosy ass off to France before I change my mind and join you!"

We embraced for a long time, and I recall hoping that she'd say something instead of just letting me go away. Her tears flowed down my chest and she used my yellow shirt to wipe her nose and eyes, yet said nothing. I was so strongly moved by the silence and her warm body that it left me breathless. Seeing no way out, I just mounted my bike and,\ saying nothing, set off toward the French border. I felt Jessica staring at my back but I didn't look back.

It took me just a week to fall in love with France's people, nature, and – of course – the baguettes, as well as all the other items of local cuisine I had a chance to taste.

One day, a few hours after the rain had stopped, I met Roger and Emily, a French couple. I had just ordered a cup of coffee and they were parked near my heavy bike outside the café in Aix-les-Bains, a pastoral town on the shore of a great lake.

Noticing my bike, they waited for me to leave the café. While inside the café, I dried off and changed my clothes, yet all the gear left on the bike was muddy, making it obvious that I'd spent quite a few days outdoors in wet weather. Approaching me, they just invited me, in a cocktail of French and English, to stay at their house that night. Losing no time, I told them I'd love to.

The next morning it was raining again, but I had to leave the French couple's house as they were heading north for a few days off. Once again, I had to depart from kind people who befriended me and generously allowed me to sleep in their home.

From Aix-les-Bains, I turned south toward Grenoble, the gateway to French Alps. I planned to try some of the most renowned climbs, riding on roads that the Tour de France competitors had covered just a few weeks before I had entered France. I wanted to end every cycling day in a place offering a view of the climb that I had just conquered. These climbs, each about 10-15km, should be called "climbing walls" and are well-known not only among European, but worldwide cyclists, as well. The best known is probably the Alpe d'Huez, which rises to 1860m above sea level. Though not the highest, it is certainly a worthy challenge. That section of road saw quite a few serious battles between Tour de France champions. When I started to climb it, I understood why the winner of this rough part of the Tour was often the winner of the entire tough, three-week race several years in a row. I'm talking about a 14km climb with 7-15% gradients. It is just one long, leg-wrecking cycle due to both the steep road and the blazing heat of the local summer.

On the other hand, cycling tourism offers a lot of advantages, such as having your hotel room with you. It avoids searches for a parking space, always offers a room with a view of your choice – either upwind or downwind – and even has the sun waking you up precisely at the time of your choice.

I set up my tent a few meters from the road descending from the ski site exactly opposite the sun and, as planned, the sun woke me up early on a tranquil, alpine morning. The night before was cold, very near to freezing point and despite the blue morning sky, the tent walls were ice-coated and the road was still wet with the night's rainwater and melted ice.

I let the sun warm the road, as well as my body for an hour before starting off. I planned a cautious descent toward the valley and then a left-hand turn to Route D1091 toward Col du Galibier, another leg-wrecking, legendary peak to conquer that day.

The downhill ride was fast and reviving. The cool, morning air burnt my lungs, yet my spirits were high due to my smooth progress as well as the local hospitality. I was in my element, feeling I could go on like this for years.

At one point, I rode by a tiny village only consisting of a few houses standing by the road, yet they were so colorful, each decorated with a window box full of red and white flowers – the classic alpine village. About 20m further on came a right-hand bend. On my right was a high, rocky terrace,\ and on my left, a guardrail that kept me from slipping into a stream running only 20m from the road. I was slightly intoxicated with the view and the good old smell of soil and rain.

It hit me like lightning. Traveling at 35 kph, my tires lost traction. Due to the melted snow, my distraction, and the high speed, I slid toward the guardrail. Noticing that I was running out of asphalt and the guardrail was speeding toward me, I applied the brakes as hard as I could. Realizing I must act now to avoid disaster, I abandoned my bike, letting it slide away from under me. Falling on my butt, I slid along for another 5m down the road, while my bike disappeared under the guardrail and straight into the gorge.

My shoes hit the guardrail hard and I felt a sharp pain in

my right heel. Fortunately, the guardrail stopped my slide when I was just a few centimeters away from hitting a big rock that would probably have broken both of my legs instantly. Examining my body, I happily found all my parts intact and detected no serious injuries, just a few painful grazes along my ass and on my knees and another open wound on my left palm.

Thirty seconds later, when I fully regained my senses, it sank in that my bike had plunged into the gorge along with almost all my gear, money, passport, and cell phone.

I was now stuck on the shoulder of a French alpine road, cursing everything – my bike, the dealer who sold it to me, the roads, and the guardrail manufacturer. When I ran out of curses, I started praying, unintentionally, to any cosmic power that might happen to hear me, even to God. I started uttering a prayer in a stuttering voice, stopping and switching to cursing and back to praying, a cocktail only possible under extreme circumstances, I guess.

It sounded a bit like:\, "Hey, you, out there, whatever you call yourself! Universe, Supreme Being, God Almighty, or any other creative scum, can you hear me!? Fine, I got your point! Any chance of you giving me a break?! Just any way out of the shit I've got myself into!" Pausing and closing my eyes for a few seconds, I went on mumbling. "I guess that's how you get your kicks, right!? Seeing us mortals in need of your help, and playing the savior at the very last moment?! No wonder I've always taken you for a sick mind!"

My breathing intensified and my ravings grew worse, but not because I failed to find God. On the contrary, it was exactly because I realized that he had been there all the time... and that God had no motivation to help me out of the mess I was in. God, instead of granting our wishes, is just a

bloody observer of our miseries who laughs at them while
he plays with his gray beard.

After several minutes of such ranting, I fell silent. There
was complete silence all around me except for the singing of
the birds and the rushing of the stream below. By now, pain
had spread through my legs and back, driving me to rage
against the whole world but mostly myself for being such a
damn fool. Then I got to my feet to see how my limbs coped
with my bodyweight, completely ignoring the loss of my
bike with all my precious items.

Standing up, I saw that my pants were torn at thigh level
and a piece of the cloth was missing. Through the hole, I
could see a deep graze reddening my pants. The cycling
gloves had taken most of the shock, saving my hands from
many wounds. Even so, one wound was bleeding and conta-
minated with shreds of asphalt during the fall.

After cleaning up and stopping the bleeding by pressing
my hat against the wound, I spotted one of my bags that had
been torn from the bike. Its contents – a pack of pasta, a
bottle of cooking oil, salt, a cooking pot, and some utensils –
were scattered across the road. When I started recovering
the items and assessing the damage to the bag, I saw, fortunately, that the hole was repairable. I then remembered the
sewing kit, along with my bike, that had dove into the
ravine. The small bottle was broken and all its contents lost.
Most of the pasta remained in the pack, but all my spices,
kept in a separate box, had spilled out.

Once I had finished gathering the scattered items, I had
to face the question I had been trying to avoid: what had
happened to my bike and the other bags? What were the
consequences of the loss of my possessions? Would I have to
travel on foot from here?

Anxiety made my pulse skyrocket, so I sat on the

guardrail for a few seconds and breathed deeply a couple of times, running through several scenarios, none of which looked at all encouraging, though each offered some way out. I coolly resolved that, before resorting to desperate solutions, I must get a clearer picture of my situation and make no decisions before I tried to recover my lost bike and gear.

Jumping over the guardrail at the point of the skid, I gingerly approached the edge of the gorge where my bike had dove into the stream rushing below, which was swelled by rain and snowmelt and showed various hues of gray, white, and green. Looking down, I could see no trace of either my bike nor the bags on it. It didn't look good, so I descended about a meter to get a closer look. Then I saw it. The bike lay on a big rock, the handlebar twisted completely backward and the saddle crooked, yet one bag was still attached. Another bag lay on the ground a meter away, torn, with my Leatherman multitool and the rest of my tools scattered around it.

I breathed with relief and much of my anxiety disappeared: I had found my bike and, as it seemed at first glance, most of my gear as well.

About 200m down the road was a pedestrian trail leading to the site of the crash by the stream. Packing all my recovered food items into the torn bag, I started down the trail toward my bike. Thirty minutes later I was back on the road with my bike and bags. The rough terrain compelled me to salvage them in two rounds: first, I brought my bike back up to the road and then, leaving my bike behind, I went back down to recover my bags.

The climbing up and down exhausted me and reopened the cuts on my palm. My thigh started bleeding again as well and stained my socks. Luckily, I found all my money, cell phone, camera, tent, and sleeping bag. Now I had to assess the damage to my bike and see if it was rideable.

When I reached the lowest point of the ski slope, it was nearly 12:00. The descent, with me pushing my bike with all my gear secured to it, took nearly an hour. However, it made me feel good, making me realize that not all was lost and that a day-long repair operation would get me in the saddle again.

I decided to camp for the night by Route D1901, a few hundred meters from Le Freney d'Oisans, a picturesque little village in a valley surrounded by dense forests, towering cliffs, and snowcapped mountains. I decided to set my tent up by the stream to ensure a water supply for the next twenty-four hours.

On top of that, my wet dream (pun intended) for a couple of days was to plunge into a stream, and this was the first thing I did right after I set up the tent and checked my stuff.

I planned to leave all my stuff there and go to the village for medical supplies, food, spices and, if I happened to find an internet café, send some text messages. However, upon reaching the village after a five-minute walk, I realized I was once again outside civilization and couldn't even figure out what day of the week and month it was.

Typical of my kind of luck, I happened to be there on a Sunday when everything was closed except the local church and gas station. I had mixed feelings about it. On the one hand, it sucked because I could get no fresh food. On the other hand, knowing that I was not bound by any external schedules, I felt like a modern-day Robinson Crusoe for a moment.

I had several such incidents throughout my European tour, and they always made me realize how boundlessly free the cycling tourist is, enjoying total independence from his surroundings and the rules that others had made for themselves and, most importantly, free to explore new ways of life. True, I used the public facilities of the countries that I traveled through, but often for as long as a week, I would encounter no people at all or have any conversation of more than two words at a time.

Returning to my riverside campsite empty-handed, I started to patch up the torn bags. As for the bike, it was tightening the axles, oiling and stretching the chain, and of course, repairing and replacing the spokes twisted and broken by the fall took a little time.

Intact wheel spokes are critical to a bike's function. They are secured to the rim radially and are supposed to sustain many forces to keep the wheel from twisting or breaking under extreme conditions. A spoke is a thin, steel wire processed in such a way as to prevent expansion or contraction either during the riding or when resting. During the ride, the spoke is subjected to enormous strains, especially when the bike's carrying several heavy bags.

Due to all that, riding on with twisted or broken spokes was out of the question. If I had damaged my wheels beyond repair, I'd be forced to replace the entire rim instead of those little steel rods. Luckily for me, I had some spare spokes and a spoke wrench specially designed to adjust them, although I knew, of course, that I should get my wheels adjusted by a specialist once I happened to reach a cycle shop. However, I did a good job of patching the torn bags using a shirt cut into pieces.

At twilight, the weather was still perfect but the cold reclaimed the valley once the sun had set behind the surrounding ridges. At about 21:00, I slipped into my sleeping bag. Making sure I had no text messages, I turned

my cell phone off to save the battery and added a few lines
to my blue diary to record this definitely unusual day and
my route for the next couple of days. The next day, I would
advance toward the nearby mountain pass, Col du Galibier.
Laying down my diary on my belly, I fell asleep with my
hand still grasping my pen.

What a surprise I had the next morning when I
emerged from my tent: a dense, white mist shrouded the
land all around me like a white tablecloth resting on a
dinner table. The verdant ground was overlooked by
mountains towering to nearly 3000m above sea level. The
sun, eventually shining through after the light showers of
the night before, revealed the full splendor of the forest
with all its rich wildlife. The heavy rains in the region
had produced a dense, lush forest comprising layer upon
layer of vegetation. Creepers covered the trees under
which grew a variety of shrubs above another layer of
grass and moss. This view made me feel that that day
would be completely different from the previous disastrous one.

A few minutes later, I was already busy with my usual
preparations for another day in the saddle – folding my tent,
some exercises, and brewing up my morning coffee – when I
detected a car approaching me. It was a new blue Peugeot,
freshly washed by the night rain.

The bathing in the stream had left me relatively clean,
yet my several months' beard and my heavily laden bike
gave me the vagabond look. The car stopped and a French
lady of about fifty stepped out. In her black high heels, black
tailored skirt all the way to her white knees, and a tight
black jacket, she had the look of a classy businesswoman.
Her chestnut hair was gathered in a bun and dark glasses
rested on her head. As she came near me, I noticed the

broad smile accentuating her lips and her ivory-white teeth. To me, she looked like Michelle Pfeiffer, yet prettier.

"Bonjour, monsieur. Comment ça va? Je suis Joséphine." She addressed me in French, in a calm and pleasant voice.

"Great morning, madame. I don't understand French well, but I'm okay. I hope I didn't do much damage or make too much noise yesterday or this morning," I answered in a cocktail of English and bad French.

"Oh la la! You really did not disturb us!" She cut me short, raising her hand, before going on in fluent English. "On the contrary, we were really glad to see you reach the stream last night, but were worried about you since you were slightly injured and bruised all over. I guess you'd had a fall or something. We were also very happy to see you this morning. We, and all our family, are also bicycle lovers and very much sympathize with what you are going through on your tour, carrying all these bags. We, too, went on such a tour twenty years ago, when we cycled across Australia for nearly a year. It was unforgettable!"

A little embarrassed, I replied, "Thank you, madame! I really appreciate your sincere care."

Now we both fell silent, just looking at each other, having nothing to say, the only sound being the rushing of the stream a few meters behind me.

Suddenly, this freeze-frame scene ended and the movie went on: Michelle Pfeifer went back to her car, returning with a big, white disposable cup on which "Bonjour!" and a big smiley were drawn on with a black marker. It was even wrapped up in a white napkin decorated with a small French Tricolor and was full of hot cappuccino that smelled strongly like a newly-opened bag of coffee beans. Before my mind could absorb it, her other hand held out a hot croissant, the chocolate filling of which was oozing from the

sides, and had probably come straight from the local patis-
serie. This was an unforgettable moment.

Later on, I commented on it in my diary: "This trip is a
forerunner of a project I want to carry out soon when I'm
back home. Will I get to enjoy a similar gesture of kindness
in my country as well?" I got my answer a few years later, in
the form of the most delicious lemonade I had ever tasted
near the Dead Sea shore."

"I wish your day will be as sweet as this croissant, and as
invigorating as this coffee," she said as I walked her back to
her car.

"Oh, thank you, madame," I said, all excited. "It looks and
smells so delicious. How could I ever thank you?"

"It's okay, just take care and get home safely," she advised
me, turning her back on me and getting into her car.
Opening the window, she waved me goodbye with a smile
that I will never forget.

I stood there for a quite few moments after she had
driven away, staring at my cup of coffee and croissant, trying
to analyze what had just happened. The main point was that
I couldn't have wished for a better start to the day. Suddenly
it struck me: such kindness and friendliness to me all over
Europe stemmed from the only thing we all love – cycling.

8

DAY 8

"Better to have a glorious failure than leave your dreams in a drawer."

Dudu Tassa

April 7, 2016
Starting point: Jerusalem
Destination: Tzemah Junction, southern shore of Lake Tiberias
Distance: 155 kilometers

I was awakened by a tickling vibration along my spine at the end of my second and last night in Jerusalem. Throughout that night, my cell phone had been wandering all over the double-size mattress I was sleeping on, finally ending up under my back. Getting up, I heard noises from the living room. It happened to be an argument between my nephews. Giving up all hope of sleeping any longer, I just got dressed and went out. I had completed all my preparations the night before, so all I had to do was get on my bike and start for the Golan Heights. Entering the living room, I was happy to see that one of my nephews, Nadav, who was wearing his sports outfit as well as his naughty smile, had decided to join me on my ride along Route 90.

Shir was angry with me for leading her children astray by encouraging them to join me, but eventually she succumbed on two conditions: the first was that Nadav must take the first bus back to Jerusalem from the Jordan Valley Monument Junction at 12:00, and the ride was to start not from Jerusalem, but from Beit Ha-Arava Junction. I accepted, of course, being happy that fourteen-year-old Nadav wanted to come along with me. He was Ari's second-oldest son. An energetic and curious boy with wanderlust in his blood, he took every opportunity to go hiking in new places.

Wasting no time, we ate breakfast and covered ourselves in sun protection cream. Before embarking, I inspected the gears of both of our bikes and made sure we had enough water and other supplies necessary for several hours' ride in the Jordan Valley's sweltering heat.

After saying goodbye, we piled into the family car and my brother gave us a ride to Beit Ha-Arava Junction, where the northbound Route 90 meets the westbound Route 1. I used the half-hour drive for texting, checking the weather report for the next couple of days, and double-checking my route. The forecast was for very hot weather, though less than the heat I had suffered on southern Route 90 a couple of days ago. The temperature was expected to rise to about 40° by midday, so it was essential to know the location of every possible watering point along the route.

Five minutes into the car ride, my cell phone was flooded with messages, some sent the night before and just then received, while others had been sent that morning from people commenting on my social media post about my planned route. Some I answered at once, while others I decided to answer later. Among them was a message from a local newspaper reporter:

Hello, I'm Shay, a Jerusalem News reporter. I heard about your project and you being in Jerusalem for the next few days. I'd love to interview you over the phone for this weekend's issue. Please reply. Thanks.

I replied instantly, agreeing to talk to him later. Another intriguing message was from Maya:

Good morning, sweetie. How I loved getting an early morning message from you! I see you're on Route 90, north-bound. From 1 to 10, how much would you like me to join you for a few hours? I promise not to be too much of a nag. It's the weekend, so I have a couple of days to kill.

Her message made me smile, so I texted her that I'd call her later to arrange a place to meet.

Toward 09:00, we started cycling slowly north, with me leading and Nadav trailing five meters behind on his heavy, off-road bike. The road was perfectly maintained with broad shoulders and little traffic. The weather was comfortable, yet the hot north wind indicated it would get hotter. However, we had sufficient water and decided to make a stop once every thirty minutes to drink and rest. Most of the route was flat, running between Jerusalem and the hills of Samaria on one side and the River Jordan on the other.

Passing the left turn to Jericho, we decided to make a stop. Nadav was riding at a good speed, keeping up with me despite his bike being an off-road type that wasn't designed for asphalt roads. While we rode, he told me how he had been doing in school and how he couldn't stand his teachers' bullshit. He couldn't wait to join the army and start hiking all over the country, like I did. He had, I thought, inherited Ari's genes with his love of backpacking and the outdoors, which he regarded as more important than sitting in a classroom. On top of that, he was also interested in my project and kept on asking me where I planned to ride to the next day and what I would do with all the money that I hoped to raise. An hour later, we had already spotted the Jordan Valley Monument Junction where we planned to make a lunch stop, after which Nadav was to take the bus back to Jerusalem while I would ride on north.

We said goodbye at about 12:00 after I had made sure his cell phone was on and that he had enough water for the bus ride back home. Then I texted Shiri that her son was on his way home and having done all that, I folded my camping burner, cleaned the glasses we had used for drinking Elnakhla black coffee, and prepared to ride north. I was aiming for a small spring called Ein Sukkot near Moshav Shadmot Mehola, where I had arranged to meet Maya. While I was preparing, she texted:

Tzuriel, you won't believe the message I just received – so don't you dare think I don't care about you! A couple of days ago, I told some friends and people I know about your project. They were very impressed and want to donate 5000 USD, so just give me the bank account info and I'll transfer the money right away. Besides, I think I deserve some reward for my help and the support I'm giving you in general. (C'mon, you nerd! I was just kidding about the reward – in case you took it too literally...) Anyway, I'm on my way to Ein Sukkot, hope to see you soon. xx.

A few minutes later, after completing my preparations for the ride, I texted her briefly:

1. What great news! You're Number One, I'm really speechless! A million thanks to your friends!

2. Didn't you make a promise not to be too much of a nag? So far, you haven't tried very hard to keep to it.

3. Get your cute little butt over to Route 90 and I'll think of a proper reward. See ya!

Ein Sukkot was nearly 40km away from the Jordan Valley Monument Junction, so my estimated arrival time would be 14:00. Riding was practically impossible during the hottest hours of the day, so the spring at Ein Sukkot would make the perfect place to rest before riding on to Tzemah Junction.

Leaving my previous stop – where Nadav and I had eaten our lunch – I took the left turn and noticed the distinctive, conical Mount Sartaba west of Route 90, north-west of Moshav Yafit. It rose to about 650m above the Jordan Valley and stood up high above all other peaks in the valley. Thanks to its height, anybody traveling along Route 90 can recognize it.

The sight of it threw me back to my army days, to my team's final stretcher-bearing exercise before graduating from the grueling Special Unit training course. It lasted all night long with one man on the stretcher. Its climax was climbing Sartaba all the way to its peak. It followed a hellish training week (which not everybody could sail through) of marching over 100km all over the country in a series of forced marches and land navigation sessions, carrying all your food, water, weaponry, and camping-gear on your back.

Stopping by Route 90, I rested my heavily laden "truck" against the guardrail and took some pictures. Spotting a shady, deserted bus stop nearby, I decided to have a few minutes' rest in order to text a few messages to my fellow servicemen's WhatsApp group. This triggered a volley of

cynical jokes from my brothers-in-arms about our early
service days.

A few minutes later, an army Humvee stopped by me.
The officer sitting next to the driver asked me how I was
doing. I was amazed at how easily it threw me back to my
army days. The sight of soldiers in helmets and dusty
uniforms, the odor of gasoline in the air, and the tarpaulin
sheltering the troopers from the sun made me recall all the
despair, danger, and exhaustion of my combat service in
South Lebanon.

It did have a bright side to it, though, in the form of the
fellow-servicemen who became my lifelong friends, the
likes of whom I would never have found otherwise.
however, all in all, military service was hard on me – so hard
that I recalled how, quite a few days after my demobilization, I wrote for days on end in my diary just to get this
heavy burden off my chest.

I recall those trips on the serpentine road between the town
of Metula on the Lebanese border and the infamous Reihan
outpost. It was a scenic road easily matching any in
southern New Zealand, running across the Litani River
amidst the pine and cedar woods and green meadows
stretching all the way to the foot of the Shouf Mountains.

When we traveled by day, we would occasionally see
shepherds waving to us in the ravines. In January 1997, the
winter hit us with all its might – a combination of snow,
rain, and cold that only Lebanon could offer. I recall just

how slowly the twenty-vehicle, cumbersome convoy moved.

I was in an old armored truck with steel sides designed to stop missiles. Its roof, however, was made of cheap tarpaulin. I was loaded up with my full combat kit: bullet-proof vest, a short-version M-16 with a bullet in its barrel – to be on the safe side – a tactical vest filled with seven magazines, four hand-grenades, an assault knife, a bar of milk chocolate, a grill-flavored wheat snack, a soft drink, a flash-light, and a first-aid kit.

We were all crammed into the truck and the dark was so dense that it felt like a sauna. You had to feel your way around before making the slightest move. I couldn't even recognize the face of Ariel only about fifteen centimeters away. He had saved me from a sniper's bullet a couple of days earlier. Like everything else in Lebanon, darkness pressed you hard and devoured you mercilessly.

The heavens opened, making us feel as if we were driving through an endless shower. We all feared that the tarpaulin roof would give way. The rain not only made a terrible noise but also dripped through a hole in the roof, down my helmet, and into the space between my neck and my uniform, which started to spread the cold water all over me.

We were already deep inside Lebanon. The silence was absolute and the tension at its highest. All we wanted was to reach the base renowned for being the deepest-located outpost in Lebanon. It was situated about 20km north of the Israeli border. The rain filled the air with an unforgettable odor: army tarp covered with oil, and Lebanese mud. It made me feel sick. It was at this early stage that I realized how much I hated anything to do with the army and the place called Lebanon.

I also recall an ambush assignment during which thirteen of us – tired, hungry, and horny – hid inside a thorny bush, sometimes falling asleep even as we were talking. War seemed to give everything its own peculiar character, so we ate, longed for home, talked, and pissed as one does in wartime, and we also killed as one does in wartime because these are the rules of war. If you don't play exactly by the rules, you will be dead meat. Pure and simple. I remember us coming back from that operation caked in sticky mud, faces covered with green and black camouflage paint. We stank of sweat, gunpowder, sausages, wheat snacks, and, of course, blood – not ours, but of those who had tried to kill us.

Yes, we saw a lot of blood, especially when some of my fellow soldiers lopped off terrorists' ears. It was not unusual, back then to wear lopped-off ears around your neck as victory trophies, just as pilots paint an enemy symbol on their plane's nose for every shot-down aircraft, and just as scholars brag about their papers being published in prestigious journals. For the same reasons, combat foot soldiers used to lop off their enemies' ears and mark a big cross on their rifle for every kill. Even some officers embraced these customs back then.

After thirty-five days in Lebanon, I was so damn eager to go on leave. Once home, I recall feeling dumbfounded and deeply insulted by civilians' comments on the operation we had just carried out. Those civilians had never carried arms, eaten anything but milk chocolate, or had to relieve themselves into a Coke bottle for an entire week. They had no idea. Needless to say, they had never encountered at close quarters men whose eyes flashed hatred at them just for being Jewish. They had never carried a friend with a bullet in his head on their shoulders. Yet they never stopped criticizing us.

I also recall that it was then that I realized just how hypocritical our world is. Oh, how I wanted to yell at those bleeding hearts who know nothing and can do nothing but tut-tut over our misconduct and scribble their carefully phrased, moving resentment. It is much easier to hide from reality behind your sheet of paper than take cover behind a spiky rock from enemy hellfire. It feels so morally powerful to write beautiful poems (or even limericks) about the dehumanization and moral deterioration engendered by the army, yet it's so easy to forget that it is exactly that immoral army and those inhuman soldiers who allow them to survive so they can shoot their poisoned verbal arrows. Since they never played our game, they could never have known its rules.

The last time I traveled across the Lebanese border toward Reihan as part of an endless column of trucks full of ammo and dead-beat soldiers, I closed my eyes, imagining that I was traveling as a backpacker far away from all that quagmire.

Well, I thought, it was about to come true, as I fell asleep after packing up my blue backpack and resting it against my bed, on the eve of my flight abroad.

After chatting with me for a few minutes, the soldiers forced into my hands several leftover cans of tuna from their rations. Then they drove off to accomplish their mission, leaving me behind them, all their Humvee exhaust gases in my face. A few minutes later, I changed into white cycling clothes that suited cycling on Route 90 in intense heat. First, I put on a white, long-sleeved shirt and a hat with a visor and a neck-flap to shade both my face and the back of my neck, pressing it down tightly under a white helmet. Then I liberally applied a white protective cream. I did this because the night before when I was staying in Jerusalem with my brother, my mother had told me over the phone that I should use more sun cream because she was worried about how sunburned I looked in my photos. I obeyed, naturally, but ten minutes of riding in the Jordan Valley heat made me regret it: all that cream streamed into my eyes, stinging them like hell. I had to stop, wash it off, and then ride on.

I rode in a sort of mindless state, attempting to detach myself from everything around me, Far Eastern meditation-style, me and my bike merging into one machine. My mind gradually drifted away from the cars driving past me and even the Jordan Valley landscape into a sort of cool, quiet cavern, where the only sounds I could hear were the gentle rattling of the chain against the sprockets, the contact of the rubber tires with the hot asphalt, and my monotonous breathing joining this symphony.

On group rides, mental detachment is quite impossible but now I felt a fundamental transformation, a rare union of man and machine. The last time I'd had a similar experience was when I conquered the challenging climb all the way to Paso del Stelvio during my European tour in the summer of 2011.

I played Queen's "I Want to Break Free" on my earphones and set myself into a quick-pedaling mood. On this nearly flat, practically climb-free road with rather broad shoulders, I could maintain a speed of nearly 30kph. The wind wasn't blowing too hard and, though the sun scorched me mercilessly, the Southern Jordan Valley had already taught my body how to ride in a temperature of 40°.

I noticed the changing landscape now that I was in the inhabited part of the Jordan Valley. Along my entire route, the road served as a kind of border between the rural Arab communities' greenhouses and the course of the River Jordan, which, flowing from Lake Tiberias to the Dead Sea, marked the border between Israel and Jordan. While maintaining my speed, I also made sure to stop every thirty minutes to pour half a liter of water over myself and to drink another half a liter at the same time

I rode past Zubaidat, a Bedouin village east of Moshav Argaman. Right after Israel's War of Independence in 1949, its inhabitants had moved to the Jordan Valley, the country's most inhospitable area, and they had lived there ever since, farming the land. Some of the local kids who had seen me rode along with me for a few kilometers. Shouting and laughing, they noticed the Go-Pro on my helmet and wanted to be photographed, so I stopped, took their picture, and then a selfie of us all together

The local adults, noticing me from afar, gestured to me to join them for a cup of tea in a palm-branch shed by the road. I saw that they had some wooden carts loaded with crates of vegetables and dry fruits that they grew and sold to travelers on Route 90. It was an offer I could not refuse, so I approached the shed but decided not to spend more than ten minutes there. It was growing hotter and I wanted to make it to Ein Sukkot by 14:00. I communicated with them in a hodgepodge of Hebrew, a little English, and elementary Arabic. Having no idea what they were talking about, I just answered, "Yes", to most of their countless questions. The tea, however, was good and strong, and the sugar cubes and dates they forced into my hands and pockets energized me to ride on.

With a friendly handshake, I thanked them for the tea and jumped on my saddle again. I got going again at a good pace, and with Queen in my ears I was soon pedaling along Route 90 again, sweating, taking a drink every thirty minutes, and mopping my sweat once every five minutes.

A forty-five-minute ride brought me to the right-hand turn to Ein Sukkot, a spring situated about 20km from Zubeidat. There was a branch road leading to the Jordanian border, and just 500m past that road, I spotted a white shirt advancing toward me. I instantly shifted to a higher gear, since cyclists on that part of the road were a sufficiently rare sight to deserve a closer look. A few seconds later, judging from the cyclist's posture, I concluded that it was a latest-model bike. Now I was even more curious about who the hell would be cycling in such unearthly heat in the Jordan Valley, and such a hellhole.

The mystery was solved in a minute and took me far away in time and space to the moment I had seen Jessica cycling toward me on the outskirts of Zurich six years earlier. This time, Maya played her part. She was even pret-tier than I imagined, sitting in her saddle, bent over her handlebars, the desert wind playing with her hair under her helmet, and very short, blue sports pants covering her body. Her white, oversized T-shirt left very little room for imagina-tion: Maya, too, chose to ride bra-free.

"Tell me, have you freaked out completely!?" I asked, dismounting and walking toward her.

"Shut up and hug me! Do you have any idea how do you look, with all that horrible cream and sweat? Be grateful for any girl who's willing to come anywhere near you!"

Resting her bike on the shoulder of the road, she

covered the distance between us in a few hops, diving on me as if we hadn't met for five decades. We laughed, feeling each other and hugging for a long time. Her unique scent, which was either deodorant, shampoo, perfume, or a cocktail of both, hit my nostrils, popping my passion like a cork from a bottle of champagne, and her soft skin made it very clear to me why I desired her. It took me a few seconds to comprehend that she was right there with me. She, noticing I was slightly dumbfounded, used her unique sense of humor to break our awkward silence.

"Well? Haven't you ever seen a bra-less girl riding a bike on Route 90 before? What's the matter, cat got your tongue? Stop killing me with your silent nonchalance! C'mon, let's move on to the spring. We need to get you cleaned up a little and make sure you drink before we ride on north!" she told me.

"We?"

"Yes, I'm coming with you. I feel like riding alongside you a little," she replied.

"You're insane! As if I wasn't shocked enough by you bumping into me out of the blue, now you tell me you'll ride with me! Well, you've definitely made my day, Maya. To make things absolutely clear, I'm the happiest man on Earth having you here, and you can't imagine how much I appreciate that," I told her, kissing her cheek.

At first, when I realized that I wasn't actually dreaming and that Maya was really here next to me, I sort of got cold feet, because I didn't want to be a party pooper and tell her that she didn't fit into my present plans. All my life, I've been my own master, so this situation put me out of focus, and I thought, amusingly, that if Maya was here, anything might happen, good or bad. From now on, I was afraid things could only get worse. It was only a few hours later that I realized how wrong I was to ignore my hunch.

Mounting our bikes, we rode for another five minutes to Ein Sukkot. It had a nice little sitting corner by the pond, and it was deserted. Dismounting, I rested my bike against a rock. Turning around, I noticed Maya was already walking to the pond, shirtless, with only her undies on.

"Are you coming!? We should wash off all your sweat and dust. Let's pick up from where we left off in the Ramon Crater pond," she ordered me, plunging into the water. I watched her swimming on her back with her eyes closed and her white breasts protruding out of the water, letting the sun warm her naked skin. The warm wind gently shaking the green reeds seemed to play tranquil music, enhancing the effect of her floating.

"Are you going to keep staring at me, or are you going to have some fun as well?! C'mon, take those clothes off and come over, it's been a long time since I saw your clothes-free anatomy next to me... well!?" she complained, gesturing to me to join her.

I took all my clothes off, not worrying about possible peeping toms. I was exhausted from the ride and felt as hot and sweaty as a workhorse. To make matters worse, I was horny, terribly horny. "Okay, you nag! I'm coming, cool it!" I told her, approaching the edge of the pond.

"Well, I see somebody's really happy to see me, not just talking about it...Come on, gorgeous!" she laughed, splashing water all over me.

It was only when I got out of the pond later that I noticed what a beautiful, rare oasis it was – a watering hole without which neither local humans nor animals could have survived. On top of that, it was surrounded by a thick wall of reeds three of four meters tall, growing right out of the water and concealing the pond almost completely. The Gilead Mountains, towering over the Jordanian border, provided a majestic background.

Nonetheless, I pulled my towel from a rear side bag and started preparing to ride. By then, Maya, too, had got out of the water. She had left her towel in her car, so she asked me to let her use mine.

"Come over here, I'll dry you off," I told her.

"Lucky me!" she cried, coming near me and turning her naked back to me.

Her long back was marked with a bright white tan line and her tight little butt was perfectly attached to the small of her back, making every centimeter of her body a unique explosion of feminine beauty. I wiped her back slowly, letting my towel slide down her spine. While I was wiping the small of her back and her perfect butt, she gathered her hair in the front, squeezing the water out of it.

All of a sudden, she turned around, smiling at me, and my body came alert and flooded with desire for her once again. Pressing herself against my naked body, she thrust her tongue into my mouth while her hand gently pushed me toward the bench behind me. "Sit down!" she commanded. "I want it one more time!" she whispered in my ear while mounting me, stark naked, her right hand making sure I slid inside her.

Her erect breasts drove me totally crazy, making me want her once again, but then another desire commanded me, making me say, "Listen, Maya. I've had a great time with you, and I love every moment with you...but I must ride on soon or I'll never make it to the Golan Heights by tomorrow."

All of a sudden, she assumed an angry look. Closing her

eyes a little, she got up, walked away from me toward her bike and started dressing. I, too, started to dress.

Suddenly, she broke the thundering silence building up between us:

"I see it's okay to text me, asking me to come, and then fuck me – but a little love and attention, if it disrupts your shitty project, is too much to ask?"

"It's not like that, Maya, and you know that damn well! Why ruin everything we have?" I protested.

She started to sob while putting her helmet on and pushing out her green road bike. Approaching me, she pierced my eyes with a furious look, telling me, "You're a cowardly nobody, selfish, and full of yourself. There are no other words to describe you! I mistook you for a different kind of man, who could feel for me and understand what I'm going through. I guess I was wrong – again. I've just broken up with my boyfriend and revealed my deepest emotions to you but, when I ask you for a little tenderness, and for you to open up your heart for me, you turn me down!" She stopped to wipe her tears and running nose. "Know what? Fuck you! What the hell am I doing here? Screw you, and screw your incredibly shitty trip, Tzuriel! Goodbye!" Pushing her bike to the road, she rode away very quickly toward her parked car.

"Hold it, Maya! This really wasn't what I had in mind! Wait!" I called after her.

She stopped just where she was, frozen to the spot and then, twisting round, holding her handlebar with her left hand, with her right hand she gave me the bird very provocatively, adding another "Fuck...you!" stressing every syllable with her lips. This whole scene – the combination of her gesture, her fieriness, and her openness – made me desire her even more. It definitely did the trick. I shouted at her once again to stop, but she was already too far away for me to catch her. I hesitated between chasing her to try to straighten things out and just letting it be.

A few minutes later, I felt so sad and frustrated about the foolish and unnecessary argument. On one hand, I had no intention of hurting Maya, and wouldn't have imagined I could, but on the other, I could not allow any disruption to my schedule, which would mean failure for my project goals. If it meant hurting someone along the way – well, I'm sorry, but let her be hurt. I had been planning this project for years, and if Maya failed to realize how important it was to me, maybe we weren't meant for each other.

It was 15:00 and I had nearly 50km to go to Lake Tiberias' Tsemah Beach, where I planned to spend the night before the climb to the Golan Heights.

The following day's plan was to cross the Golan Heights, starting off early in the morning from Kibbutz Hamat Gader in the southern Golan, handling the Mevo Hama climb, which many cyclists consider one of Israel's five toughest climbs, and then ride north to Neve Ativ village near the peak of Mt. Hermon, where I would rest for the weekend at my relatives' house.

I had been looking forward to riding in the north despite knowing that it involved tackling roads no less remote and challenging than those I had tackled in the south. That morning's weather report once again predicted inhospitable weather, complete with a heatwave that was forecast to carry on beyond Sunday. It meant another ride in extreme heat, compelling me to carry an additional load of water. This would make the climb to the Golan Heights, especially to Mt. Hermon, an unusual challenge.

In April 2016, the expected sunset time in northern Israel was a little past 18:00, which left me nearly four daylight hours, barely enough to reach Tzemah Beach. I knew that unless I started out right away, I would have to spend the night next to Route 90.

Ten minutes later, I was in my saddle again, all edgy and pepped up, eager to reach that day's destination. I assumed my normal pace although the temperature in the Jordan Valley was at its peak – nearly 40° – which didn't make it any easier for me. On top of that, I had to deal with northerly winds hitting my face and leaving my lips dry and cracked.

Two hours of non-stop cycling brought me to the town of Beit Shean. To save precious daylight time, I drank and poured water over myself while riding. The sun set at about 18:10, and the darkness engulfed me quickly. A little past Kibbutz Gesher, I set up the front and rear lights to allow me to cycle at night.

Luckily, a few years previously, a cycle lane had been built along that part of my route all the way to the Tzemah Junction, so I could avoid practically all of the bustling traffic on Route 90.

Toward 19:00, I reached my haven in the form of a small, remote piece of Lake Tiberias' shore east of Tzemah Beach and near to Kibbutz Maagan, which was recognizable by the many banana, date palm, and mango plantations surrounding it. I set up my tent behind a patch of dense grass, locking my bike to the tent, and headed on foot to Tzemach Junction – more specifically, to the local Aroma Café. Reaching it, I ordered an iced coffee, my regular drink throughout this trip, and a small supper.

The coffee was delicious as usual and chilled me just like I had imagined it would. Even better, the place had Wi-Fi so I could send and receive messages from friends wishing to ride with me the following week in the Upper Galilee, where I planned to give some lectures.

The total donation so far cheered me up: it amounted now to nearly 20,000 USD, thanks to the generous donation Maya had arranged and the quite considerable money transfers made by some generous people I had happened to meet in Jerusalem.

On receiving this good news, I made a shopping list in my blue notebook of how the donations could be spent, the blue notebook also serving as my diary.

Walking back to my tent, I recalled that day's twists of fortune: one moment I was riding alone in the Jordan valley, and the next moment had a rendezvous with an enigmatic woman I had only met a few days earlier and who had told me all her life story and shared with me her shapely body. I could hardly forget Maya's "farewell speech" or our strong mutual desire, which was much stronger than we had antici-pated. For a moment, I considered texting or calling her just to say hello and thank her for the time and effort she had spent in meeting me. Having decided against it, I turned my cell phone off and chose to sleep on it. I was too exhausted to engage in endless conversations all night long and was preoccupied with the climb to the Golan Heights and the intense heatwave threatening to attack the entire northern part of the country.

 Preparing my tent for the night and before slipping into it, I brushed my teeth and opened my diary again. Briefly reading the previous week's records, I was overwhelmed with satisfaction and could already envision the successful conclusion of the Heart to Heart Journey. The next day, I was to reach Mt. Hermon and by Sunday, Kibbutz Rosh Ha-Nikra on the Lebanese border. From there, I would go south on Route 4, returning to my Ashkelon home after a two-or three-day ride.

Before falling asleep, I wrote this in my diary: "A few

minutes ago, I closed my eyes, listening to the singing of the winds blowing over Lake Tiberias and gently stroking my tent walls, the waves breaking on the shore in calming unison, harmonizing with the wind, sending me to sleep at the end of an extraordinary night that concluded an even more extraordinary day. For a moment, it crossed my mind that I may be the loneliest man on Earth. Can I call myself a loner after all my life's adventures over the last couple of years – and more so after my last meeting with Maya? I guess so, but it's perfectly okay to be one."

9

DAY 9

"Thou shalt love thy neighbor (even when he's not such) as thyself."

Lev. 19:18 paraphrased

April 8, 2016
Starting point: Tzemah Junction
Destination: Mt. Hermon
Distance: 110 kilometers

That Friday was one of the most challenging days of the entire trip. I woke up a little before the basalt rocks of the Golan Heights started to absorb the sun's heat and left my tent with only my underwear on to check that all my gear was intact. Then I exercised my legs and pelvis, which were cramped from the previous day's rid, and, of course, made sure to empty my bladder and start brewing up black coffee.

I sat on the dark ground next to my tent waiting for the water to boil in the pot, the base of which had blackened with use. Black coffee was the inevitable prelude to nearly every riding day. Caught up in the bizarre plot of *Kafka on the Shore*, I read nearly thirty pages that morning. While making my coffee, I was drawn into the surreal reality of the main character, Kafka Tamura, who runs away from home at the age of four in search of his sister and mother. The intricate plot defies any logic, combining reality and fantasy from start to finish while shattering myths and Western social taboos. I was so engrossed that I was almost oblivious to the sun's appearance over the Golan Mountains, blinding my eyes and forcing me back to reality. Eating up my break-fast– a mixture of a little long-life milk, granola, and dried fruits – I cleaned and folded my camping gear. Suddenly I noticed that the towel I had used for years to mop my perspiration was gone.

"Noooooo!" I screamed, looking around. Even the thicket around me seemed to wonder why the hell this maniac was screaming over some dirty old towel.

Turning all my bags inside out, I searched through all my clothes but failed to find it. I took it for a sign of trouble. I didn't mind some girl cursing me and walking away from me for no reason, or sunburn all over my skin and blisters all over my hands and feet due to the endless riding...but the loss of my good old towel was really unbearable.

"Dammit!" I cried again upon realizing that I had left it in Ein Sukkot after my fight with Maya. That little towel was nothing short of a sacred object to me as even Suleiman, a 75-year-old Bedouin sage I'd met in Sinai several years earlier, had observed.

Its very presence next to me throughout that journey connected me to the elements and all living creatures around me. It had been with me through challenges and countless mop-ups, the very essence of my trips. To this very day, I can't say if I really believed it was sacred, but that little towel had become much more than just a towel...it had assumed an iconic meaning for me.

Nonetheless, once I mounted my "truck" and started out toward the Yarmouk River, I forgot everything and got into a cycling rhythm. The temperature was rising quickly, and the weather report predicted an intense heatwave all over the Golan Heights by 11:00. I wanted to complete the roughest of the climbs before the heat peaked, so I pedaled as hard as I could to the start of the climb, heading for Kibbutz Hamat Gader, where a sharp bend to the right marked the beginning of the rough climb to the Golan Heights.

Kibbutz Mevo Hama, situated high above me, nearly 10km from the bottom of the climb, would be my next long stop in conjunction with the short stops during the climb that started 37m below sea level and ended 372m above it. The slope was nearly 6km long, and the climb was slow and exhausting even if you used your lowest available gear. Handling the Golan Heights required excellent fitness, an intelligent use of the shifting mechanism, and maximum attention to bodily alerts.

By 08:00, I was on Route 98. It would lead me to the peak of Mt. Hermon. It was an uphill route, climbing from the Yarmouk River across the entire Golan Heights. A few kilometers before I took the north turn to the Golan Heights, I spotted the impressive Yarmouk River canyon and the brand-new, dark asphalt road – probably repaired recently – leading straight to the Yarmouk Reserve, one of Israel's most beautiful and unique reserves. That day, the river gorge was clothed with the colors of spring, a rare, beautiful mingling of the yellow grass and green trees. As I found out later, the Yarmouk is the major tributary of the Jordan, and its drainage basin is the entire northern part of the Biblical provinces of Bashan and Gilead, which are currently part of northern Jordan and southern Syria.

After cycling for ten minutes above the riverbed, I noticed to the east in the Jordanian and Syrian parts of the reserve their white-yellowish limestone cliffs tens of meters high. Opposite them, to the west near Kibbutz Shaar Ha-Golan, the banks sloped moderately and the river widened slowly. I also noticed lush vegetation that included the chisel-shaped leaves of the Moringa Peregrina plant on the riverbed. It had originated in Sudan and can now be seen on Israel's northern border. Its main habitat in Israel is the Jordan Valley and Dead Sea areas.

The climb up the yellowish crag was harder than I had expected. I had underestimated its steepness but, after five minutes of slow, hard pedaling, I figured out the right strategy for conquering the climb: a few minutes' ride, a thirty-minute rest, and so on.

Heat radiated from the asphalt and the hot wind rising from the Yarmouk skyrocketed my body heat. My face felt on fire. My lesson from the rides near Eilat and southern Jordan Valley was that to complete the climb intact, I must maintain a low pace and keep my body heat from rising. To achieve that, I took my red cycling shirt off, leaving only my cycling bib on.

After a few bends, I stopped for a few minutes at one of the most pleasant spots of my entire trip. Looking ahead over the guardrail, I saw the entire Yarmouk Reserve stretched out before me. Paradoxically, the warm wind rising from the bottom of the cliff I'd just climbed cooled my sweat. Route 98 wound beneath me between the cliffs of the Golan like a colossal snake with a white stripe along its back. Then, looking up and behind me to see how long the climb ahead of me was, I realized that the steepest part had just begun. I loved that sensation of a new challenge, which motivates my body to act and focuses my mind on telling my limbs exactly what to do to accomplish the mission.

Just before I mounted my 45kg truck, I filled my water bottles with a pink-colored isotonic powdered drink. It looked and tasted really disgusting–like children's medicine– to the point of making me want to throw up. Well, I thought, desperate times call for desperate measures. Pouring a half-liter of it straight down my parched throat, I started out. The ride was still rough, yet bearable. I knew that the steepest part would be over in a moment.

I was riding standing up to stretch my strained limbs and my bike was swinging left and right like an overloaded truck that the driver cannot control. The standing up relaxed my pelvis a little and increased my legs' push and pull by a few centimeters. While increasing the momentum, it also exhausted me and made me fear my quadriceps might get cramped. To avoid this, I switched to a sitting position once every couple of seconds, which allowed a more relaxed ride.

The almost non-existent traffic made the climb to Mevo Hama easier, allowing me to zigzag across the road. This cycling technique makes extreme cycling easier by practically canceling the slope.

The silence around me was so complete that the only sounds I could hear were my heavy breathing, the occasional tweeting of birds above me and next to the road, and some unclear yet alarming metal clicking from various parts of my bike.

At a certain point, I noticed that the landscape was changing; the open spaces were starting to assume the good, green color of the Golan Heights. About a kilometer away, a small grove and a few scattered eucalyptus trees indicated the end of the climb. When I stood up once again in the saddle, I heard some cars – probably approaching me from the Yarmouk. This forced me to stop zigzagging and restrict myself to the road shoulder.

When the motorcade was about 100m behind me, I noticed its noise was different and twice as loud as any other vehicle, which meant somebody had tuned the engines or modified the exhaust systems.

"Hey, amigo, what's your game?" one of the passengers shouted at me. "Want a ride?"

He was in a white Subaru Impreza with a sunroof. It was occupied by three guys in undershirts and baseball hats, smoking cigarettes. It slowed down and kept pace with me, with two of the three passengers lowering their windows, laughing and calling to me. When I told them that I was okay and didn't need a ride, they drove on with loud honking and overtaking me on the left.

This was followed right away by another car – a black Seat Ibiza with dark windows and two red length stripes. It was occupied by two girls: the driver, and a redheaded passenger next to her. The latter asked me, through her lowered window, if I was all right and if I needed any help. As soon as I told her I was okay, this car also drove on uphill.

The motorcade was made up of about ten vehicles of all kinds, and their owners seemed to be harmless travelers who had decided to take their tuned vehicles on a trip to the Golan heights.

Suddenly they stopped a few hundred meters ahead of me, probably due to the smoking bonnet of the Subaru. As I approached them, they all clapped their hands and took snapshots of me on their cell phones. Suddenly, as I cycled past, one of the gang cried, "Hey, Tzuri, you shithead! Stop and say hello! I'm Avi, your next-door neighbor! Pull over for a sec, you loony!"

At first, being preoccupied with the grueling climb, I didn't catch what he said but once I heard, "Avi, your next-door neighbor," the penny dropped. He was a good-looking guy of around 25 who worked out a lot, was lean and tall, and always kept his long, black hair neatly combed. His appearance and way of talking reminded me of John Travolta in Grease. He lived with his parents in Apt. 10 of my building and drove a tuned-up 2009-model Honda Civic. Whenever we met, we talked about cycling trips, motorbikes, his new girlfriends, and that it sucked how the Ashkelon Football Club never won. A couple of months earlier, when I had told him about my planned trip, he had been very excited and wished me good luck.

I recognized him the moment I stopped to look back. He was standing next to the two Ibiza girls, with his arm around the waist of one of them, while his other arm waved me to come near. Getting closer, I also recognized those who had overtaken me a few minutes earlier, nodded to them, and they nodded back.

"It can't be true! What are you doing here!?" I asked Avi.

"Haven't I told you!? I'm on my monthly trip with the group. This time, we decided to take our beauties to the Golan," he explained, his gesture making it clear that he meant the cars, not the girls. "I do remember you telling me about your trip," he went on, "but I didn't imagine you were that crazy. Where did you ride here from? By the way, meet Meital and her friend, Lin."

"Nice to meet you, Meital and Lin," I said, shaking their hands. Just as I was, with only my bib on, I explained, "Today I've come all the way from the shore of Lake Tiberias, but I started off two weeks ago from Ashkelon, passing through Eilat and Jerusalem, and right now I'm on my way to Mt. Hermon."

"What did you say? Ashkelon? Eilat? Say it again! I didn't really get where you've come from!"

"Ashkelon. I've cycled nearly 1000km nonstop and will probably make it home next week."

"Listen, you're one hell of a nutcase! Are you for real about the 1000k? You must be kidding me! My Honda can hardly cover 2000 kilos in a row...are you alone? Nobody to help you out? No escort?" he enquired, while his companions, who heard us talking, approached us.

"I'm all alone, just me and my bike, nature, and whatever God gave me: my legs, lungs, and heart. What an amazing coincidence for us to meet here! So, where are you heading?" I asked in an attempt to change the subject.

Instead of answering, Avi went to his car to get his cell phone, then started videoing himself as though he was a live TV news reporter. He started describing the landscape, location, and his fellow-travelers. Then, standing next to me, he started "interviewing" me, interrupting the interview to describe my adventures so far.

We walked a little away from the group, and after we exchanged jokes and banter for a couple of minutes, he asked if I needed any help, offering me a seat in their car. As far as he knew, as he put it, the girls in the Ibiza would be more than happy to see me join them for a ride.

"That thing you're wearing almost made me laugh myself to death. You look like a farmer," he laughed. "Is this shirt comfortable? Those strange tights make you look like a wrestler!"

"What's your game, you idiot?! I took my shirt off because I was too hot, and nothing else mattered," I countered.

A few minutes later, Avi came back with a cold beer from his car's picnic fridge and told me they were heading for the town of Kiryat Shmona (on the eastern tip of the Israeli-Lebanese border) and planned to spend the night in a B&B on a local kibbutz. He tried to talk me into joining them for a few hours' rest, hinting that Meital, the curly-haired girl, was rather thrilled with the rag I was wearing and she'd be happy for me to join them.

When I told him, referring to her by name, that there was no chance of me joining them, as tempting as it may sound, she suddenly surprised us from behind. "Hi, I see you've been talking behind my back. Want some?" She offered me a long, white joint, rolled with perfect symmetry.

"Hi to you, too. No, thanks. I might, perhaps, later at the end of today's riding. Right now, it's a bit of a problem."

"Well, I'll keep it for you until you finish riding. I promise not to smoke it without you," she told me, handing the joint to Avi, who stood next to me smiling naughtily. Meital had brown, bouncing curls that reached her brown shoulders, and honey-colored eyes. As she talked, I noticed that she was short enough for her head to reach my neck level. She wore a short pair of jeans and a shirt that flattered her curvaceous body. She was sexy and she knew it and spared neither looks nor touches to show it.

"Hey, don't be such a nerdy stuffed shirt! Why turn me down this way when we rarely meet like this on a trip?" Avi tried some emotional blackmail.

"Enough!" I replied, with a wink. "Meital, I definitely didn't expect to run into anyone like you in the middle of today's ride," I commented, "let alone be flattered and invited by you. However, I must turn you down, as tempting as it sounds. We can exchange numbers and get in touch some other time if you want."

"Forget it. You're sweet and all that, but you're not for real. Happy riding!" she informed me harshly.

After kissing my heated cheeks, she went back to her friends, lighting up the joint.

Fifteen minutes later, I was riding my "truck" along the final leg of the rough climb to Mevo Hama. When I reached the flat part of Route 98 on the southern Golan Heights, the air was rent again by the noises of the tuned engines of their cars closing in on me. Once again, Meital's Ibiza came alongside my bike and slowed down. The wind rolled down and the passengers took my picture, laughing.

Meital, now in the seat next to the driver, waved at me to stop, shouting that if I changed my mind, I should just signal her. Reaching out from the open window, she handed me a little yellow note. I took it with my left hand, smiling at her. After the two girls waved me goodbye, Lin, the driver, suddenly pressed the gas pedal all the way down, gunning the car forward to join the rest of the motorcade, which had by then disappeared over the horizon.

The note read, "Hey, I like you. Here's my number, call me. Meital."

Folding it with my left hand, I pushed it into my half-open handlebar bag. Well, I thought, smiling, maybe this pair of tights didn't look as awful as I thought.

I had over 80km to go to today's destination, but my spirits were high. That day had an excellent start: I had successfully accomplished one of the country's toughest climbs and, despite my sweaty face, long stubble, and kinky-looking black tights, got the phone number of a beautiful stranger.

A little past Kibbutz Kfar Haruv, I made another stop to re-examine the map of my route along Route 98 and to drink another half-liter of the disgusting pink liquid, which

I should be finishing soon. My morning pep made me completely forget the extreme heat stress predicted in the weather report that I had still a long day ahead and that the heatwave hadn't reached its peak yet. I took another gulp of water to wash away the disgusting taste then cooled myself with a few drops over my head. Finally, I swallowed an energy snack that crumbled apart in my hand, letting its chocolate chips melt on my cycling gloves.

I was so preoccupied with eating, drinking, and thinking of Meital that I forgot to replenish my water supply, or even check the amount of water left...and, for the first time on this entire trip, I failed to check the location of possible watering points along my route, which proved to be a dangerous mistake later on.

When I reached the intersection of Routes 808 and 98 near Kibbutz Ramat Magshimim close by the Syrian border, the route seemed more isolated from civilization. The nearby border worried me even more than the heat, although it reminded me of the extreme heat I'd had to face during my last day on Route 90.

After changing into my white, long-sleeved shirt, which suited riding in intense heat, I carried on north along Route 98 passing by deserted army bases. The only suitable places to rest were Moshav Alonei Ha-Bashan and the community of Keshet. To make matters worse, I couldn't have imagined how rough that road was.

As I found out, all the northbound routes of the Golan Heights were constant climbs. You'd hardly notice it when driving a car but for a cyclist, especially with the north wind blowing the heat and haze into his face, such climbs are as challenging as the one I'd conquered that morning.

This time, I was caught unprepared. My legs struggled with the slope and the wind, and the air I breathed felt like fire consuming my insides with every breath. Therefore, I decided to be cautious and stop once every thirty minutes to allow my legs and lungs to recover and to overcome this rough slope slowly but safely.

Between the turn to the communities of Keshet and Ramat Magshimim, I had to make a stop to wet my lips a little after the harsh wind had hit and dried my face up completely. Only one vehicle had driven by during the past hour. Looking around, I saw no sign of a human settlement or even an army outpost – nothing but grassy plains with an occasional cow looking for a cool place to rest, and some rusty pieces of barbed wire and minefield warning signs. I was all alone with my bike.

Maybe the heat had started to addle my brains but, for some reason I decided, most foolishly, to take a shower right there and then. Resting my bike by the road, I took all my clothes off, letting the hot wind cool my naked, sweaty body for a few seconds. Then, pulling the 1.5-liter water bottle out of my rear rack bag and the dishwashing liquid bottle out of my front rack bag, I walked, stark naked and barefoot, into the middle of the road. I turned on my cell phone speaker, rested it on my rear bag, and pressed Play.

I took my shower to the sounds of "In the End" sung by Linkin Park. While soaping myself and pouring water over my head, I joined the late lead vocalist, Chester Bennington, in the refrain – the only part of the song I'd ever managed to memorize:

I tried so hard
And got so far
But in the end
It doesn't even matter
I had to fall
To lose it all

But in the end

It doesn't even matter

The lyrics cleared my mind, suddenly elevating me to another, more sublime sphere away from the here and now, in a sort of mild drug trip. Anybody happening to see me like that – standing stark naked in the middle of an empty road near the Syrian border, covered in soap and screaming in English – would have taken me to a mental institution right away. Once I'd had my surreal shower, I got dressed and rode on as if nothing had happened. It refreshed me and made me feel better, just as happened that morning at Tzemah Junction. After thirty minutes' riding, I realized what a mistake I had made: I had no water left and I had nearly 40km to go, that is, nearly another two hours' cycling.

I was thirsty, my lips felt parched and I grew weaker. In short, that shower proved to be a grave mistake that I had no way of correcting. Desperate, I opened the rear bag where I kept a half-liter bottle of water for emergencies. Now, for the first time since day one, I had to use it. Riding on for another few hundred meters, I saw a small eucalyptus grove around a mound of rocks indicating a long-deserted human settlement. Stopping off, I took off my shirt and my shoes to cool myself as best as I could. The shade cooled my body down to normal, but I was still pissed off by the heat and the stupid situation I'd gotten myself into.

I checked my location on the map and the cell phone reception in case I had to be evacuated or call for water supply. Although there was no reception, I still texted my location to my family. My body was emitting intense heat and I felt my strength leaving me. I could not believe that I'd been such a fool! Why hadn't I learned my lesson from previous near-fatal dehydration and heatstroke incidents?! I felt like a stupid boy who always gets into trouble. The possibility of having to call for help once again upset me.

A few minutes later, still burning with frustration, I nonetheless started to make myself a small lunch, mostly of vegetables I'd bought the night before: five cucumbers, three thinly sliced tomatoes, tahina, and crackers. Since the vegetables contained a lot of water, I devoured the entire meal ravenously, hoping it would save me from the predicament I had gotten myself into.

I had several more hours of riding ahead of me and less than one cupful of water, or about four mouthfuls, in my emergency bottle. The heat showed no sign of abating and the situation was on the verge of being life-threatening. My options were to either hitch-hike or ride on with practically no water. I decided to run the risk and ride on, realizing that if I wanted to get to my relatives in Neve Ativ in one piece, I must act rationally, avoiding unnecessary stops and foolish outdoor showers.

Suddenly I some message alerts came in from my cell phone, which was connected to the solar charger. Grabbing it instantly, I read them all. The first was from my parents, asking if I was okay. The next was from the Jerusalem News editorial staff, who sent me a PDF version of the flattering report about my trip. The third one was a few words from Maya: "Are you still alive? Sorry for what happened." The next was from Ehud, who continued to support this project with his surprise money transfers. He wrote that he was amazed that I'd kept on riding against all odds and that he'd transferred another 1000 USD to my project.

I was so absorbed in reading the messages that I didn't notice an approaching car until it had passed the grove where I was resting. Once I heard it, I was really pissed off at being so absent-minded because getting that lift would have been very helpful. Realizing I must ride on again as soon as possible, I packed up all my utensils and put on my hot-weather riding outfit.

I felt that I was doing the right thing. Despite losing focus for a couple of hours, I was determined not to let it affect my riding. For the time being, I chose not to answer the messages before I knew how I was doing. I was very happy, of course, to receive Maya's message. She had kept her silence for an entire day, and I decided to answer her as soon as I reached my day's destination.

When I reached Alonei Ha-Bashan after a ninety-minute ride, my emergency water bottle was empty, but I happened to meet a friendly local who told me where the nearest cold water tap was. I finally overcame my second water-shortage crisis during this trip. I also called my relatives in Neve Ativ, Michael and Rachel. Michael was the younger brother of my sister-in-law, Shiri. He and Rachel had moved from Jerusalem to Mt. Hermon seven years earlier, choosing to build their home in what I consider the most European spot in Israel, at least as far as its remarkable landscape and weather are concerned.

I still had nearly 40km to go on Route 98 before I reached Neve Ativ, passing by Kibbutz Elrom, the Druze village of Masadeh, and Moshav Nimrod. Most of the road ahead was a long, but rather gentle climb running through rural communities with apple and peach orchards. Now, my concern was not water shortage, but traffic and darkness.

Michael and Rachel happily agreed to pick me up wherever I happened to be, saving me the unpleasant experience of cycling up the country's toughest slope. During my stop, I noticed the changing landscape around me. From the grass-covered basalt plains of the southern and central Golan Heights, I was now surrounded by grassland dotted with eucalyptus groves and occasional deserted minefields, cherry and apple orchards, and deep gorges. The road climbed all the way to the Jabal Al-Sheikh (literally, "the Old Mountain," referring to its snowcap that resembles an old man's white hair) the Arabic name of Mt. Hermon.

The suddenly-changing landscape threw me back in time to the happy days of my cycling tour across Europe, particularly to my endless climb up the Swiss Alps. The sight of my country's highest mountain, still snowcapped, restored my energy and willpower, driving me to fight on a little despite my painfully weary feet.

Nonetheless, before resuming my northbound ride, I decided to rest a little, exercise, double-check the route to Mt. Hermon, and check the time when the Sabbath was due to begin, since my local relatives were observant Jews. Realizing I could not make it to the top on time, I was deeply disappointed and my only consolation was to consume the remains of my food. Too exhausted to handle the remaining vegetables, I settled for the tiny, crumbling crackers, which I covered with sardines and spread tahina on top of them to keep the fish from slipping off.

However, a couple of minutes later, the sardines seemed to pop up in my throat, giving me severe heartburn. As this was the only food I had at the time, and no matter how much I regretted eating it, my muscles begged for protein to shorten their recovery and to resume the ride. A few minutes after swallowing that hodgepodge, I rode for another hour north, the Hermon growing larger in front of me with every passing bend. At the same time, I noticed unusually dense, gray clouds to the west. I had been looking forward to that sight all day and couldn't remember the last time I had seen clouds during my journey. I concluded that the heatwave's end was just an hour away and that even some rainfall was possible. With the changing landscape, narrowing road, and the signs of the weather changes, I realized that I was starting a new phase of my project after nearly completing a 1000km ride around Israel. Advancing to my country's highest point, I could look back with pride over the distance I had covered.

Now, Heart-to-Heart was beginning to fulfill the vision I had when I embarked upon it. Despite all the hardships, mishaps, crises, and uncertainties, I knew that my own safety was a mere instrument, a means to raise funds for the sake of the have-nots. The project was a powerful, mighty goal, unbeatable by any adversity. Throughout that journey, I felt at one with nature: whenever the weather changed, I had undergone an inner change as well to the point that any change in the wind direction or intensity had good or ill effects on my mind as well. Nightfall dragged my spirits down, while at daybreak, my spirits were high. I felt the natural cycles of the universe running in my blood – a magical sensation, transcending all reason.

At about 18:00 when I made it to Neve Ativ, I was so exhausted that if I had closed my eyes for just a second, I would have fallen asleep right away. Michael and Rachel, noticing my fragility, took good care of me as if I were one of their children. Without me saying a word, they guessed I desperately needed food. The smell of the dishes, especially the soup, reaching my nostrils all the way from the stove, served as a shot of adrenaline and caused my stomach to emit some most embarrassing noises.

I had known Rachel since her childhood in Jerusalem when I worked as a security guard in the Old City. She had impressed me as a friendly and optimistic person, and I don't remember ever seeing her not smiling. She had count-

less questions about my journey and was evidently very
curious about it.

Michael, though as curious as Rachel, was exhausted
after a day's work at the Mt. Hermon ski resort, so most of
the time he just listened while handling the kids, who gave
him no respite. Michael was an old acquaintance (through
his sister) and at every family reunion we would talk about
Mt. Hermon, ski gear, and the places of interest near Neve
Ativ that were worth visiting.

The next day was Saturday, so we all took a morning
walk. Michael, Rachel, and their three children lived in the
touristy part of Neve Ativ on the main road between two
major hotels. Their house was rather isolated, surrounded
by a huge courtyard, and only a two-minut' walk from the
deep gorge of Wadi Guvta that flows from Mt. Hermon to
the Banias River. During this walk, the rocky wadi was
coated with green grass, above which occasionally rose
groups of splendid-looking, violet-colored Mesopotamian
iris.

A few minutes before boarding easyJet's low-cost flight from
Geneva, having cycled for more than six months across
Europe, I visited the airport's bookshop. The dealer, who
probably noticed both my unusual look – namely my
unkempt beard – as well as my odor, may well have thought
me a nutcase. Instead, in English with a heavy German
accent, he offered me some Swiss postcards to buy. On one
of them I saw an eye-catching phrase which fourth-century

Christian theologian, St. Augustine, supposedly wrote in his travel log: "The world is a book, and those who do not travel read only a page."

This statement sent me down memory lane to the tasty cappuccino and croissant I received from Michelle Pfeifer's French lookalike a month previously. My memories of the tour stirred mixed feelings in me: a combination of great sorrow that the tour had ended and an immense satisfaction with the challenge I had just overcome. Only then did it strike me that this was not the end, but actually the beginning of my journey. It was just Chapter One of the book of my travels.

As St. Augustine put it, I had completed merely one page of the great book of the world, one of many more that I planned to read.

Exactly five years after coming back from Europe, on the first Saturday of September 2015, I decided to go on a trip unprecedented in Israel and perhaps anywhere else. In spirit, I had been in Europe nearly every single moment since I had left it, roaming the same roads, endless mountain passes, lakes, and, of course, meeting the very same people I had met then and there. Now, I decided I was ready for a long, solo cycling trip with no support or escort for the sake of the disadvantaged and unheard who struggle to make a living.

I started planning a 1200km road-cycling tour around Israel to attract public attention for the needy and, practically speaking, raise money for them to buy food for the Passover. It was to be a touring ride on a bicycle fitted with bags filled with all the items necessary for a long trip without having to use hotels, public transport, or shopping centers. This non-competitive tour could be limited to one country, though I had previously gone on tours across entire continents, crossing numerous countries, and even involved crossing seas. The point of the tour was mostly about absolute self-reliance with no escort or external support, and a reconnection to nature. My tour was planned to start in late April 2016 and to end a few days before Passover.

However, there had already been some obstacles. A year earlier, my bike had been stolen from Tel Aviv Central Train Station. I was heartbroken because that was the very bike on which I had cycled all over Europe. I could have never imagined that the loss of my bike would depress me so much. It felt as if all my memories from that tour had been stolen. Moreover, it was as if a part of me had been torn off. To me, my bike was priceless – a treasure worth much more than the 500 USD I might have sold it for. Living without that bike was like living without an arm or a leg.

For a long time, I couldn't even think of buying another bike and felt I terribly disillusioned. Only when I started preparing for my Heart to Heart Journey did I look for a new one in an attempt to get over it.

Finally, I got my new bike and little-by-little grew to trust it. A guy advertised a second-hand bike for sale on a sale site and a week later, after carrying out all the necessary checks and taking it on a test ride, I was the proud owner of a Dawes Galaxy touring bike, a British brand with decades of reputation. It combined the qualities of a road bike and an off-road bike: a black aluminum frame with the brand printed on it, thin road tires with French-made valves, a

Shimano shifting mechanism consisting of three front sprockets and another eight rear sprockets, black aluminum rims, and a strongly-built rear rack designed to carry the two trunk bags I bought for my European tour to contain my clothes, sleeping bag, tent, and other lightweight items.

Unladen, the bike weighed about 14.2 kilograms. The burden on the bicycle greatly affects riding during tours, so the weight must be properly distributed. Most of the rider's weight rests on the rear of the bike, so I had to carefully make sure all the heaviest items were packed in the front bags. Therefore, the only item I lacked was a strong front rack for the two front bags in which I planned to pack my food, as well as cameras, solar charger, repair tool kit, and utensils. It took me a week to carry out training rides for the tour and to find an aluminum front rack in a bike shop in Kibbutz Beeri.

I also had a handlebar bag fitted right above the front wheel for my wallet, cell phone, camera, map, protective cream, sweat-wiping towel (R.I.P.), pen, notebook, dark glasses, earphones, headlamp, speedometer, Mentos, energy snacks, and a few tour information cards. With foresight, I had prepared some cards in advance.

With the help of my sponsors, I started to prepare my gear an entire month before Day One to make sure everything would be in place. To achieve this, I even took a day off. Back in 2016, I worked as a swimming teacher and fitness trainer for kids and adults. Earlier that year, I had also completed my part in the development of an application with some partners.

Consulting friends and professionals, I made a checklist of all the items I would need. During that preparation period, I came to fully recognize the fact that in a few weeks, I would embark on a special kind of journey that might change me entirely – the sort you can never predict. During the few days before Day One, I had that sensation I always had upon entering an airport, which always speeds up my pulse and spreads a big smile all over my face. It was that addictive sensation of knowing that, in a moment, I would take flight in more than one sense to a place totally new, where I could encounter sights, tastes, wildlife, and people found nowhere else in the world.

My experience from previous trips, as well as my friends' advice, had taught me that I must use the lightest, best-quality, and easiest-to-use gear available. Touring trips usually involve sleeping outdoors away from any human settlements and are carried out with no escort or resupply personnel. Due to all that, I had to prepare for a month on the road, on my own, facing extreme weather conditions away from civilization.

Finally, after a few days of deliberations, I completed the necessary checklist, down to the type of straps and the number of snacks. It looked like this:

Bike accessories:

A speedometer; a yellow bike lock; two racks; a lightweight kickstand; four trunk bags; a handlebar bag; a helmet with a GoPro camera mount; a puncture repair kit; two spare tubes; a Leatherman multitool; a spare brake cable; a toothbrush for cleaning the mechanism; chain oil; spare brake pads; one red rubber luggage strap; ten small straps; ten large straps, and a small air pump.

Clothing and footwear:

A pair of Brooks jogging shoes; a pair of flip-flops; a green raincoat; a black down-filled coat; a Nature Valley visor hat; two pairs of bibs; cycling tights; two white, sweat-wicking shirts bearing the journey's logo; two cycling shirts, one red, one yellow; a pair of long, black Nike tights; two balaclavas; two bandanas; a pair of long hiking pants; a pair of jogging shorts; one buttoned shirt; one long-sleeved thermal undershirt; one short-sleeve thermal undershirt; one pair of training pants; one thin white undershirt; a long-sleeve undershirt for the night; three pairs of socks; three pairs of boxer shorts; a small, quick-drying microfiber towel; two pairs of short gloves and a pair of long gloves.

Camping gear:

A tent with six stakes; an inflatable mattress; a solar charger with cables and adapters; a washbag; a pack of 100 moist towelettes; a roll of toilet paper; a compass; a camp burner; a coffee kit; two gas cylinders for cooking; two lighters; two boxes of matches; five small candles; a box of sugar, black coffee, and tea bags; small packs of salt, pepper, olive oil, and basil; dishwashing liquid and dishwashing cloth, all packed in one plastic box; a pot with a lid; a coffee pot; a knife, a fork and a teaspoon; two water bottles of 500mls capacity; four water bottles of 750mls capacity; fifty Nature Valley energy snacks; five meal-in-a cup units; a kilo of muesli; one liter of long-life milk; five bags of noodles; 500 grams of tahini; 500 grams of honey in a tube; a 500g bag of mixed almonds, cashews, pecans, and Greek nuts; a 3m long tying-up rope and a black rubber rope for drying laundry.

Additional items:

GoPro camera; 100 cards presenting the project's vision, wrapped in plastic; 10 waste bags; 10 watertight bags; a pair of earphones; a pack of dark glasses; 6 AA batteries; a head-lamp; insulation tape; a rag for wiping the hands, and kitchenware.

A week before Day One, I had gathered all the afore-mentioned items, arranging them on a cloth on the floor of my Ashkelon living room, and checking every single item on my list before packing them in the bags. With every "check" I made on the list with a black marker, my stomach murmured with thrill and tension, and I grew edgy and sleepless, fearing I might have missed something.

In an attempt to cut expenses as well as attract public attention, I decided to share my vision with several leading companies in their respective industries to get them to promote my journey and also provide me with necessary items.

First, I approached the folks at PayBox, an Israeli start-up business founded in 2014 in south Tel Aviv. They had devised a user-friendly money transfer app for specific events. The young and energetic founders were instantly thrilled by my vision. They printed their logo on the shirts I would wear on the journey, next to the Heart to Heart logo designed by Nirit, my good high-school friend. They also promoted the project on social media. Naturally, their app significantly contributed to the success of the project, since most of the donations were transferred via that app.

After that, I won the sponsorship of General Mills, the food-import giant that among other things, imports into Israel brands such as Pillsbury, Haagen-Dazs, and Nature Valley. They, too, shared my vision, and got straight to the point: "Okay, Tzuriel, just tell us how many and what kind of energy snacks you need, and you'll get them." They also bought me some beige visor hats suitable for extremely hot weather. They, too, asked for visual documentation of my trip that could serve them for marketing purposes.

My third sponsor was DAA, importers of GoPro cameras and advanced bicycle drivetrain systems. They, too, totally sympathized with my vision and liked the idea of combining extreme sport with philanthropy. After meeting Dan, the head of their sales department in their logistics center in Tel

Aviv, he checked whether they could lend me cameras and colorful cycling clothes. Eventually, they lent me two of the latest model GoPro cameras back then – a HERO5, and a HERO Session, complete with chargers and a hardpack, plus two sets of red and yellow cycling shirts and a high-quality black cycling bib.

Right after I'd said goodbye to him, my hands full of bags filled with clothes and camera equipment, that very friendly fellow called me back to give me a white cycling helmet with a cool device on it – a small lamp on the back that I could turn on with one button while riding.

I had already tested the bike's durability by riding for two hours with the bike fully laden to make sure it worked smoothly and the aluminum racks could stand the load. To test the bike's performance under extreme conditions, I rode on roads with pits, rocks, and bends. This increased the strain on the bike's systems. As I kept telling myself: better to get something broken 500m from home, than 5000m away. When I returned from the ride, I replenished my energy with some fruit, a smoothie, and some yogurt to provide much-needed protein to my aching muscles.

Knowing that there was much harder work ahead in two days, I decided to end my training and dedicate the time to resting and making sure everything was packed up. After that test ride, I took a shower and brushed my teeth, looking at my naked body in the mirror.

I thought about asking Dana out that night. I had met her at the Tel Aviv Marathon. She was 29 and a newly-qualified architect who had always enjoyed many sports. Back then, it was running. Running at the same pace, we kept each other company for nearly the entire length of the marathon. Crossing the finish line together three hours and twenty minutes later, I asked her for her cell phone number.

After that, we agreed to be there for each other, whatever help was needed. She had asked me several times to help her. Once, when she moved house two years before after dumping her boyfriend, we spent the whole night carrying, unpacking, and boozing a little until everything was in place. A few months later, I texted her, asking her to spend a week with me in Sinai, and two hours later we were crossing the Egyptian border. That night, however, I chose not to call her. I fleetingly entertained the thought of finding a new girl just for the night before starting out, like a soldier who goes looking for a girl on the eve of a battle.

I had spent the years after my breakup with Noa in an endless feast of one-night-stands, occasionally several times a day. Now it felt terribly stupid but nonetheless, I craved the touch of a tender and aroused body next to mine to drive away all my troubles for a couple of seconds.

I craved Dana's curves, remembering what happened whenever her naked body had pressed against me. She had the most beautiful eyes and whenever she gave me that look, I would be overwhelmed, letting her enchant and tame me completely. This thought quickly sent me to the bathroom to wash away all those fleeting longings with a cold shower.

Following the advice of Johnny, an American friend who had cycled all over the world, I slept for the couple of nights before Day One in my tent indoors. There were several reasons for this: first of all, to make sure the tent was intact and stable, and none of it was missing; secondly, to air the tent before the trip; and last but not least, to get used to sleeping on an inflatable mattress, since I hadn't done it for a couple of years, and had to get used to sleeping not in my bed.

Setting up the tent next to my bed, I spread the mattress

and sleeping bag out on the floor. On the first day of practicing, I felt like the world's greatest loony...sleeping in a tent inside my own house, half a meter away from my bed. Two days later, once I'd gotten used to it, it made perfect sense to me.

In addition to preparing my gear, I constantly checked the weather forecasts. It was March-April, which in Israel is a transitional season. On the same day, you can have rain, fog, a heatwave, and high humidity. The forecast for March 27 didn't look good since a short, cold front was expected on the night of 26th March. To be on the safe side, I checked all available forecasts – the Greek, American, and finally the British. All of them predicted a cold front exactly on my planned Day One, which did little to calm me down. The last thing I wanted was wet roads in Ashkelon when I started off. I was prepared, of course, for riding in the rain but would prefer a dry start. However, two days later, when my Day One finally arrived, all my fears – and the forecasts – proved groundless. Though the rain did come, it stopped a few minutes after I had started off south to Eilat.

My final inspection of all items, concluding my preparations for my 2016 around-Israel tour.

PART III

10

DAY 10

"To be doing good deeds is man's most glorious task."

Sophocles

April 10, 2016
Starting point: Neve Ativ village
Destination: Kibbutz Rosh Ha-Nikra
Distance: 104 kilometers

"'Never close your eyes,' Johnny Walker said clearly. 'This is another rule. Never close your eyes. Even if you close your eyes, things will not get any better. Nothing will go away by you closing your eyes. On the contrary, when you open them, everything will only get worse. This is the world we live in, Nakata-San. Open up your eyes wide. Only softies close their eyes. Only cowards look away from reality. Even when you close your eyes and cover your ears with your hands, time keeps running, tick-tock.'" (Haruki Murakami, *Kafka on the Shore*)

On Sunday morning, April 10, 2016, a few minutes

before I started my journey's final week from Michael and Rachel's place, I had time to read a few pages of Murakami's book. Stealing another look at the back cover in the hope of finding out how it ended, I learned nothing.

Then, after Michael helped me load my bike, I said goodbye to Rachel and their kids, who waved me goodbye from the balcony. I pushed my bike toward Route 989, which runs across the village steeply descending to the Saar Waterfall Junction.

Michael followed me in his car all the way to the magnificent Nimrod Fortress overlooking the entire Galilee and the Hula Lake. Reaching the junction near the fortress and after giving me several farewell honks, he U-turned to drive back to the Mt. Hermon ski resort.

After he left, I rolled down the steep descent at an insane average speed of 60kph, struggling with both the fierce wind as well as the slope, having to stop several times because my hands ached so much from the constant braking. Thirty minutes later, I reached a T-junction with a right turn to the town of Kiryat Shmona and a left turn to the Odem Forest reserve and the Druze village of Masadeh. Taking the right turn onto Route 99, I followed it all the way to the Saar Waterfall, which was north of the road. Locking my bike under a bush a little distance from the road, I took my handlebar bag, which contained my camera, wallet, and cell phone, and climbed down through the thicket to the large pond at the bottom of the waterfall.

Taking my shoes off, I sat down at the edge of the pond, dangling my legs in the water and watching the water rushing over the basalt rocks. This tranquility was the complete opposite of the storming, downhill ride from Mt. Hermon. The only sound was of the rushing Saar stream. The breeze hardly disturbed the pond's surface. It was my first stop since I had left Neve Ativ, and the realization that this was the last week of my journey kept haunting me.

The weather was autumnal, the sky almost completely covered by clouds with only an occasional glimpse of light blue. The humidity was high, which meant that rain was very likely.

Taking my cycling outfit off, I realized that my body was as fit as on Day One, despite cycling 1000km, and it felt great. However, the ride to Eilat along Route 90 had taken its toll: the skin was peeling off my arms and I spotted a few sunburn blisters on them. On top of that, my knees ached whenever I had to cycle up a steep climb, and the pains in my hands suggested possible arthritis due to gripping the handlebars. My lower back ached as well, probably as a result of sleeping on a thin mattress and staying too long in the saddle.

Because of all that, I had mixed feelings about the road that lay ahead. But, before my worries overwhelmed me, I decided to wash them away in the pool and refresh myself before riding on to Kiryat Shmona. After all, I thought, I was there to ride the road and was determined that these complaints would not affect my state of mind, especially as I was facing a long climb all the way to the Upper Galilee followed by a long ride all the way to the Mediterranean coast.

After bathing, I dressed and started climbing up back to Route 99. While climbing, I decided that I must be more available on my cell phone in the coming days both for friends who might wish to pay a visit, as well as for a more intense fundraising campaign.

Once I regained reception after reaching the top, I had a call from a fellow ex-serviceman, Amikam, who asked how I was doing and wanted to meet up that night. I was really thrilled by his willingness to visit me, and especially by the tons of meat he promised to bring along. As he put it, "It's up to me to get the meat, and it's up to us to eat it up. Okay?" Naturally, there was no chance I could resist such an offer. The very thought of a well-done, thick, fat-soaked steak motivated me to make it to the Mediterranean coast by that evening, so we decided to meet at Hanita Junction at 20:00, in case we had no contact over by phone.

Thirty minutes later, the downhill slope was behind me and I was riding up a moderate slope from Kiryat Shmona to Metula. Reaching the town, I stopped for a few minutes to have a coffee and a croissant with almonds and lots of sugar, and to check messages and weather reports before riding on north.

Good old Route 90 took me all the way to a turning a little past the Tel-Hai College. There, I took the left turn onto the uphill road leading to Kibbutz Manara. The humidity kept rising, which, combined with the effects of my earlier week's riding didn't make the climb any easier and my legs hardly seemed to work, which made me very frustrated and doubtful as to whether I could make it to the coast by the evening. Right from the start, I realized that I was going to shed a lot of sweat on this climb – as much as during the good old ride along southern Route 90. My new sweat-wiping towel, which replaced my old favorite, was soaked after twenty minutes.

I had to take my shirt off once again and spread it out to dry on the rear bags. Here, just as I'd done while climbing to Mevo Hama, I switched between riding and resting every few minutes. This slowed me down, and my face was covered with sweat that kept flowing and stinging my eyes.

Finally, I decided to speak my mind: "Dammit! Where

the hell's the predicted rain!? Where's the goddamn temperature drop the Greek forecast promised?!" I cried out loud.

The climb to Manara Ridge took me by surprise. I was completely caught up in thoughts about the steaks waiting for me that night and about ending my journey that I ignored what I had to go through before that: Israel's most rugged terrain, which included a 100km climb all the way to the Mediterranean coast.

The sun emerged from behind the clouds during the last kilometer of the climb, inevitably raising my body temperature and once I got onto Route 886, the ride became an endless nightmare, driving me to use abusive language more frequently. All I wanted was to get that damn climb over with. I tried to avoid stopping since every stop only weakened me and made my knee make alarming noises.

Finally, after a 14km climb all the way from Kiryat Shmona, I read WELCOME TO KIBBUTZ MANARA and smiled with the last ounce of energy left in me. I was riding south now with the Lebanese border a few meters to my right, and the breathtaking view of the Golan Heights, Mt. Hermon, and the north of Hula Lake to the left.

Well, just when I assumed that my trials for that day were over, a white Isuzu pickup truck happened to stop near me. On its roof was a red and blue light, plus a loudspeaker, and a 1.5m-long aerial. Its doors were covered with red stickers inscribed in thick black letters: SECURITY. I noticed that the driver wore red-rimmed Oakley sunglasses and had an unkempt, gray mustache.

"Good morning," I greeted him as he lowered his window.

"Do you know that this is a restricted area? Please go back to Kiryat Shmona!" This order came from the fat and edgy cartoon sheriff.

"Why should I?" I tried to reason with him.

"Because I tell you to! Stop arguing!" was his aggressive response.

First I dismounted, rested my bike against the guardrail, and wet my towel with water. I wiped my face with it, then drank some water, and poured the remainder all over myself. Then, after several deep breaths, I counted to ten and gave the security guy the following speech: "Look, I don't know you, but, with all due respect to your position, could you please tell me why can't I ride on? I see no check-points or any armed forces personnel around here. Look – there are cars driving past in the same direction as me. So, what's the matter?"

"Hey, boy, don't be so cheeky! You're not in Tel Aviv anymore! Getting out of your big city bubble of snobbery doesn't make you any big boss, so just move your ass and your weird bike away, or I'll call the police!" he informed me, turning his engine off.

"Okay, call them! You're not authorized to detain me or give me orders. Good day!" I told him off, walking back to my bike.

When he saw me pushing my bike toward the nearby bus stop shade and realizing that I was not going to obey him, he got out of his pickup truck and approached me with his handheld radio. He had a huge belly, a football fan's red cap, the blue, sweat-wicking shirt of a local relay-race partic-ipant, and a Gluck 17 pistol in a plastic holster on his belt. I started running through a variety of scenarios in my mind.

I could not stand such people, certainly not after the leg-wrecking ride I had just made. The last thing I wanted was to face some gung-ho guy who might force me to stop my trip for no apparent reason. Only the police had such authority. Knowing my legal rights, I knew he couldn't do anything except shout and make empty threats, so I just kept ignoring him.

After eating a few energy snacks and checking the amount of water I had left, I mounted my "truck" and headed for Kibbutz Yiftah. Seeing that I had ridden off, he ran back to his vehicle and came after me.

"Hey, are you deaf or something?" he shouted from his lowered window as he kept pace with me. "Stop or I'll force you off the road!" he ordered me, starting his siren.

The noise did annoy me and to demonstrate my disregard for him, I plugged my earphones in. This was too much for the mustached sheriff, and it made him stop. I wondered if he was calling the police.

Meanwhile, I rode on past Kibbutz Yiftah along a road running across farmland and oak groves, a landscape like no other I had ridden through on that trip. I kept riding south on this road along the Ramim Ridge, which stretches from the Keren Naftali Lookout in the south to Mt. Zofiya, near Metula, in the north. After that section of the ride, I read a most accurate description of that ridge in my guidebook: "This ridge is the northern extension of the main anticline ridge that runs between Mt. Turan, Mt. Kamon, Mt. Meron, and Kibbutz Misgav Am. This anticlinal ridge, sloping moderately westward, falls eastwards in a steep fault 700m below to the Hula Lake. The entire east side of the ridge is interrupted by the Hula Valley Fault, and its main cliff, Ramim, is part of the Hula Valley Faultline. The falling of this ridge from the Manara-Yiftah watershed line down to Hula Valley is one of the most impressive features of Israel's morphology. The ridge itself reveals the oldest rock outcrop in both Upper as well as Lower Galilee."

This passage looked impressive enough for me to copy it into my diary.

Riding south for an hour, I reached Route 899 and turned west. Right after that, a police car sped toward me. The policeman used his public address system to tell me to pull over, and then overtook me and blocked my way with his patrol car. Getting out of the car, the policeman gestured me to stop and dismount. The Isuzu pickup truck had arrived too and now stopped on the road shoulder, which made me feel like a fugitive running from the law. I had a hunch it had been unwise of me to respond to the mustached guy the way I had.

"Good morning, Officer," I greeted him. "Is anything wrong?"

"Yes. May I see an identity document?" he asked me, carefully examining my bike.

Dismounting, I rested my bike in the shade against a bus stop and searched for my wallet. I knew it was in my handlebar bag but decided to search through all my bags, one by one, to bide the time.

"Where have you come from? And what's all this stuff for?" the policeman demanded while I was searching for my wallet.

"Ashkelon. I've been cycling around the country for the last two weeks, and now I'm on my way home," I told him.

"If you're pulling my leg, you picked the wrong guy! Now, down to business. What are you blabbering about Ashkelon? That's a long way from here! Either you get real, or follow me to the station!"

"I AM real," I told him, handing him my driving license and cell phone with my selfies from Mitzpe Ramon, Eilat, and the Dead Sea shore. The policeman, about my age with receding hair, looked like he could not wait for his workday to end. Suddenly, he took two steps back and I thought that

I'd had it: he was going to detain me and fuck up my trip, for sure.

"Hey, wait a sec! Aren't you the guy who's raising Passover donations for needy families? I read something about that in the newspaper when I visited my sister in Jerusalem. If it's you, it's insane! Tell me, where did you come from today?" He took his sunglasses off, revealing a pair of brown eyes.

"From Mt. Hermon. I'm on my way to Rosh Hanikra, from where I'm going to head south on the Coastal Road," I explained, sipping water.

"Listen, Tzuriel King – is that your real name?" he inquired, examining my driving license. "That's the deal. I'm Menachem." We shook hands like two businessmen closing a deal. "I'll tell the Shlomi station you're heading their way, and they'll make sure you're okay. Right then, I'll escort you for the next hour until you're out of my territory. As for him- he gestured at the pickup - let me sort it out with him."

"Come on, Menachem! Seriously? I really don't need an escort. I'll move along, but anyway, thanks for the offer. You're number one! You've made my day!" I answered, some- what embarrassed.

"Forget it, " he said. "It's an offer you can't refuse! You've no idea how thrilled I was last week to read that there are still people like you, capable of completing what you're doing. I'm even more thrilled to offer you any possible help!"

As we spoke, the wind suddenly picked up and the Greek promise of rain seemed to be coming true. A few minutes later, raindrops started falling on our heads and he offered me a ride as far as Shlomi. While he ran for cover in his patrol car, I gestured to him that I was okay. Putting my green raincoat and helmet on, I set off again after a nearly thirty-minute enforced stop.

After escorting me for about 45 minutes, Menachem got out of his patrol car to shake my hand, hug me and ask me to take care, and then drove back. A few minutes later, I wondered whether "soaked to the skin" adequately described my situation then and there. I felt as if some thunder cloud was deliberately hovering right between Kibbutz Sasa and the community of Mattat, with me as its target. On the bright side, it was not cold, and it felt like a tropical rainstorm.

Torrential rain fell on the road and soon covered the centerline with rushing water and mud carried in from the roadsides. The thunder all around me only intensified the drama. Paradoxically, the rainstorm boosted my morale, as if all the earlier morning incidents were being washed away. Screaming with joy, I started singing Dana Berger's hit once again: "You probably won't say, but this is unimportant. Imagine it's abroad, and that's okay."

I slowed down, though, to avoid sliding on the wet road, but the fragrance of wet soil hit my nostrils, lifting my spirits even higher. Ten minutes later, the rain had reduced to an eye-irritating drizzle. Toward 15:00, I reached the gates of the community of Tzuriel, where I decided to change my plans and stop for lunch. I thought it would be nice to take a few triumphant selfies with the local WELCOME sign before heading west. Now it seemed surreal that, a few hours earlier, I'd had to ride shirtless due to the unimaginable heat and humidity. As usual, no matter how carefully you plan your route using the best maps, set your destination, and fix your schedule, you can never guess ahead and are powerless to know what trick nature's going to play on you.

At 18:30, I reached the southern approach to the town of Shlomi and started looking for a decent campsite where

Amikam and I could "stuff ourselves to death with meat!!!!" as he put it. He had a civil engineering business and was a year older than me. He had asked to join me for an evening at the very beginning of my journey, but only now did the time suit both of us. He had texted me to say that he'd be a little late due to a long workday, but once it was over, he promised to fill his Land Cruiser with a food cooler, a ton of entrecote steaks, and a few cold beers, and bring all this supply north to our meeting point.

A little past Shlomi, I took Route 8990 to the Hanita Forest, which covers the cliffs overlooking the town. The long climb allowed me to study the magnificent-looking Mediterranean flora of oaks, pistacia, and Judas trees. The view impressed me enough to convince me that I should spend the night in that forest.

After a fifteen-minute uphill ride, I found the perfect camping spot where we could set up our tents and feast like civilized people. It was a small parking lot connected to the main road by a dirt road. Next to the parking space was a wooden picnic table and a leaking, meter-high water tap with a puddle under it. Right next to the table was a perfect rectangle of flat, brown, damp ground enclosed by a wall of Clematis Cirrhosa and mastic.

At about 20:30, long after the woodland of the Upper Galilee had been shrouded with darkness, the temperature suddenly dropped to 10°, forcing me to light a campfire to keep warm. Enjoying the heat, I was suddenly blinded by the headlights of a gigantic Land Cruiser invading my space like an elephant breaking through a shop window. Amikam finally appeared.

Thirty minutes later, we had already finished off our first steak and second beer. Right away, Amikam served me another steak on a bed of sliced onion and roasted red peppers, geometrically arranged on a disposable plate, and lavishly sprinkled with coarse salt.

After setting our tents up and placing our sleeping bags inside them, we sat deep into the night by our small, private campfire that gently illuminated the woods surrounding us. We feasted eagerly on nothing but entrecote – no wasting precious stomach-space on salads or, God forbid, pita bread!

11

DAY 11

"When I had no roof, I made audacity my roof."

Robert Pinsky

April 11, 2016
Starting point: Kibbutz Rosh haNikra
Destination: Yokneam city
Distance: 65 kilometers

That night, the temperature had dropped to nearly 2°C. On the bright side, the rain had subsided a little past 06:00, and I unzipped my tent flap to see if I could crawl out without getting soaked. Amikam had set up his tent a couple of meters away, opposite mine. A puddle of brown water with pine twigs floating in it separated our tents. The night before, the rain had turned the ground into thick brown mud, and to make matters worse, water dripped with big, loud splashes from the tree above us.

It looked like General Winter had invaded the Galilee, so

it would be advisable to use the rainfall intermission to pack up and start off south along Route 70.

Amikam and I chatted for a few minutes from inside our tents, bantering with each other and agreeing that it sucked to leave our cozy sleeping bags. Inevitably, we were carried away back to our army days, especially to the similarity between then and now. Both of us thought it surreal that we were once again near the Lebanese border, in mud, under a bush, with our asses frozen.

Nearly an entire hour passed before we ventured out of our tents. The rain had started again with a vengeance. It had refilled the puddle separating us from one another and the sleeping bag seemed just too cozy to leave at that moment. Nonetheless, I finally plucked up the courage to get out of the tent and stretch myself, only to find myself barefoot in the cold puddle, my feet covered with mud. Ignoring the harsh cold piercing my feet all the way to my bones, I was consumed by the intense pain in my knees and thighs. Suddenly, just like on that cold morning in Shaharut, my left quads stiffened like a rock and when I stepped on the ground again in an attempt to get out of the puddle, I screamed like hell.

A terrible pain shot straight up my spine. It was unlike any other pain due to the cold, the overstrained muscles, and the lack of movement for several hours. This time, the pain was sudden and strong, like the one you get when your big toe hits the table, only a hundred times worse.

Instantly grabbing my cramped leg, I tried to uncramp it with a few stretching exercises. Hearing my screams, Amikam popped his head out of his tent. He saw how much pain I was in, but he burst into laughter, hitting me with a hail of sarcastic remarks, hinting that maybe I should retire now at my peak.

When the pain had gone, we had to tread carefully on the muddy, brown ground while folding up our wet tents quickly. Then, after drying ourselves, we completed our preparations inside Amikam's white Land Cruiser. After he had helped me load my stuff on my "truck" we decided to meet fifteen minutes later in the gas station café on the southern approach to the town of Shlomi, which would just be waking up after the rainy night.

We spent about an hour in the café, devouring coffee and croissants with chocolate and almonds. I told him about my planned route for that day, and he suggested helpful alternative routes with less traffic. While we were speaking, the ongoing drizzle turned into a shower. Having spent an hour-and-a-half on morning coffee, we left the café and after a couple of warm hugs and selfies, said goodbye, promising to go on another trip together someday.

Avoiding the rain, I walked quickly back into the café, wrapped in my green raincoat, and ordered a big espresso with a hot cheese pastry. Sitting down at the table where I had chatted with Amikam, I started planning my route and schedule for the days to come. I also turned my cell phone on, having been out of cell phone contact since the previous afternoon, and wrote down my previous day's adventures in my diary. While the rain kept raging outside, a waiter brought over a tray with my coffee and pastry.

"Enjoy your meal," he said. "I'll be over there for you," pointing at the counter. I was all alone in the café and the smell of coffee and pastries only made me more resolved to delay the beginning of my wintry journey. I had also started receiving message alerts. Some messages were from friends and family asking how I was doing, and others were from followers of my trip.

"To be sure," I wrote in my diary, "the dramatic weather change has brought good news."

Those new messages kind of infused me with a belief that nothing could stand in my way, be it rain, painful legs, bike malfunctions, or whatever. The first message was from my sponsor, PayBox:

Hi, Tzuri, what's up? I'm Avi. We've been following you, and we're speechless! Your project is an incredible success! As far as I can figure out, it'll be over in a couple of days and, according to our app, your donation account comes to nearly 30,000 USD. How about letting us hand out some packages to needy families in our Rishon Le Zion Compound? It's a huge area that's perfect for such an event. We'd love to help out, just tell me what you decide. Have a great day and take care out there on the roads!

I texted back that I thought it was a great idea, promising to contact him once my trip was over. The next message was from Maya:

Hi, man, what's up? Can I come visit? I can spend a few hours with you between shifts, over a cup of coffee or the like, or even take you to my place, but I'm not sure if that suits you. Somehow, I miss your nonsensical talking as well as your new beard. Besides, I've managed to find some doctors and nurses in the hospital willing to donate to your project. Is money transfer by PayBox still possible? As I read on your journey's Facebook page, it'll be over in a few days. Could you move over your cute little butt to Tel Aviv after? So, don't be snobbish, and send me a sign. Big hugs, Maya

At first, I hesitated to respond. On one hand, she hadn't been on my mind recently, and I'd been pissed by the row we had at Ein Sukkot, so much so that every message from her just brought her furious curses to my mind. Nor could I forget our pleasant moments as well: her warm body wrapped around me in my tent by Wadi Tamar, and her naked back when she invited me to join her in the pond. Therefore, I finally decided to text her the following:

Good morning, my edgy yet gorgeous doctor! What's up? I'm okay. How in the world can I turn you down!? However, right now I'm in the northern town of Shlomi, and it's been raining cats and dogs since last night. I plan to reach Yokneam today and be near Netanya or Tel Aviv by tomorrow. I'll be on Route 70, then Route 4. (You're more than welcome to surprise me, as you always do so well.) Yes, of course you can still use PayBox. Thanks! P.S. It seems I've forgotten what you look like, so if it suits you, please remind me. Thank you!

A few minutes later, she texted me back:

Here we go, just because you asked so nicely. I'm trying to get some time off, and I'll update you about our date. P.S. You're so cheeky!

Attached to it was a side-view selfie of her in green scrubs with her name tag on her chest (which she tried to push forward), a stethoscope around her neck, and her hair gathered up in a bun. Judging from the wink in her left eye and her stuck-out tongue, her spirits were high.

At 09:00, when I took to the road from the gas station, I looked up to check on the weather. To the east, the sun was still hidden behind approaching gray clouds, while to the west were large patches of blue, cloudless sky. The wind and rain had ceased completely. The only traces of winter were the water flowing along the road gutters and the water droplets dripping from the adjacent vegetation. Nature seemed to have started its slow yet persistent regeneration by being washed by the rain which, in turn, was entirely absorbed by Mother Earth.

Before heading south, I decided to pay the Mediter-

ranean coast a brief visit at Israel's northwesternmost tip,
namely Kibbutz Rosh haNikra, which is on the Lebanese
border. According to my cell phone map, it was 6km away.
Putting my helmet on, I set off west. The air warmed up a
little as I rode and, little by little, the familiar smell of the
Mediterranean started to tickle my nostrils. The closer I got
to the coast of the Western Galilee, the more strongly I felt
the salt and humidity in the air.

Of course, there was also that overwhelming landscape
stretching out below me. It compelled me to stop a few
minutes after I had started climbing toward Rosh haNikra,
pull my camera out of my handlebar bag, and snapshot
myself with that piece of the Galilee landscape.

I didn't remember ever having seen a similarly magnificent composition of blue sea and green grass growing so
close to the shore anywhere else in Israel. That high-alti-
tude vantage point at the country's northwesternmost tip
allowed me to see my route for the hours to come right from
where I stood. The Coastal Road ran nearly straight through
the sandhills that the spring had clothed with green grass.

Looming on the horizon was the city of Nahariya, and I
could see the fishponds scattered east of the Coastal Road,
where many locals lived. Somehow, this landscape made me
recall the beach town of Byron Bay, New South Wales,
Australia, where I had traveled after my demobilization.
Famous as a Mecca for surfers from all over the world, as
well as for healthy and spiritual lifestyle seekers, its endless
pristine beaches and impressive waves have given the locals
their easy going nature.

Once I'd taken pictures of the landscape far below me, I
felt the need to share this intense experience, but since
there was not a soul in sight, I wrote in my diary:

I've been riding around the country for over 1000km on

Israel's most remote roads for more than a fortnight, attempting to raise money for the needy. Today, I finally reached my beloved Mediterranean, breathed its familiar smell, and feasted my eyes on the inspiring Big Blue. The magnitude and power of the sea never fail to overwhelm me. This time, I've found a new, unique meaning in the words of pop-singer Ehud Banai's song, North Winds: "Listen to the waves, to your heart and pains."

Reciting those words today, I have that same feeling I had back then when I traveled in the Far East and Europe – a feeling of being intimately connected to and synergized with nature and the universe, which is only possible deep in the wild. It makes me feel like, with a little effort, I could communicate with the plants and animals. All of a sudden, it strikes me that I share that same sense with Native Americans, Incas, indigenous Australians, New Zealand's Mauri, and many other tribal peoples who live in practically perfect harmony with nature by sharing her treasures. They realize that whoever you are, wherever you live, and however rich you may be, you must obey the laws of nature and respect her if you want to win her favors. Otherwise, she will overcome you.

I've always been fascinated by their lifestyle, their ability to communicate with the universe, and their intimate understanding of it – an understanding that Western civilization has yet to achieve.

I've had countless rocking adventures, ups and downs, and challenging crises, yet I always meet angel-hearted people who help me get back on my feet and move on.

My legs may hurt after my travels along Route 90, across the Golan Heights and the Galilee, but my heart and mind are alive with endorphins and oxytocin thanks both to nature, which surrounds me day and night, as well as all the moral support I've received from my friends and relatives.

It is with great joy and immense satisfaction that, as hard as it is to accept the fact, I only have 200km ahead of me. I'm southbound on my way home!

After two hours of exciting feelings and devouring two completely crushed honey-and-cinnamon energy snacks, I got into the saddle yet again, starting off toward Route 70, which runs parallel to the Coastal Road, most of which is off-limits for cyclists.

During the last days of my journey, I had to deal with bustling roads running through urban centers, rural communities, and countless intersections. In addition, when I started along Route 70, the road was slippery and the visibility occasionally limited, so I decided to finish this piece of my route quickly as possible, which meant making fewer stops. On top of inhospitable weather, I also had this coming-from-the-outback syndrome. Until then, most of the roads I had traveled were in nearly uninhabited areas with hardly any traffic, where proper places to rest were a rare treasure. This road was completely the opposite, with a gas station every ten minutes and a small community every thirty minutes. It all reminded me of Europe, and once I was past the eastern turning to the magnificent Crusader fortress of Monforte, I realized just how European the Upper Galilee landscape was.

Shortly before arriving at Kibbutz Kabri Junction, I noticed that I had been following a road that marked the boundary between the Mediterranean flora and the coastline. The entire Western Galilee is nothing but a tricolor of green, white, and blue. Once again, the unique landscape I was traveling through – incomparable to any other in Israel – forced me to slow down and look. To the west, that is, to my right, a multi-cove coast stretched away, while to the left, that is, east of me, I faced moderately steep mountains, sliced through by green valleys and wadis. Such scenery definitely made me feel as if I was cycling through Switzerland.

Once I spotted the village of Kafr Yasif and the gray clouds creeping across the sky once again, I sped up, fearing another torrent of rain that might flood all the roads, and started to look for a proper place for a lunch stop.

Kafr Yasif, a predominantly Christian and Muslim village with a Druze minority, has made its name mostly due to its excellent hummus eateries. Remembering that I hadn't had any decent food since the night before, hunger struck me and I started dreaming of sitting in a local eatery with a waiter serving me a dish of hummus with olive oil and paprika, a pile of pitas and fresh, brownish-green falafel balls piled in a perfect pyramid on a separate dish.

I rode into the village a little before 12:00, wearing my long, black cycling gloves, a balaclava, and a raincoat covering my head and upper body. A few minutes later, the rain grew too strong for me to keep enjoying the ride through the village, and I looked for a possible place to stop. On one side of me was a sidewalk on which I could not ride, while on my other side there was dense traffic with many cars driving very close to me.

Suddenly, on the left-hand side, behind a green fence, I spotted two signs indicating that my search was over. They read "Al-Tanur Bakery" and "Al-Fawzi, the best hummus in the country!"

I instantly dismounted onto the nearest traffic island and then carefully crossed the street to the opposite pavement. Once safely there, I hid my bike under a red tarp sheet and took my winter outfit off. Then, resting my "truck" against the eatery wall, I stepped in.

The warm air and cocktail of intoxicating smells shot a shiver up the back of my neck. The place was brightly lit and decorated with a large mirror. Following me in were a family with two children, and two men. The family took seats at the other end of the eatery, while the two men sat down near me.

The space was dotted with about ten brown tables, each with four matching chairs set around it. Each table proudly presented open menus displaying the images and prices of the humus and salads served there. I, however, needed none of those, knowing exactly what I wanted. When the waiter approached me to take my order, he was surprised by my quick response.

"Good afternoon, I'd like a dish of hummus with a hard-boiled egg, parsley, and a lot of olive oil. I'd also like seven falafel balls, two hot pitas, and a thinly-cut green salad. Finally, I'd also like a glass of lemonade, please."

"Wow, bro, that was fast. You've been here before, right?" the waiter asked me with a heavy Arabic accent, bending toward me. "No problem, but the hot pitas will take a little time because there's something wrong with the oven, okay?"

"Fine, anything goes. Thanks."

A minute after the waiter had gone, he was back with a rectangular brown tray loaded with four dishes: one of humus drowned in olive oil, another smaller one with a quarter of an onion, twenty green olives, two pickled cucumbers, and half a tomato. Seven falafel balls as green as the mountains of Galilee and as hot as the desert roads I'd been traveling on two weeks before were piled up in a perfect pyramid on the third, exactly as I had dreamt. The fourth one was piled high with a thinly-cut green salad sprayed with olive oil that glowed under the fluorescent lamp.

"Here we go," the waiter told me. "It's all yours. Enjoy your meal."

A few minutes later, he came back to place two pitas in a wooden basket on my table. "Your pitas and lemonade, bro. I'm Adel. Call me if you need anything," he informed me, moving on to the next table to take an order.

Ten minutes later, it was all devoured to the last crumb. Sitting back in my chair, I stared at my bike. Despite the continuing rain, my stuff was safe under the yellow water-tight covers of my trunk bags. Noticing that I'd eaten up everything he had served me, Adel cleared my table right away. I ordered nothing else, as I was now preoccupied with planning my schedule for the days ahead. However, like a regular mind-reader, he came back with a black coffee in a glass in one hand, and a small plate with two honey-colored pieces of baklava.

"Help yourself, bro."

He only looked fifteen-years-old or at most, eighteen. His black mustache made him look more like a man, helping him to conceal his boyhood. He wore blue jeans, worn out at the front, and a white buttoned shirt tucked into his pants. Judging by the frenzy with which he worked the tables and his constant smile, he definitely loved his work. It felt as if he gave me more attention than other customers, and he knew what I wanted without me having to ask.

Either way, I finally had time to plan ahead and send pics and messages. Yokneam was 45km away and according to my information, most of the road was flat and obstruction-free, so I was in no hurry to get out of Kafr Yasif and decided to use my lunchtime break to accomplish as many unfinished tasks as possible.

First, I texted Avi, my man at PayBox, to tell him the date I'd like the food to be handed out – somewhere around the Passover night, which was ten days away – so I wanted as many food packages as possible to be handed out before the Passover began.

Suddenly, I remembered that Nissan, the Jewish month when Passover is celebrated, had started two days earlier. Amusingly enough, I only remembered it now thanks to the smell of the falafel balls. Back in the 1980s, my kibbutz used to celebrate the beginning of every Jewish month with a feast made mostly of falafel. We kids used to sneak into the dining hall an hour before the festive dinner to be the first to scrounge some falafel balls and taste them before the adult in charge kicked us out. Now, somehow supernaturally, Adel left on my table a bag of five falafel balls for the road.

Shortly after, my cell phone rang. It was Adina, director of Rishon Le Zion's City Welfare Department. Avi had given her my number and she asked whether she could give me the names and addresses of, as she put it, "... hundreds of families in severe economic distress who would be glad to receive a food package next week."

Her call made me feel awkward at first, but then it struck me that in a few days, I could really make a difference to the suffering of the needy, and I was strongly moved. Suddenly, I considered cutting my journey short since, after all, it was for them I had started it, and meeting their needs was more important than the fulfillment of my own dreams.

Right after the call, I asked for my bill and started preparing to leave. Taking my money, Adel could see no reason why I was in such a hurry. "Can't you see it's raining out there?" He pointed outside, trying to reason with me. "Stay here a little while. You must be insane to cycle out there now! Trust me!" he told me, picking up my glass and plate.

"Well, Adel, my motto is, 'start as fast as possible, and gradually speed up,'" I replied, smiling.

Toward 13:00, I was all set to head south and the weather, too, was looking more favorable. The rain had abated a little and although it looked as if another raincloud was on its way, the roads were bustling with traffic and their shoulders full of puddles. But no matter how rough the ride ahead of me seemed, only one thing was on my mind now after the call from Adina: I must end this journey as soon as possible to help those needy families. Just before leaving, I texted Maya to let her know my current location and my planned stop for that night, inviting her to meet me near Kibbutz Ha-Zorea, by Wadi Ha-Shofet. She just replied, "Hi, sweetie, see ya later. Too busy. Ride safely."

That day Route 70 was far from fun due to the heavy traffic typical of highways, so I had to keep well over on the shoulder. Rainwater had accumulated in the roadside ditches and because of it, I nearly fell in. Finally, I reached the Kibbutz Yagur Junction and turned left to Yokneam.

The rain, which had fallen incessantly throughout that day, stopped seemingly for good. The sun, about to go off-stage, suddenly appeared, blinding me for a moment, until it was concealed by Mount Carmel. I rode on for a few more kilometers until I found the turning I was looking for. Though the road was slightly muddy, I kept going. I felt at home in the wild, where the roar of traffic gave way to the twittering of birds and the babbling water of the nearby stream.

I rode for fifteen minutes through the Menashe Forest along a sandstone trail that became a paved road then turned back to sandstone again...all of it coated with thin, sticky, beige mud. I passed by the ruins of an Ottoman flour mill and a cave, which, according to a sign, had also been an Ottoman mill.

Once the sandstone trail parted from the stream, I stopped and rested my bike against one of the dry, upright pines along the trail. The moment I approached the stream, I knew I should camp there.

I saw some old willow trees, the roots of which went all the way down to the stream, while green weeds with gray leaves grew on the other bank. I stood on a patch of flat ground between the willows. What charmed me most was the lovely composition of the little green pond and the oleander, with its beautiful pink flowers that served as a kind of natural barrier between the stream and my planned camping site. I started unpacking my stuff straight away before the light went, and in ten minutes my tent was set up with all my stuff safely in it, the rain cover stretched over it in anticipation of a rainy night. Now I had to find some firewood, so I started searching for twigs that were not too wet.

My supper consisted of falafel leftovers, pita bread, tahina, and herbal tea. A little past 20:00, I had a good fire going and was enjoying the peaceful silence. I sat down about half a meter away from my campfire. Reclining on a bag I had pulled out from my tent, I opened my diary on my folded knees. I could hear the babbling of the little waterfall flowing into the green pond behind me mingled with the crackling of another piece of wood transformed into a glowing ember. I occasionally detected stars shining through the forest canopy. The sky was cloudless, promising an extremely cold night.

Suddenly, the silence was broken by unidentifiable engine noise.

"Dammit!" I thought. "God, let it be no nagging, bored

ranger asking me to put my fire out and leave!"

The car stopped, the engine stopped, and footsteps approached. But, instead of some nagging ranger, Maya appeared, wearing the very same outdoor clothes she had worn on our first encounter: jeans, Australian boots, a coat, and an orange-and-black striped balaclava.

"Have you ever been told you're surreal?" she asked, smiling, leaping toward me over the campfire. I got up slowly and we came together. I felt her breath on my face as I placed my hand on her cute little butt and gently pressing her pelvis against mine.

"Yes, I have. Does it bother you in any way?"

She replied with a naughty smile, pressing her plump lips against mine, instantly reminding me how strongly I desired her. That good old taste of her lips and the scent of her body permeated me deeply, making me want her to keep doing that on and on. My body, exhausted after my wintry journey throughout the Galilee, sprang to life at once. Being a doctor, Maya must have noticed that. She invited me to join her in her Jeep for a few minutes.

"After you," I accepted.

She took me by the hand to her car.

About thirty minutes later when we came back to the fire, it had nearly died out so I threw in some more twigs. Using our headlamps, I quickly showed her the campsite, pond, and nearby stream, and then I brewed up tea for two. We sat down next to each other as close as possible to the fire, cuddling under her blanket.

First of all, she gave an apologetic speech for her words to me last time we'd seen each other, saying she was just too frustrated, thinking of nothing but her selfish needs, and admitting she acted like a jerk.

"So how are you?" I tried to show some sympathy. "I

guess you've had a busy day in the hospital. Is that how it usually is?" I asked, pouring her tea.

"It's been insane for the last couple of days. Some doctors have told me that it always happens just before Passover. On top of that, two resident physicians went down with the flu, so the rest of us had to bear the brunt. We didn't even have time for a proper meal. To make things worse, the head of my department's a real schmuck. I have twenty-four hours off duty before I start another 26-hour shift."

Hearing her plight, I told her all about my cycling adventures since our previous encounter and my plans for the couple of days ahead.

Toward 22:00, my eyes started drooping but, whenever I fell asleep, Maya woke me up by touching my beard.

"What's that scent you're wearing? It should be sold as a freshening-up cologne!" I declared, pressing my nose against her neck and sniffing her.

"What the hell are you talking about!? It's just how I smell!" she told me, resting her head on my shoulder. "Let me tell you, you're getting better day by day on this journey of yours. I guess you had some fun with other girls, right?

So, just keep cycling and letting your beard grow for a week and then when I visit you, you'll be a real kick-ass with that Robinson Crusoe look," she declared, thrusting her icy hands under my down-filled coat.

"How about we go to bed? I'm exhausted, and we both have a busy day tomorrow. Which side of the tent do you prefer? Regarding your question – yes. I had scores of girls, every day a new one," I told her, standing up slowly. Putting out the fire with the remaining tea in the pot, I took her hand and we slid one by one into my tent.

"I'm sure you did. After you," Maya replied.

12

DAY 12

"What is the proof that one is alive, sir and madame? Him eating, drinking, moving around? No, not at all! Scores of people walk among us, sleeping at night and rising in the morning – yet they are dead, unaware of their own death. At least I am aware of it. Living, sir and madame, means taking part in the action of this world, either enthusiastically or disgustedly, motivated by your own will. And if that is absent, you are dead. Am I in the right?"

Lea Goldberg, The Lady of the Castle

April 12 and 13, 2016
Starting point: Yokneam City
Destination: Ashkelon
Distance: 147 kilometers

After sunrise, deep inside my sleeping bag with only my eyes showing, I opened my eyes and had no idea where I was. Unzipping my tent and removing the balaclava from my eyes, I saw Maya's orange balaclava resting on my mattress. This instantly reminded me that I had fallen asleep with Maya in my tent.

A few minutes later, still lying on my back deep inside my sleeping bag and mentally preparing to get up, I heard a woman's voice singing the words of Dudu Tasa's hit, "Better have a glorious failure than leave your dreams in a drawer."

Upon leaving the tent, I saw her sitting by the camping stove wrapped up in my down-filled coat, singing that song as she waited for our tea to boil.

"Here, I made you a strong mint tea with lemon and the verbena I brought along," she said, handing me the cup.

"Thanks. When did you get up?" I asked, sitting down next to her.

"Fifteen minutes ago, and I took a little walk around. This was a fine place you chose, next to the stream. Are you planning to reach Ashkelon today? I thought that maybe you'd like to stop off at my place in Tel Aviv for a shower and a rest before riding on."

"I'd like to, but it depends how well today's ride goes. Anything can happen before I reach Greater Tel Aviv. I've found it's unwise to make any promises on such a trip because so many things may go wrong."

We kept sitting there silently, pressed against each other, the only sounds around us being the lazy flow of the stream nearby and an occasional crow's croak.

"Have I told you that I joined the Israel Climbing Club?" she asked all of a sudden. "Anyway, I've signed up for some expeditions to some of the world's highest peaks, doing whatever it takes. I'm telling you this because I've met travelers from all over the world and heard their countless stories and – I know I've told this already – but I *swear* you've got a hell of a story to tell and you must share it with the world." Resting her cup of tea on the ground, she pulled a brush through her hair. "You're too absorbed with your trip – traveling all alone away from the world, riding all day and sleeping by the roadsides – to realize just how powerful and inspiringly rare it looks to a bystander. For you, it's just another day of cycling but you've no idea how outstanding what you've done really is. You've risked your livelihood, your health, and your life for the sake of helping the needy. I can't imagine where you draw all that energy from, what drives you to fight through another day. If I didn't know you better, I'd mistake you for some insane daydreamer who should be locked up. Listen here! You *must* write down all your experiences!"

I did listen, and her words went deep inside my mind. I could do nothing but keep silent and observe how beautiful and arousing she was, speaking to me in such an imperious tone. Just then, I noticed that when she brushed her hair and pulled it back, her body stretched with feline flexibility. She caught my eye, laughing. "I'm talking to you about your future, while you keep undressing me with your eyes... you're shameless!"

"I plead guilty on both counts. Interestingly, you're not the first to tell me I should write down my adventures. Trouble is...I'm not sure I have the ability to write even a few lines, let alone an entire book. I can write a short blog or a news report but I've always considered that writing a book's beyond me. That's only for those who are, well, gifted, those endowed with exceptional imagination and the endless patience to sit on their butts day and night. As for the second count, I definitely undressed you with my eyes. Aren't I allowed? Will you file a complaint?" I defended myself, smiling.

"Of course you're allowed, you fool! Too bad you only

did it with your eyes..."

She handed me her brush while she was gathered her hair in a bun and went on, "A good friend of mine writes for a daily newspaper and is also a gifted literary editor. He'd love to help you if you ask him to."

Taking another sip of her sweet tea, I rested the cup on the ground and went away to take a leak. Only then did I realize just how heavily I'd slept the night before. Usually, I awoke to take a leak in the night. While emptying my bladder, I wondered why I didn't need to pee last night? My thoughts were about planning today's ride and whether I could make it home by the end of the day. I also thought over Maya's suggestion about writing. And yes, I even gave her undressing a little thought...

Back in my camp, my legs were so cramped that I limped and a sharp pain shot through my knee. I was powerless to ride on and really wanted to carry on sleeping for a few more hours. However, I knew that this weakness always disappeared within the hour, leaving me ready to ride in body and spirit. Noticing my limp, Maya gestured to me to come near her. She examined me while I stood above her, like a doctor examining a patient.

"Wow, your skin's a mess! You've got sunburn all over – on your legs, arms, and even on your nose! Don't you ever apply a protection cream, or wear a long-sleeved shirt or anything? You're limping, too, and that doesn't look too good. My initial diagnosis is that you're falling apart. Can't you have a few days' rest before riding on?"

"I really appreciate your concern, Doctor," I replied as sarcastically as I could, " but I'm all right, thank you. It'll go away. Sorry for forgetting you're a diligent resident doctor and, yes, I do use protection cream, but it gets washed away by my sweat and the water I pour over myself to cool down, so I usually ride cream-free."

Preparing to ride, I noticed that the ground, as well as my bike, was wet, so I checked the weather report and informed my friends and relatives about my planned route. I was thrilled when checking my donation account...it had reached the 40,000 mark. Suspecting some mistake, I exited the app and went in again, and what I saw put such a big smile on my face. It was no mistake! I had collected US$40,000. Unbelievable! Now I had to figure out how the hell I could manage all the food and clothing that I could buy with that money.

Maya helped me pack up and prepare for the ride while I changed into cycling clothes. Putting on my green raincoat, I started loading my "truck" with my stuff.

"So, what are your plans for the rest of the day?" I asked her while tying everything to my bike frame.

"To be honest, I want to spend some time with you. It's so fun and enjoyable. So, if it's okay with you, I'll escort you today since I'm free until midday," she whispered her reply.

Standing between me and her Jeep, she looked at me, waiting for my response to her sincerely expressed feelings. I came near her, giving her a long kiss, and she let her tense body relax, closing her eyes and letting herself indulge in the moment. As I gently pressed her back against the car door, she wrapped her arms around me. I felt her body become aroused and her breathing grow heavier. The scent of her body and body lotion aroused me to the extent of being unable to get in the saddle again.

"Why did you stop?" she wondered as I broke away from her slowly.

"Because all things, good and bad, must end, Maya. From here, I ride alone, so please don't escort me. I just like it this way...it has nothing to do with you. Please try to see my point." Upon saying that, I feared she would react as I remembered from our last encounter.

"I see," she said, falling silent.

Then she came near me, persistently pressing her head on my left shoulder for a few seconds. Then she made me an offer: "Can I at least offer you a tempting massage for when you finish all this insanity, or do you have any plans already?"

"No, I have no plans. But again, I'll make no plans until this trip is over. Sorry, I can't focus on anything else right now."

"I understand perfectly. Well, just give me one last hug for the road, a little warmth before we say goodbye... something to think about on my long shift today," she begged.

Her wish was granted, of course. A few minutes later, Maya was driving south and I was far behind her, facing another day's ride.

Ramot Menashe National Park, where I had spent the night, is a part of Menashe Heights. To the north, its boundary is Route 70, which runs along Wadi Yokneam, separating it from Mount Carmel. Its eastern boundary is Route 66. To the south of Route 66, on Route 65, the road runs along Wadi Ara, separating the Heights from the hills of Samaria. To the west, where there is no distinct boundary, the road slopes moderately toward the valley between the wine-making towns of Binyamina and Givat Ada.

That morning, the roads themselves were clear, but their shoulders were strewn with shards of glass, metal, and other objects washed down by the heavy rainfall. These threatened punctures that could befall me at any moment.

Leaving the sandstone trail, I returned to Route 66 and rode a few kilometers until it met Route 70. From there, I headed west and planned to keep going until it met Route 4, on which I would ride south to my final destination.

By the end of that day, I planned to ride through the cities of Hadera, Raanana, Herzliya, Tel Aviv, Bat Yam, and Rishon Le Zion, before reaching my hometown, the provincial capital, Ashkelon, locally nicknamed Ashkel-town.

I rode slowly for ten minutes to warm up my cramped legs before the long climb to the rural community of Eliakim. Finally reaching the outskirts of Yokneam, I turned west on the highway, starting the moderate climb toward the Carmel ridge. Although the road itself was well-maintained and free of pits or grooves, here, too, the roadsides were covered with tons of debris that I did my best to avoid.

Advancing, I saw a large yellow metal plate with a white, A4-size paper notice announcing in black letters: "To the blooming fields. Left at the next junction."

As the owners of my bike shop informed me later, each year during the winter and spring, Menashe Heights becomes one big, blooming field of spring flowers, which is a rare sight in Israel. Even during my short time there, I'd occasionally noticed wonderful, multicolored carpets of anemones, buttercups, yellow asphodel lines, irises, orchids, and other wildflowers. The colors of spring popping out everywhere flooded me once again with that sense of reconnection with nature.

Harsh reality, however, promptly shattered my elation, as if some evil force were watching me from high above, making sure I could never soar to higher spheres, clipping my wings the moment I started.

I got my first flat tire that day 500m past Eliakim Junction. Tough luck, I thought, but a ten-minute repair could get me back on the road, so I bought a tube at a nearby gas station and replaced it. Ten minutes later, I had another flat tire, which made me even more pissed, though not too much. At worst, I thought, I'd curse a little, hate myself a little, and after letting off some steam, I'd fix it and ride on. So I bought another spare tube in a gas station, spent another ten minutes unloading the bags, finding the puncture, replacing the tube, and putting everything back. When I took to the road again, I wasn't as happy as when I'd been near the sign to the blooming fields, but at least I felt relieved that the run of flat-tires was over.

Exactly fifteen minutes later, I got my third flat tire in a row, in the middle of the downhill ride from Fureidis Junction. That made me *really* frustrated. All of a sudden, my bike was thrown off balance, started zigzagging at over 40kph. I was sure I was about to be thrown over the guardrail into the ditch. It was unbelievable! On top of that, a raincloud had chosen to target my head and the road directly around me with annoying drizzle. Finally, after nearly losing control and crashing, during thirty nerve-wracking seconds, I managed to stop my "truck."

After dismounting and glancing at the contact between my rear tire and the road, I realized that Lady Luck wasn't smiling on me that day. I had yet another flat and had run out of spare tubes.

"Dammit! Dammit! Dammit!" I screamed, taking a few brief and quick breaths before letting off more steam. "This can't be happening to meeee..." I yelled in the general direction of the Carmel Ridge.

For the first time on this journey, I hurled my bike violently into the ditch north of the road. It landed with a loud metallic crash then slid down with a screech. A bitter sense of defeat overcame me and the self-accusation started. All it took to avoid these flat tires was a little more attention to the position of my bike on the road! When it struck me that the state of my body and mind was preventing me from riding on, I grew dispirited. This despair triggered my greatest fear – of quitting mid-way due to a mental break-down – with no wish to get in the saddle again. On top of that, the rain intensified, flooding the ditch where I'd thrown my bike and wetting my bags.

I sat down at the edge of the ditch, facing the road, resting my elbows on my knees, with my wet forehead in both hands. I was so enraged that I had to break something apart. It just couldn't have happened to me! Only then did I realize just how much stress I'd suppressed deep inside in order to accomplish this journey, and it finally erupted like a volcano. I spotted a nearby bus stop and started dreaming of the hot shower, clean clothes, and cozy bed I could be enjoying within ninety minutes – if only I decided to quit.

Ten minutes later, I was standing in the shelter of the bus stop, clearing mud from my feet and bike when, some-how, the song that Maya had hummed that morning managed to cheer me up: "Better have a glorious failure than leave your dreams in a drawer."

To snap is only human, I reassured myself. At least I'd tried. There's no law compelling you to fight till the finish. Waiting for the bus, I gradually regained my even-headed-ness. I happened to have, among other things, two dates that Maya had left that morning in my bag.

Checking my cell phone for the bus timetable, I saw two messages. The first was from Adina, who wanted to know what day I'd chosen for distributing food parcels, and whether I needed volunteers from all over Rishon Le Zion to help me with the task. The second one was good news: a high-tech company, on learning about my project from social media, had donated about $5,000.

After reading these messages, I had a revelation: I remembered that Shay, my best friend, lived nearby, so I called him, asking him to rescue me. He, however, was at a business meeting near Tel Aviv and couldn't help. Merely twenty minutes later, though, a silver Honda Civic stopped by me. Galit, Shay's partner, lowered the window and told me with a big smile, "The cavalry has arrived. Can I help?"

Shay had been an old acquaintance for nearly two decades, ever since we had worked together as security guards in the Old City of Jerusalem. He met Galit later while traveling in South America, and they have been together ever since. So far, it was unclear who had seduced who. The point is, they might have been out of my sight, but they were always on my mind.

Opening her trunk, Galit begged my pardon for the mess – like I cared a bit – blaming it on their kids, and started loading my stuff. All of a sudden, she asked me if something was wrong, as if she had keenly sensed that I was in the middle of a hell of a breakdown.

"All's well with the world," I lied and went on, "I've just had too many flat tires today, so it would be very helpful if you could drop me and my bike in Karkur, by the nearest repair shop."

As she drove me to the shop and my clothes were drying out, I recalled Amy Cuddy's moving TED talk, Fake It Till you Make It, in which she speaks of the necessity to fake a state of mind even when you don't genuinely feel it. With compelling examples and eyes full of tears, she explained that your mind can eventually adapt to the fake mood and it becomes a reality.

Even after helping me unpack my stuff at the shop, Galit still wanted to help me even while the repair was being done. Finally, after lying to her that I was all right, she bought into my perfectly performed fake mindset and drove home to Binyamina.

That cycle shop, a franchise of an Israeli chain of bike shops, was only second to my best wish. The staff instantly discerned my trouble and the shop manager, Yossi, was kind enough to ask me where I had cycled from, where I was heading to, and why I was carrying all those heavy bags.

After hearing me out, he disappeared inside his shop, saying nothing, and came back a couple of minutes later holding two cups, one of double espresso and another of cold water. Then he promised me that his repair expert would be with me in a minute at my service. On top of that, he stuffed two spare tubes in my shirt pockets.

By midday, the rain had stopped, all the roads along the coast had dried up, and the cloudless sky promised that the rest of the day would be bright. After saying goodbye to Yossi and his amazing staff, I found myself on Karkur's main street with three cups of espresso in my blood, two Snickers bars in my belly, and four spare tubes in my shirt pocket. Overjoyed and reassured by all these gifts, I jumped in the saddle and set off south on Route 4.

Given the circumstances, I chose not to ride directly to Ashkelon but to spend the night at Kibbutz Shfayim with Yaara and Irit, two friends who were very glad to see me. Irit, my companion on my first marathon ten years earlier, welcomed me warmly with open arms and a smile only she was capable of, while the rest of her family also made me feel at home. Irit had always shown an interest in everything

I'd done, and now she bombarded me with countless questions about what I'd been through.

I was less focused on her questions and more interested in the pot of hot pasta on the table. Having been literally starved, that dinner was my first civilized meal since that Sabbath dinner in Neve Ativ. It was only the next day as I left the kibbutz that I realized how strong our friendship was.

I was really reluctant to ride out of the kibbutz, but finally mounted my bike and rode on, not looking back. Ahead of me lay 80km of urban roads and highways swarming with short-tempered Israeli drivers, but I was already making plans for the week to come from the very first moment I started pedaling.

When I reached Ashdod at about midday, I paid my younger sister, Talya, a brief visit for a ten-minute coffee, a piece of cake, snapshots, and endless hugging before riding on. At that point, I was eager and homeward bound. Despite the strong headwind slowing me down, exhaustion, aching legs, and cramped muscles, I could see that the end was near. I had that inevitably human sense of slackening off a few minutes before reaching the goal – that "It'll soon be over, so I don't give a damn," feeling.

At that moment when my mind absorbed that I had done it and had really cycled around Israel all alone, overcoming all the hardships, I was left with mixed feelings about it all. Feelings of pride and satisfaction skyrocketed my confidence on the one hand, but on the other hand... there was a sort of emptiness. What was next? What would my next goal be?

I came to the right turn toward Ashkelon. My starting point, which I had left eighteen days ago, was 500m away. I was slowly flooded with a sense of immense satisfaction.

Like the heat of a bath, it started from the tips of my toes, slowly spreading up my entire body.

I had to cherish that moment, so I stopped and dismounted. A few minutes later, a black Mazda 3 stopped by me and a little girl with long braids got out. She obviously needed to pee and went off behind a bush followed by her father. After she was hidden, her father started to walk back to the car, but she called to him not to leave her alone. I clearly remember how I smiled when her father came back to her straight away, staying with her until she was done.

Pulling my last energy snack out of my back pocket, I sat down at the roadside and looked once again at the girl and her father and then started to examine my aching legs. I massaged them a little.

That little scene showed me how much love fills this world, and that it's just there for the picking. All of a sudden, I was thrown back in time to the winter of 2009 in Nepal, when I met Arjoon, that ten-year-old Nepalese orphan who had broken my heart. Recalling all the sadness and fear I had seen in his eyes, I thought how lucky that little girl was to have her father watching over her and how we all take our happiness for granted. This made me burst into tears.

Those tears were neither of grief over what I had lost for a decade, nor of joy over what I had gained. I cried out of gratitude for all the goodness engulfing and overwhelming me. At that moment, I realized that I had become a billionaire: I was enriched by priceless emotions and experiences that I would cherish forever.

Until then, I had imagined life to be a regular orbit like the moon circling the Earth, but now I realized just how beautifully unexpected life can be. No matter how much good or evil there is, everyone can change their life dramatically with a single act or thought of compassion.

I slowly rode on a little further, feeling no physical pain at all at that moment. Toward 18:00, I arrived home, relaxed and resolved, full of humility, and conscious of all the good my world had to offer.

EPILOGUE

I remember it as if it were yesterday. A couple of days before the Passover Night of 2016, I saw dozens of volunteers from all over the country, gathering at the Rishon Le-Zion's free food distribution point to give hundreds of needy families the food purchased with the money people had donated during my around Israel, Heart to Heart tour.

Thanks to the tens of thousands of dollars I had raised, hundreds of families managed to have a decent Passover and many homeless people had a hot meal that year.

It would have been impossible without the cooperation of my outstanding friends, who I'd rather call angels. Those big-hearted people helped me achieve both my charity project as well as my mind's child: *Alone I Did It.*

I would like to thank them here.

First, my parents, who texted me every couple of hours throughout my journey, just to ask how I was doing. During the weeks preceding the completion of this book, they were even more thrilled than I was, realizing that their shy son was about to become the family's first writer.

So I dedicate this book to you alone, dear Mommy and

Daddy. What you are, your unconditional love, and all you've given to me all my life defies all description and so a thousand thanks. I hope I've proved deserving of such a rare treasure.

I also thank the rest of my immediate family – my siblings who were always there for me. Knowing that you will always stand by me is the wind that helps me sail to new horizons.

I also thank all my friends, Ital Wegschel, Amos Duke, Gilli and Yishay Granit, Yuval Friedman, a staff member of the Karkur bike shop, and of course, all the staff of Amin's Bike Shop in Eilat. Some rescued me from some seriously difficult situations while others just supported me with a smile and a compliment, or had a cup of coffee or a glass of beer with me during my trip. A thousand thanks to you all.

Special thanks go to Sagi and Avivit of Be'er Ora for their warm hospitality on Day One of this trip. Words cannot express my happiness being in your company.

I also will never forget the matchless Dana Danos, who called me in the middle of the desert, near Uvda Airport, practically forcing me to call on her sister, Michal, who lived in Israel's remotest community, Shaharut. A thousand thanks, Dana and Michal, for all your help, hot meals, sweet tea, and warm hospitality.

I will never forget Avichai Jackson for coming to my rescue in his tiny car on the roads winding through the Eilat Mountains in intense heat, like the US Cavalry. Thank you, dear Avichai, for what you are and what you did for me.

Nor will I forget Izi, father of my good friend Tal Bloch, or my stay in Ein Yahav. Though he could not see the tears flowing down my cheeks, I was overwhelmed with his boundless warmth when I stopped by his farm. Thank you for the world's best scrambled eggs, Izi!

I am also much obliged to all the drivers who bothered to stop alongside me on Route 90, just to ask how I was doing.

I also express gratitude to my older brother, Aryeh, and my sister-in-law for their outstanding hospitality that surpassed any five-star hotel in Jerusalem. I also thank you, Yiska, for allowing me to take my nephew, Yonadav, for the 60km ride along Route 90. I really appreciated your company, Yonadav.

I am also much obliged to Sarai and Rafael, my northernmost relatives who brought me into their Neve Ativ home at the foot of Mt. Hermon, pampering me for an entire weekend as if I were their son coming back from a war. The time I spent with them was as pleasant as a never-ending dream. I clearly recall how it saddened me to leave them when I cycled down the hill to Kiryat Shmona.

I will also never forget the welcome that I was given in Kibbutz Shfayim, for which – as well as for the great food and all the other extras only they could offer – I am deeply grateful to Orit Ram-Nof and her family.

Nor will I ever forget all the artists whose works inspired me to fight on throughout this journey: Queen, Pink Floyd, Shalom Hanoch, and all the other international and local singers, as well as Haruki Murakami.

During my cycling tours all over the world, I have met many people, some of whom only spent a few hours with me. Nonetheless, all these encounters enriched me, inspired me, and drove me to love, think, laugh, cry, and experience both pain and pleasure. Most of all, they inspired me with their acceptance of all humans, since all humans are born good.

I send my thanks and a Namaste to all those I have encountered on my travels.

Finally, my deepest gratitude to my friends since childhood. There are too many to mention by name; so all I want is to send you a thousand thanks and apologize for all my nagging on social media while I was writing this book.

I thank the matchless Amihai Shalev, the toughest and most British editor I have ever met, who kept pushing, encouraging, and showing an interest in me - always arguing with me professionally. Many thanks for Liron and Ifat from Bethaorchim company; your escort and advice were just perfect.

Also Julie Phelps, the amazing English consultant and proofreader who sprinkled some magic powder while upgrading my words and vision. she helped me to make my book so unique. Thanks a lot, Julie!

From now on, I will never do it all alone, but with you.

I love you a lot,

Tzuri

9 798577 864934